Classification in Social Research

Classification
in Social Research

Ramkrishna Mukherjee

State University of New York Press
Albany

Published by
State University of New York Press, Albany

© 1983 State University of New York

Printed in the United States of America

For information, address State University of New York Press, State University Plaza, Albany, N.Y., 12246

Mukherjee, Ramkrishna.
  Classification in social research.
  Bibliography: p.000
  Includes index.
  1. Social sciences—Classificaiton. 2. Sociology—
Classification. I. Title
H61.2.M84   300'.12   82-682
ISBN 0-87395-607-9   AACR2
ISBN 0-87395-608-7 (pbk.)

To
Immanuel, Terry, Hayward

Contents

Chapter 1
Perspective

1 OVERVIEW

Classification is concerned with the population of a schematically conceived universe. The population may be human or any kind of inanimate or animate objects: for example, the population of Bengalis, bees, birch trees, bolt-making industries, banking institutions, Brotherhoods (sacred or secular), and so on. We identify the universe of the population by space-time coordinates, for example, the Bengalis in the State of West Bengal in the Republic of India in the decade of the 1980s or the Bengalis in Bangladesh in the same decade. Now, if the characteristics of a population were the same (i.e., a constant), there would have been nothing to classify. For example, it is not a matter for classification that the Bengalis have one nose each, but the shape of the nose can be classified qualitatively as sharp or flat (narrow, medium, broad, etc.), and the process of classification will be precise and comprehensive when the shape of the nose is classified quantitatively according to the metric values of the nasal index. The Bengalis, or any other population, can thus be classified by a set of *variable* characteristics which may be developed from qualitative distinctions into quantitative measurements.

The role of classification is, therefore, to present in a consolidated manner our knowledge about the characteristics of variation in a population belonging to a specified universe. Hence, it is a perennial concern of scientific investigation, the task of which is to elicit the variable properties of the phenomena with which the populations are involved: the phenomena defined as things that are perceived but the constitution and the cause of which are not known—fully or partly, precisely or comprehensively. A scientist, accordingly, categorizes certain series of variation in such a manner as he or she considers suitable to (1) describe a phenomenon or a set of phenomena, (2) explain concomitance or causality regarding the phenomena, or (3) diagnose and predict, on a probability basis, the future possibilities regarding the phenomena.

Classification is thus seen to be inherent in any course of scientific investigation. At the same time, it does not seem on its own merit to require any specific attention by the scientist. Why should we therefore discuss classification as a subject in itself? This is the first question we must answer before proceeding with the methodology of classification.

The question, as the title of the book states, is to be answered in the context of social research. Is it necessary, therefore, to elucidate what is "social research"? Activities labelled as social research have been on the agenda of scientific investigation for a long time and have received academic recognition for more than a century. Social research is, however, seen to be distinguished from economic research, psychological research, historical research, and so on. It thus seems to be the specialized concern of the "discipline" of sociology as the other kinds of research on society are distinguished by their "disciplines."

The field of social research, however, is also seen to cut across the social science "disciplines" and, in that context, a distinction is drawn by the terms *"societal"* and *"social."* This brings us to the controversy on the formulation of the branch of knowledge dealt with by social research: Is it to be characterized as "social science" or "social sciences"?

By the expression "social sciences" we mean that there are different bodies of knowledge organized as different disciplines, i.e., distinctive branches of instruction on, and understanding of, society. The distinctions among such subjects as economics, political science, sociology, psychology, history, etc., can therefore be regarded as of crucial importance while their interrelations attain an auxiliary status as being helpful for developing a comprehensive understanding of society. *Thus the social science subjects would be considered as analogous to each other,* i.e., the subjects are parallel in origin and development out of the world of society they represent.

By the expression "social science," on the other hand, we mean that there is one organized body of knowledge for understanding society and, therefore, there is one discipline. It follows that different aspects of society are examined as *specializations* in the discipline by means of the subject categorization according to economics, political science, sociology, psychology, history, etc. *Therefore, the social science subjects can be considered as homologous in character;* i.e., they have a common origin in the world of society although they are dealt with separately because of the inherent constraints on grasping the whole of society comprehensively as well as precisely. From this perspective, therefore, the interrelationship among the social science subjects would be of primary relevance, their distinctions secondary.

The difference between two formulations may appear as quibbling. One may ask: Does it matter whether we regard the subjects like economics, sociology, political science, etc., as different social science disciplines or as specializations within one discipline of social science? The answer would be that it matters because we should not be equivocal about the *generic* and the *specific* roles of these subjects for understanding society. In the present context, moreover, we must be clear on the scope of social research so as to discuss the role of classification in consolidating our knowledge of those characteristics of variation in the population relating to society as an organized whole; with which we shall be concerned.

In introducing classification as a subject, therefore, we should examine the following two issues: (1) whether the terms "societal" and "social" are to be equated or whether the two must be distinguished while at the same time being interrelated on substantive bases; and (2) how the solution of the first issue resolves the controversy on "social science" or "social sciences," which is reflected in contemporary developments in social research.

Beyond the demarcation of the field of social research in this manner, we should be clear on the focus of our attention in conducting research. Are we concerned with the *search* for information or data (i.e., the information collected with a particular objective in view) or with *research* on the basis of all theoretically possible arrangements of the data space? The methodology of classification will be different according to whether we adopt one or the other mode of investigating social reality, that is, by searching for information or data, or by researching in the data space.

We should, therefore, discuss these two issues of search and research with reference to what we can conceive as (1) the information space, which is constituted of *any* item of information on the *enumerable* properties of all *possible* things constituting a phenomenon or a set of phenomena, and (2) the data space, which is constituted of particular *sets of information* considered as data with respect to the stated objective of examining a phenomenon or a set of phenomena. A data space is thus conceived of as emerging out of the information space in the light of a prior selection of things to represent a phenomenon or a set of phenomena and, correspondingly, the specifically chosen properties of these things.

Our interest may be restricted to a mere description of *what* are the structures and functions of a set of phenomena and *how* the phenomena operate within and among themselves. In that case, we collect and consolidate out of the available information space whatever information we consider relevant in these contexts. Theoretically, this space contains infinite but enumerable points of information. The collated information, therefore, may provide us with a description that would differ from other possible descriptions of the same set of phenomena according to the relevance one attributes to the sets of information collected. For example, Robert Redfield's (1956) portrayal of peasant society was different from that of Oscar Lewis (1951), although both were based on observations of the life in a single Mexican village, Tepoztlan. All these variations, however, may emerge from mere search for information.

In addition to describing a phenomenon, we may wish to explain its causality with reference to an established theory or a hypothesis formulated on the basis of prior knowledge about the phenomenon. In that case, we must answer the *why* question about the phenomenon, which we do by collecting and consolidating the particular information necessary in the *context* of the theory or hypothesis adopted as the yardstick for explanation. We thus now attend to a data space, instead of the overall information space from which it emerges. As one adopts one or another established theory or previously formulated hypothesis as the yardstick for explanation, corresponding data spaces will, of course, emerge from the same information space. In all such cases, however, we are concerned with the search for a particular set of data in the given context.

Thus, so long as our focus of attention in conducting research is restricted to description or explanation on the basis of a theory or hypothesis, we are concerned with mere search for information or data. Each one of us, of course, may deal with different information sets in descriptive investigations, as illustrated by Robert Redfield and Oscar Lewis. We may also deal with different data sets in explanatory studies. In the latter event, the data sets may refer to the same data space for a set of homologous explanations, or to different data spaces (but all belonging to the same information space) for analogous sets of explanations. For example, Karl Marx's descriptions of the Asiatic mode of production vis-a-vis European feudalism refer to the same information space on the phenomenon of feudalism, but their explanations refer to analogous data spaces constituted of "particular kinds of labor", its "craft mastery and consequently property in the instrument of labour", and whether or not the respective kinds of labor equal "property in the conditions of production" (Marx 1964: 101-102; R. Mukherjee 1974: 143ff). Marx's and Max Weber's explanations of the origin, development, and persistence of the Indian caste system, on the other hand, refer to the same data space but different data sets (R. Mukherjee 1979: 66-68). All the same, in all these cases our focus of attention is not research on data sets available from the same or different data spaces but the search for items of information which may be particularized as data.

If, on the other hand, we are interested in diagnosis and answering the *what will be* question of prediction, we must arrange different explanations of a phenomenon in a series of alternate hypotheses. These hypotheses will include also those explanations which are not propagated as established theories but are formulated on the grounds of prior data as tentative hypotheses. As we shall illustrate in Chapter 4, all these hypotheses are to be tested in order to ascertain their relative efficiency in drawing an inference on the probable course of existence, change, or disappearance of the phenomenon in the immediate future. In this case, therefore, we proceed beyond the search for a particular set of data to explain the phenomenon. *We now undertake a course of research with reference to various ways of constructing data-sets from the information space.* As noted, these data sets may belong to one or more data spaces, all of which emerge from the same information space with which the phenomena are concerned.

We are not concerned here with the scope, limitation, and the methodology of different modes of investigation, which are discussed elsewhere (R. Mukherjee, 1979). As we shall point out in this chapter, however, contemporary developments in social research require us to deal with alternate explanations about a phenomenon or a set of phenomena. We should accordingly be engaged in diagnostic investigations on the relative efficiency of these explanations and, therefore, with various ways of constructing data-sets. This means that the procedure of classification must be completely flexible, to accommodate all possible (and not merely all immediately available) variations in datasets. Such is not a necessary condition for the merely explanatory investigations, which are restricted to search for data, and is not even relevant to the descriptive investigations, which are concerned with the search for information. The methodology of classification for dealing with alternate explanations will accordingly be different.

In this connection the title of this book suggests that we should attend to the following three points:

1 What is classification?
2 How should classification be viewed in the context of social research (which follows from an answer to the question: What is social research?)?
3 Why should we discuss classification in the context of research (i.e., research as distinguished from mere search for information or data)?

We propose to discuss these three points in this chapter with specific reference to the present state of our accumulation of knowledge about society and the consequent role of classification in systematizing the process of appraising social reality.

2. CLASSIFICATION

Before we discuss the structure and function of classification, we must specify what we mean by "class" and how a set of classes (and not one class by itself) enters into the process of classification.

A class is formed of a number of specimens exhibiting the same characteristic. The specimens are the constituents of the population with which the classification is concerned. However, we do not always describe the grouping of specimens specified in the above manner as a class. Furthermore, the term has acquired a theoretical meaning in the Marxist schema and in the Weberian understanding of "social class." It is also rather loosely employed to denote a particular group: for example, the nineteenth century social reformers spoke of "the female class" and we speak of the "working classes" or "the working class." In the context of classification, however, "class" must be defined in a precise and, at the same time, comprehensive manner.

We therefore identify, for example, a set of human beings (specimens) engaged in the gathering or production of fish as forming the class of "fishermen." The families (specimens) exhibiting only the conjugal, parental-filial, and/or sibling relations among the family members will be regarded as forming the class of "nuclear families". A number of nation-states (specimens) exhibiting a particular form of consolidation and distribution of political power will, in the same manner, form the class of "people's democracies." And we commonly describe a number of human beings (specimens) exhibiting the same economic, political, cultural, and ideational characteristics as forming the "middle class."

The characteristics that a set of specimens thus display may be treated as constant or as the variable properties of a common trait. Under the first condition, all the specimens form one class; if variability in the trait is known and cannot be totally ignored, we regard the unaccounted properties of the trait as referring to an amorphous class of "residuals." Under the second condition, on the other hand, the specimens will form mutually distinct but analogous classes according to the discerned variable properties of the trait. We shall illustrate the two possibilities with reference to the examples cited.

Fishing may be regarded as the only enterprise of the population in a specified universe with respect to the production of material goods. In that case, the specimens (human beings) classed as fishermen will not have an analogue. Alternatively, in terms of the variable properties of the trait under consideration (viz. the production of material goods), the specimens may be classed as hunters, animal breeders, fishermen, agriculturists, miners, handicraftsmen, workers in machine industries, and so on.

If only the conjugal, parental-filial, and/or sibling forms of kinship characteristics are considered for the families under examination, the specimens will be classed as nuclear or residual. Otherwise, in terms of variable kinship properties of the family members, the families will be classed as nuclear or as different forms of extended family according to the nature and extent of the lineal and affinal relations exhibited by the specimens.

With reference to the consolidation and distribution of power in the nation-states, the specimens may form the class of people's democracies and the residuals. Alternatively, they may be placed in analogous classes of people's democracy, parliamentary (bourgeois) democracy, military dictatorship, theocratic dictatorship, fascist dictatorship, dictatorship of the proletariat, and so on.

And, in the context of a set of economic, political, cultural, and ideational characteristics, the middle class may be examined exclusively or with reference to the upper and lower classes.

The mutually distinct but analogous classes are thus turned into categories of classification with reference to the grouping of specimens in various manners. Classification is therefore conceived to involve the following three operations: (1) placing a specimen in the group of specimens exhibiting the same characteristic of a trait which is common to all such specimens; (2) distinguishing groups of specimens according to variable properties of that trait; and (3) arranging in a serial order the groups thus constituted of specimens.

All the three operations depend on a systematic arrangement of the variable properties of the trait common to the specimens to be classified. The arrangement begins with a *nominal* distinction drawn among the variable properties in order to *identify* the differences as "this" or "that." Next, the arrangement proceeds to the construction of an *ordinal series* of the nominally distinguished properties according to a systematic relationship drawn among the *identity differences*. The arrangement, then, undergoes transformation of the ordinal series into *numbers* (e.g., 1, 2, 3, . . .) in the light of the systematic distinctions drawn among the identity differences of the variable properties as "more" or "less." Finally, the arrangement culminates in an *interval scale of measurement* of variations in the properties of the trait: The arrangement stipulates *unit distance* between successive pairs of ordinal numbers, viz. between 1 and 2, 2 and 3, and so on. Thus the traits used to classify specimens produce the *measure variables* for classification.

An appreciable number of social scientists, however, may not agree with this formulation of measure variables. They are inclined to think that quantification must precede measurement even though the dictionary meaning of the term is to "ascertain extent or quantity of [a thing] by comparison with fixed unit or with object of known size" *(The Concise Oxford Dictionary)*. They disregard this description of measurement and its implication that from the moment we specify the comparable extent (and, not yet, the quantity) of a thing, measurement begins. It begins with the nominal distinctions drawn with respect to a thing, attains precision with the formulation of ordinal series in that respect, becomes unequivocal when the ordinal series is turned into numerals, and, ultimately, becomes comprehensive when the numerical series is transformed into an interval scale. Moreover, besides disregarding the precise and comprehensive meaning of measurement, these social scientists generally take the view that most of the social traits cannot be reduced to quantities, and that even an attempt to order the properties of a trait into a series may jeopardize our awareness of the intrinsic qualities of that trait.

We may point out the fallacy in this sort of argument by citing examples from those branches of knowledge which also, at one time, were regarded as not amenable to quantification and measurement. For example, within the scope of physical anthropology, the skin colors of the human world population was, at one time, nominally distinguished from observation as white, yellow, brown, red, and black. Later, an ordinal series was formed according to a color chart and the series was turned into numerals (e.g., with reference to von Luschan's chart). Eventually, the spectrophotometer came into use to register an interval scale for measurement of the skin color of each and every human being. Nevertheless, we cannot dismiss the argument against non-contextual ordering of a discrete series of variable properties of a trait, ambiguous numeralization of such a series, and the construction thereby of a fallacious scale of measurement.

This must be borne in mind in the context of classification in social research because a large number of the traits with which we are concerned are not quantified. Moreover, we have yet to explore how they can become quantifiable from an unconstrained but systematic ordering of their qualitative properties. We may better appreciate the problem by looking further into the examples cited earlier.

For example, the ordering of enterprises with respect to the production of material goods usually follows from a consideration of the organization of productive forces in society. It is expressed by a series such as cited earlier or as can be extensively constructed from the *Industrial Classification* prepared by the Statistical Office of the United Nations (1968). But whether or not such a series, expressed in codes of several digits, can be translated into an interval scale of measurement is a moot point.

However, corresponding to the UN classification of industries, the International Labor Office (1949, 1958) has prepared a 6–digit code of occupations, i.e., the jobs performed in any and all economic enterprise. An exhaustive ordinal series of occupations can thus be constructed and systematized in terms of, say, the manual and mental components of labor involved in performing the jobs. This moreover may make it easier to formulate an interval scale of measurement through consideration of the intensity of manual and/or mental labor involved in the jobs performed.

We may point out in this context that those who are against quantification in social science (or even producing an ordinal series of variations of a trait) make a nominal distinction between the nonmanual and manual occupations. Furthermore, many of them distinguish the nonmanual occupations as of high grade (e.g., managers, executives, etc.), middle grade (e.g., white collar workers), and of low grade (e.g., janitors). Correspondingly, they distinguish the manual occupations as of high grade (e.g., a foreman in a machine shop), middle grade (e.g., a skilled worker), and of low grade (e.g., an unskilled worker). A more detailed ordering of occupations is also sometime attempted. Clearly, the classification of occupations follows the sequence from the nominal to the ordinal and, possibly, to the interval scale of measurement.

On the other hand, an ordinal series of nation-states with respect to the consolidation and distribution of political power has yet to be formulated systematically and comprehensively. The substance of the trait, however, refers to the nature of the consolidation of political power, as we have briefly indicated. The trait is also characterized according to the flow of political power from the center (constitutional and actual) to the subjects or citizens, and with respect to the interest groups the subjects or citizens form in this context in the nation-states and for their world perspectives.

We notice that these distinctions in the classification of nation-states apply to the First, Second, and Third Worlds. Such distinctions are also drawn on the same grounds within the Third World, between, say India and Tanzania, Tanzania and Argentina, Argentina and Ethiopia, Ethiopia and Iraq, Iraq and Malaysia, and so on. Differences are correspondingly noted in the Second World between, say, Czechoslovakia and Poland, Poland and Yugoslavia, Yugoslavia and Albania; in the First World between, say, the United States and France. And a sharp contrast is drawn in these respects between the United States and the Soviet Union, or the Soviet Union and China. The preparation of an ordinal series of nation-states and, eventually, an interval scale among them according to the nature and extent of their centralization of power may not therefore be an impossible proposition.

As regards the classification of family structures, an ordinal series according to the kinship characteristics of the family members has been formulated in a rather exhaustive manner (Murdock *et al.* 1950). We shall show in Chapter 3 how such qualitative demarcations in a series from being discrete can be made virtually continuous. We shall also demonstrate how the course of classification can sequentially pass from quality into quantity without affecting the intrinsic merit of this trait for classification. And we shall examine how the kinship network of family members can be transformed into an interval scale for measuring the kinship distances among them.

We find, on the other hand, with respect to the middle and analogous social classes that there are sharp differences among social scientists regarding the formulation of an efficient ordinal series. By definition, the middle class falls in between other classes. It can be distinguished in detail but always with reference to these classes. The Weberians differ from the Marxists in thus ordering a series of classes. Among the Marxists also there are controversies over the distinctions to be drawn among the national, comprador and lumpen bourgeoisie, on class categorization of the "peasant community," the equivalence of sharecroppers and agricultural wage-earners as representing the agricultural proletariat, and so on. The construction of a precise and comprehensive interval scale of measurement for the Marxist class distinctions is, therefore, a remote possibility at the moment.

These examples tell us that *quantifiability* of the traits employed for classification is an important issue to be examined. We may note in this context the pertinent remark of Lord Kelvin: "When you can measure what you are speaking about and express it in numbers, you know something about it, but when you cannot measure it, when you cannot express it in numbers, your knowledge is of a meagre and unsatisfactory kind" (quoted in Mahalanobis 1950: 7). The sequential development of the measure variable from the nominal to the ordinal, and then to the interval scale, is therefore of basic importance to any form of classification, with respect to social or any other kind of research.

At the same time, however, we should bear in mind that quantification of a trait and the construction of an interval scale of measurement on that basis will not automatically determine the placement of a specimen in one class and, correspondingly, the identificiation of a series of mutually distinct but analogous classes. The *context* of classification is as important as the measure of classification, and both must be considered in as many ways as possible and necessary. We shall illustrate this point with reference to a trait which is formulated as measurable by an interval scale and of which the scope of measurement is virtually limitless because of decimalization of the numerals employed as the measuring quantities.

Income in any denomination (e.g., dollars, pounds, francs, yen, rupees, etc.) represents a continuous variable distributed on an interval scale of equal distances between the points of measurement. The placement of specimens (e.g., individual persons, their respective families, or any other relevant corporate body) on these points will therefore be precise and unequivocal along the scale of measurement. The placement will also be comprehensive because the interval scale will accommodate any form of graduation between the points of measurement within any range of their distribution.

Now, if the all the points in a particular income range contain equal numbers of specimens, that range will form an income class in accordance with the stated definition of class. That class, however, can become a category of classification only in the context of other mutually distinguished ranges of income or of the same range but with reference to other sets of the same sort of specimens. As we have explained, classification comes into operation when the characteristic exhibited by a class of specimens is a variable with respect to other corresponding classes of specimens. But, in this case, income as the measure variable has turned out to be a constant with respect to all the specimens examined within a particular range. *Clearly, the identification of the contextual reference (or references) for the range (or set of ranges) is indispensable for the production of a set of classes with respect to a measure variable.*

If, therefore, all or some of the points in an income range are represented by unequal numbers of specimens, the measure variable of income will operate to demarcate income classes and denote mutually distinct but analogous groups of specimens. In that case, however, the demarcation of income classes requires that we identify cut-off points within the range of income distribution so as to produce groupings of points representing relatively homogeneous characteristics of the specimens within the respective groups (classes), and increasing heterogeneity between the groups of specimens as these groups are placed farther and farther apart along the scale of measurement. But on what basis can we ascertain homogeneity within the respective groups of specimens and heterogeneity among the groups?

We may proceed mechanically by grouping equal numbers of income-points (e.g., 1-10, 11-20, etc.) or equal numbers of specimens (e.g., 15) located at so many adjacent income-points. But where the same number of income-points contain the same number of specimens (e.g., income-classes 1-10, 11-20, etc., each contain 15 specimens), classification would lose its usefulness because it will merely establish that income as the trait for classification behaves as a constant with reference to the 10-point gradations in the income scale; it does not register variability in the numerical placement of the specimens on the scale.

This means that classification by cut-off points becomes operative when, within the total range of income, the income-points contain unequal numbers of specimens. This is what usually happens with respect to a measure variable although it may, of course, contain the same number of specimens at certain points of measurement. In such a situation, what will be the rationale behind the formation of income classes? Can it be elicited from the income distribution itself?

Clusters of specimens may be located at certain income-points. In that case, an analysis of these clusters is useful to appreciate the nature of the income distribution. By themselves, however, the clusters will not present a systematic and comprehensive grouping of the specimens into mutually distinct and analogous classes.

The cut-off points to identify clusters in the income distribution are a matter of subjective judgment by the researchers. Should the extreme points in income distribution, accepted by one researcher as forming a cluster, be left out by another because, in the latter's opinion, these points are poorly represented by numbers of specimen? Should the small cluster formed of a few income-points be enlarged to include other points to make a substantial block? Do the poorly represented income-points in the middle of a cluster suggest the formation of two or more clusters from one? These and allied questions about classification are pertinent to the analysis of variation in income distribution as the trait for classification. And they indicate that classification must precede analysis.

In order to answer such questions, we must arrange the cut-off points in the income distribution in many different ways. These ways are suggested by various questions and indicated by the rationale which gives rise to the questions. We must therefore keep room for all possibilities in the identification of cut-off points and, thus, for the grouping of income-points in all possible ways to form income cluster classes. Therefore, systematic but variable classification of the income-points must precede cluster analysis.

However, even if we systematically identify clusters in this manner, they may not comprehensively categorize all the points in the income distribution and thus may not form a set of mutually distinguished but analogous classes. Gaps are likely to occur among the clusters of income-points, which will comprise variable numbers of scattered income-points and represent variable numbers of specimens. A gap of many income-points may include a scattering of even more specimens than in a cluster; yet all these gaps will merely be a negative analogue to the adjacent clusters.

We may, therefore, conceive an income distribution as composed of small spaces by extending the boundaries of respective clusters to adjacent points in the gaps. In other ways also we may form *continuous* series of specimen clusters or segments. The marked-off spaces will systematically and comprehensively cover the total range of income distribution and, therefore, denote a set of categories for classification. But, as for cluster formation, how will these spaces be demarcated?: Surely not on the merits of the income distribution under consideration.

We may cite, in this context, an appropriate example from biological classification. In biometric research on human remains we may come across some bones (e.g., the pelvic or jaw bones) which are not definitely known to belong to a male or a female. The bones are not found associated with undisputed evidence (e.g., some cultural material in situ, like fragments of a dress worn exclusively by a male or a female) from which we can deduce the respective sexes of the persons they came from. In such a situation what is usually done is to allot their sexual classification according to certain characteristics of the bones (e.g., the prominence of the iliac crest in the pelvic bone) which are known to be particularly marked in one sex and not the other.

Here we find an analogy to income cluster analysis and notice that the *clusters are subsumed under known characteristics of the male and female classes.* The anatomical variations among the sexually unidentified set of bones may be measured in minute detail. But, by themselves, the measure variables thus brought into account do not indicate the sex of those who left these bones. *The context of classification lies beyond the bones under examination and refers to predetermined bone characteristics of males and females.*

We may extend the analogy to small-space analysis in cases where the bones of indeterminate sex belong to such a set that for an appreciable number of bones in that set the sex is definitely known or can be deduced from associated cultural or other kinds of appropriate evidence. In that case, the spaces close to males' or females' bone measurement values will be known for some bones in terms of sexually differentiated central tendencies and ranges of metric value dispersion of the bones' relevant characteristics. By inference, therefore, the bones of indeterminate sex are placed in one of the two spaces according to their metric values for the same characteristics; that is, according to whether these values fall within the wider range of known dispersion and central tendency for one or the other sex (see, for instance, Mukherjee, Rao, and Trevor 1955: 103–111). *We notice, however, that in this case of small-space analysis, also, the demarcation of the spaces is dependent on properties beyond those under consideration, viz. bones of indeterminate sex.*

Despite these explanations and examples, it may appear that such small spaces can be identified in exclusive reference to the measure variable by reducing to a uniform base (such as, on a percentage basis) the distribution of (1) the specimens and (2) the properties of the trait for classification. The appearance, however, would be deceptive. *A critical examination will show that that which seems to be the exclusive role of the measure variable hides, in fact, the concurrent role of the context variable.* Let us illustrate this contingency with reference to our example of income as the trait for classification.

As we shall discuss in Chapter 2, a concentration curve of income (Figure 2.1) can be drawn by considering the percentages of specimens (p_x) possessing x or more income and the percentages of total income (q_x) possessed by this percentage of specimens. We shall also show that the curve can be interpreted as composed of linear segments connected at different angles, so that these segments will denote a set of complementary and contradictory categories of specimens. It would thus appear that small spaces in the income distribution can be identified in exclusive reference to the measure variable by means of appropriate manipulation of the points of measurement.

We notice, however, that the continuous series of categories evolved in this manner refers as much to the grouping of the income-points as to the division of the measure variable according to minute details. And, if we look critically into the manner of manipulating the trait for classification, we find that the process of grouping is provided with a specific context by means of the relation between p_x and q_x. *In other words, the reduction of the distribution of specimens and of the income-points to a uniform base (as, for example, by relating the percentage distributions of p_x and q_x) means that the context of classification is taken into account simultaneously with the measure of classification.*

Unlike the example above, the context variable and the measure variable do not usually synchronize although they refer to the same trait for classification. The measure variable is concerned with more and more precise, unequivocal, and comprehensive *division* of the variable properties of the trait in order that the specimens may be placed in respective class categories without any ambiguity or constraint. The context variable is correspondingly concerned with how these classes can be distinguished with respect to the specimens and, therefore, with the *collection* of the variable properties of the trait. *"Divide" and "collect" thus form two directions of variation in the properties of a trait, the coordination of which is the role of classification.*

There are, however, tendencies among social scientists to emphasize one of these two at the expense of the other, by stressing either quality or quantity with respect to the traits for classification. Those who stress the aspect of quality confine themselves to typological classification, which is inefficient, as we shall show in Chapter 2. *Those, on the other hand, who stress the aspect of quantity tend to equate classification with analysis and thus forfeit the specific relevance of classification,* as we have pointed out. We must bear in mind the following sequence: Analysis follows from classification, leads to a more unequivocal classification in the light of the results of the analysis, and classification, in its turn, provides the basis for an ever more refined course of analysis.

This sequence was clearly underlined by the scientists who pioneered the study of variations in any aspect of life and living. It was also strictly adhered to by the successors of the pioneers, who enlarged the scope of studying variations from univariate to multivariate analysis. This is attested by the construction and use of various analytical tools, like Karl Pearson's Coefficient of Racial Likeness, which was employed to distinguish racial groups, P. C. Mahalanobis's D^2-statistic applied to ethnographic and various other forms of societal classification, Paul Lazarsfeld's latent structure analysis, which is currently applied to groupings of individuals, etc. As M.G. Kendall and A. Stuart stated (1966: 336):

> The problem of classification, as we define the word, is one of determining from empirical evidence whether individuals "group" or "cluster." There are two different ways of looking at this problem, corresponding to the *two kinds of space* in which we represent the data.
> (a) Given, as usual, a *p* x *n* vector of observations, let us consider the *n* sample points in the *p*-dimensional Euclidean space determined by the *p* variables. If these points, to *some acceptable definition,* fall into clearly distinguishable groups, we may say that the *n* individuals may be *classified* into those groups. Their "nearness" is to be considered as a function of the variate values which they bear.
> (b) In the alternative *p*-space embedded in an *n*-space the variables are represented by vectors. There is some interest in how far these vectors cluster, as we have seen in canonical analysis. In this case we are concerned with the extent to which the *variables cluster, not the individuals.* [emphasis added]

At present, however, some confusion seems to prevail over the distinction between classification and analysis. In a monograph on cluster analysis prepared on behalf of the Social Science Research Council of Great Britain, B. Everitt stated that "the terms cluster analysis and classification will be used interchangeably for describing methods of analysis which seek to group individuals," although "Kendall and Stuart propose that the term *cluster analysis* be used for techniques which group variables, and *classification* for techniques which group individuals" (Everitt 1974: 1; emphasis in original). Interestingly, in the context of defining a cluster, the author mentioned later that (ibid.: 43):

> The common feature of most proposed definitions is their vague and circular nature, in the sense that terms such as *similarity, distance, alike,* etc., are used in the definition, but are themselves undefined. What is clear, however, is that there is no universal agreement on what constitutes a cluster: in fact, it is probably true that no single definition is sufficient. Indeed, it has even been suggested (Bonner, 1964) that the ultimate criterion for evaluating the meaning of such terms as cluster or similarity is the value judgement of the user.

We have also seen how, like cluster analysis, small-space analysis cannot supplant classification as the repository of prior knowledge about the context variable. And we find this to be equally true with regard to multiple classification analysis (MCA), although the label seems to supersede classification as a theme. F.M. Andrews et al. clearly stated in describing the uses of MCA that it "is a technique for examining the interrelationships between several predictor variables and a dependent variable within the context of an additive model," and that "its chief advantage over conventional dummy variable regression is a more convenient input arrangement and understandable output that focuses on *sets* of predictors such as occupation groups, and on the extent and direction of the adjustments made for intercorrelations among the sets of predictors" (1973: 1, 2).

All of this means that with respect to the population of a schematically conceived universe of variation, classification cannot be precluded by analysis. The role of classification is to consolidate our knowledge in such a manner that the best possible link can be established between prior knowledge and the posterior knowledge to be obtained from further investigation. As should be clear from the foregoing discussion, this requires a precise, unequivocal, and comprehensive accounting of the context and measure variables, and the efficient coordination of any set of these two kinds of variables. Neither of the two kinds should be unsystematically structured or unilaterally stressed in the procedure of classification. In order that classification can fulfill its role, we should therefore examine it as a subject in itself and discuss its methodology in the perspective of social research.

It follows that we should discuss next the specific implications of social research, beginning with the necessity to draw a distinction between the terms "societal" and "social".

3 SOCIETAL AND SOCIAL

Social, by consensus among social scientists, deals with the characteristics of human society. Should it, however, refer to any and all *societal* characteristics? Usually "social" refers to those characteristics which hold society together and denote it as an entity (i.e., a thing in existence). Controversies exist, however, regarding the limits of this definition, for society is need-based and all its manifestations must meet one or another of its needs to exist.

Conventionally, therefore, *social* is a *residual* subject, dealing with those characteristics of human society which cannot be labelled prima facie as economic, demographic, ecological, psychological, political, cultural, ideological, and so on. This we notice in spontaneous classifications of societal phenomena by many social scientists, and from the categorization of various kinds of statistics relating to these phenomena by the UN and other international and nation-state agencies. However, lacking a precise comprehension of what is *social* and how it is to be distinguished from, and at the same time related to, all that is *societal,* the coverage of residuals must also vary. The convention is sometimes to consider all those societal phenomena as social which are not economic, demographic, political, nor psychological in character. These variations create the problems of *identification, duplication,* and *conceptualization* of the social phenomena out of all that is societal.

For example, is the occupation of a person (i.e., the nature of the job performed by him or her in a sector of the economy like agriculture, manufacturing, etc.) an economic or a social attribute? The spontaneous answer might be that it is economic. But, then, why do we regard occupational mobility as a social phenomena? Correspondingly, does a coresident and commensal kingroup form a social unit of the family as an institution, or is it an economic unit of consumption in all societies and of production in peasant societies? Is class as defined in the Marxist schema an economic, political, psychological, or social entity in the context of the formulations of "class by itself" and "class for itself"? Should we consider the "youth revolt," a "tribal" movement, or an ethnic upsurge as a social or political phenomenon? These are all problems of *identification* in classification.

More examples can be cited, and it may be noted that often we attempt to bypass this quandary by using the hyphenated labels "socioeconomic," "sociopolitical," "socioreligious," "social psychological," "sociodemographic," and so on. But the problem remains of identifying that which is social. The family, for instance, may be the medium for various manifestations in society that would be appropriately categorized as economic, demographic, psychological, religious, etc. Class, defined in terms of relations of production and property arising out of a particular mode of production and the state of development of the productive forces, appears to be an economic entity; nonetheless, its political, ideological, and cultural connotations are clearly expressed in present-day societies. The youth revolt, a "tribal" movement, or an ethnic upsurge is the expression of, and it releases simultaneously, sets of variations that can be categorized as economic, cultural, political, psychological, and so on. In all such instances our attention is drawn to the particular nuances of the societal phenomena and not to the phenomena themselves.

If we do not direct our attention exclusively to one aspect or another, the problem of identification is transformed into the problem of *duplication,* that is, the same entity or phenomenon is labelled under two or more distinct headings. This we find in social science literature. Particularly in the statistical handbooks, both national and international, the size, structure, and distribution of population, births and deaths, migration, etc., are labelled as either demographic or social; sanitation, health, and nutrition fall under medical or social categories; employment, labor conditions, level of living with reference to income, expenditure, savings, and investment are regarded as economic or social; crime and justice fall under social or judicial labels; and even welfare, which appears to be entirely social since it is usually qualified as "social welfare," the economists claim by propagating the notion of "welfare economics."

Then there is the problem of *conceptualization.* For instance, can we conceive a phenomenon to be distinctly social and not economic, demographic, cultural, psychological, and so on, even though the distinction appears to be clear-cut? Education is universally regarded as a social phenomenon because its objective is the advancement of learning in society and, thus, an induced process of socialization for individuals. But the establishment of educational institutions and facilities is also an enterprise for entrepreneurs in many nation-states, and this may not be less profitable to them than establishing some manufacturing industries.

Appositely, while an educational establishment advances one form of learning in society, a manufacturing establishment provides another, through the various kinds of work relationships, complementary among the large number of workmates, and contradictory in terms of the bosses and the underlings. In intensity, coverage, and/or quality, the latter form of learning is less available in an agricultural community, a point which promotes consideration of industrialization as a social phenomenon. Should we, then, consider educational and manufacturing institutions as social or as economic entities? Alternatively, must we avoid the issue by labelling both as "socioeconomic?"

One may be accused of ridiculing the sanctity of education by linking it with mundane matters like the manufacture of goods instead of learned persons. But the multiple nuances of societal phenomena already illustrated occur at the same level of our comprehension and analysis of social reality as in other instances. For example, occupation, income, expenditure, consumption, savings, and investment are accepted as mutually correlated economic variables. However, empirical research has shown that with a unit rise in expenditure level the consumption pattern varies by the ethnocultural characteristics of a society, and the savings and investment pattern varies with an identical unit rise in income level (Ganguli and Sanyal 1968: 811–814). Clearly, these variations are not dictated by any single standarad subsumed under "rational behavior of economic man." Should we, then, conceptualize these variables as related to socioeconomic phenomena?

Industrialization does not involve a mere occupational change for the people moving from an agricultural to an industrial area. It affects their family organization and associations, demographic patterns, culture, politics, psychology: in sum, their way of life. Correspondingly, given the definition of an urban area, urbanization is prima facie a matter of density of population, their municipal organization, and the virtual absence of agriculture among the constituent population. Hence, just as industrialization is sometimes labelled a socioeconomic phenomenon, should we characterize urbanization as a sociodemographic phenomenon?

A detailed scrutiny of many such societal phenomena raises the question: What is social about them—is everything that happens in society to be regarded as social or is the term meant to refer only to certain *specific* characteristics of societal phenomena? The first alternative would foreclose any discussion on what is social by removing the distinction between societal and social; but in the second alternative the distinction may be useful for appraising reality comprehensively in terms of its many facets. We should, therefore, search for clues from the second alternative for defining what is "social."

We notice, accordingly, that societies may be identified by certain criteria applied singly or in any combination: for example, by people inhabiting a common territory, their shared political authority, ethnicity, language, religion, type of economic activity, way of life, and so on. These criteria distinguish one configuration of human society from another and, therefore, may be regarded as *external* to the definition of society. It follows that each configuration of human society identified by its external criteria must possess certain *internal* criteria to be characterized as a society. It also follows that these criteria must be common for all configurations of human society in order to define human society itself. Hence, these common criteria for all societies should provide us with the clues for conceiving and defining what is social.

The search for the common criteria should be based on answering the question *how* society operates, rather than *why* society is formed. The second question would prompt us to examine the basic motivation of individuals to congregate and form society. The drives behind this motivation can be enumerated, as hunger, sex, security, etc. Opinion differs on their relative importance or even the necessity to consider one or another of them. In any case, an answer to the "why" question would be concerned with the *identity* (i.e., the absolute sameness) of human society, and not with the *commonality* of different configurations of that society. The answer to the "how" question, on the other hand, is concerned with the existence of different configurations of human society as *similar but not the same,* and with the changes occurring in the course of their existence, but always as representing human society in one form or another. The internal criteria for characterizing society therefore emerge from the following facts:

1. To form society there must be interactions among persons in order for them to coexist. The nature and intensity of interactions would, of course, vary according to the *meanings* attached to them; however, for society to exist, the variations cannot be at the level of spontaneity or personal idiosyncracies. Actions of this sort cannot create precise and complementary meanings among the interacting persons. Such actions would have a personal relevance, but their effect on society would be momentary or marginal. Even charismatic actions fail to affect society unless, by repetition and concerted exposition of their intentions, they acquire precise and sustained meanings among the interacting persons. When actions thus convey unequivocal and comprehensive meanings to the interacting persons in a sustained manner, they become *social actions.*

2. Meaningfully repetitive social actions are necessary not only for the existence of each particular configuration of human society but also for its change and even disintegration. For all these purposes, however, the social actions which are homologous (i.e., have a common origin) form a distinctive set. At the same time, all homologous sets of social actions form mutually distinct but analogous (parallel) sets. Even the asocial *sadhus* (holy men) of India perform homologous and analogous (but not disparate) sets of social actions among themselves and with their disciples.

3. Each of these sets of social actions is distinguished as a behavior pattern; for example, the parental-filial, intra-caste, and inter-caste behavior patterns, patterns of class behavior within and beyond nation-states, the fraternal or hostile behavior patterns among the *sadhus* and their paternalistic behavior patterns with their disciples, the patterns of behavior among the nation-states—of which a complex instance is found between the East and the West Pakistanis during 1947—70 and 1970—71, and since then as Bangladeshis and Pakistanis.

4. The behavior patterns may be colored by the personal behavior of individuals (e.g., one father may be a disciplinarian vis-a-vis his son and another not so), but that does not alter the basic character of the respective patterns. On the contrary, once a pattern is established through a process of learning—of which the social actions are *initiators* and also the products in the sense that they *anticipate* the expected behavior of the interacting person—the pattern can determine or guide the interactions of even those persons who are not always in contact. Such cases we notice in the condescending behavior of, say, a Bengali *Babu* (gentleman) toward a *chasi* (cultivator) or of a white toward a colored person.

5. Through direct and indirect interactions, the behavior patterns thus reflect the internal articulations of one configuration of society, its linkage with other such configurations, and ultimately all of humanity. Changes in society or its wholesale transformation are recorded in its changed and/or newly emerged behavior patterns. Accordingly, with reference to "social behavior," which these behavior patterns represent, we understand society as an entity and appreciate the nature and extent of variation in societies identified by their external criteria.

6. It follows that the external criteria also are the expression of one or another range of social behaviors, the characteristics of which are less variable *within* one configuration of society and more variable *between* the homologous and analogous configurations. Social behavior, therefore, can provide the basis for us to define "social" and draw its interrelations with the other kinds of societal phenomena. To ascertain this possibility, we should examine the position of social behavior vis-a-vis other internal criteria for characterizing society as an entity.

Social behavior is not a matter of observation. It is a matter of deduction or inference from the observed or assumed social actions between specific social actors as reference points. Father and son, mother and son, father and daughter, and mother and daughter represent reference points denoting the parental-filial behavior patterns, for example. The Bangladeshis and the Pakistanis represent reference points for denoting their behavior patterns as "brothers" in the past, as "enemies" recently, and as "friends" at present. For centuries the bourgeoisie and the proletariat have represented two distinctive patterns of contradictory and, at the same time, complementary social behavior through their respective social actions.

All such empirical reference points (i.e., the specifically designated social actors) for denoting varied kinds of social behavior must be composed of more than one pair of persons. Even the simple form of father-son behavior does not refer to only one father and one son but to fathers and sons. Like others, this behavior pattern may vary over place, time, and people, but the variation would be as "fathers" and "sons." Similarly, a behavior pattern may wither away, newly emerge, or replace a previous one; however, in all such cases social behavior is represented by distinctive groups of persons and not by lone, stray individuals. This means that the reference points for social behavior are presented by "social groups."

The *social groups* are identified in terms of precise relationships between them: between fathers and sons, citizens in the two parts of earlier Pakistan or now in Pakistan and Bangladesh, the bourgeoisie and the proletariat in terms of the relations of production and property, and so on. These relationships are not personal or fortuitous in nature; instead, by summarizing distinctive kinds of behavior among the relevant social groups, they are to be labelled "social relationships."

The *social relationships,* in their turn, emerge from and are sustained through distinctive agencies of human effort and achievement, which are known as "institutions" in society. These agencies not only hold society together but also consolidate further the existing social relationships or supersede them by others. The parental-filial relationship has emerged through the institution of marriage and is regulated and sustained through the institution of the family; however, this relationship may be consolidated more by the institution of monogamous than polygamous marriage and the institution of the nuclear than the extended family. The indigenous political institutions in British India created new social relationships among the people with the partition of the subcontinent in 1947, and the political institutions of Pakistan led to further alterations and the current consolidation of some varieties of social relationships among the peoples of India and Bangladesh and the disruption of certain social relationships among the peoples of Bangladesh and Pakistan.

The institutions may thus be conceived of as forming homologous or analogous sets, and leading to the emergence of new institutions in society. The institution of marriage incorporates monogamous, polygynous, and polyandrous marriages and companiate marriage in many parts of the world, since the 1960s particularly. The institution of the family includes the nuclear, partilineal-patrivirilocal, matrilineal-matriutrolocal, and various other kinds of extended family—not all of which are clearly deciphered yet. The institution of caste in India was regarded by Marx (1964: 101-102) to be analogous to the institution of feudalism which, on a world scale, has been superseded by the institution of capitalism and is expected in the Marxist schema to be replaced by the institution of communism. Clearly, in the light of facts and expectations, institutions are the source of internal criteria by which to characterize society as an entity and to sponsor changes in it—even beyond one or another of its configurations as identified by the external criteria.

The institutions are, therefore, usually regarded as the sponsors of various kinds of societal phenomena and, according to the presumed essential characteristics of the sponsoring institutions, these phenomena are classified as economic, political, cultural, religious, etc. Some of these phenomena are also classified as social, exclusively or in duplication, in the sense of holding a particular society together while also changing it with respect to structure, function, and process. We have noted how inadequate and inefficient this classification procedure is, and we are now in a position to point out why it happens. *The problem emerges from the fact that any institution can refer to various behavior patterns, which, according to our accepted categorization of most of the social science subjects, may fall under more than one subject.*

The problem can be removed through our understanding of the role of social behavior. As noted, each behavior pattern, i.e., a *form* of social behavior, refers to a homologous set of social actions. A social action, i.e., sustained and meaningful interactions among persons located at corresponding reference points, can occur only with respect to societal characteristics: the interactions can neither emerge nor operate in a vacuum. The societal characteristics are categorized so as to represent one or another social science subject. *An unequivocal link is thus established between social behavior and the social science subjects through the relations between social actions (for the former) and societal characteristics (for the latter).*

As pointed out, however, some societal characteristics create problems if placed under only one particular social science subject, because their manifest characteristics are seen to cover more than one subject. *This implies that all societal characteristics and all the social science subjects should not be considered as at one and the same level of our analysis and comprehension of social reality.* We notice, at the same time, that the distinction in levels does not emerge automatically from either the societal characteristics or the social science subjects. This is why we face the already mentioned problems of identification, duplication, and conceptualization. The course of establishing the distinction and interrelation between the levels must therefore be engineered by a *linkage phenomenon*. As we shall explain in the following pages, social behavior is that linkage phenomenon which determines the *levels of our analysis and comprehension* of social reality in such a manner that those matters in social science usually regarded as all-inclusive or residual maintain this character but under precise conditions and not haphazardly.

4. SPECIALIZATION AND INTEGRATION

In order to demonstrate the role of social behavior in the process of social science specialization, we should first examine the *core characteristics* of those subjects not regarded as all-inclusive or residual. We should bear in mind that *specialization means more and more precise, unequivocal, and comprehensive appreciation of the characteristics of a "population."* That population can be conceived of as *schematically* representing a particular facet of reality and as incorporated in one of the mutually exclusive social science subjects at the *primary level* of our analysis and comprehension of social reality. That population, however, can also be conceived of as representing the basic characteristics of the total reality and, in that context, incorporated in an *all-inclusive* social science subject considered at *secondary and higher levels* of our analysis of social reality. The comprehensive reality can then be understood by the integration of its facets with respect to its basic characteristics.

For purposes of explaining the relation of particular facets with the basic characteristics of social reality, we should note that many forms of social behavior are clearly categorized with reference to their respective facets and as falling under different social science subjects. As these subjects are schematically distinguished from one another, a *set* of various forms of social behavior, homologous in the context of a social science subject, will be of one particular type and, thus, belong to one *class.* Analogous classes of different types of social behavior (each type being composed of various forms) can be identified. It follows that social behavior can be conceived as a *classificatory variable* with respect to the social science subjects and with reference to homologous sets of different *forms* of the same type of social behavior and analogous sets of different *types* of social behavior.

By proceeding on this basis, we shall be able to distinguish some particular homologous forms of social behavior as of such a character that they can, as residuals, be left out, for the moment, from the process of categorization. We shall see that these forms of social behavior are of a type not registered at what we have designated as the primary level of our analysis of social reality. We shall also see that while providing the scope for specialization in a particular social science subject, this type of social behavior indicates the integration of the different recognized social science subjects. And we shall find that this process of integration occurs at higher levels of our analysis and comprehension of social reality. The distinction and interrelation between the societal and the social characteristics can thus be drawn unequivocally. Let us illustrate this schema.

Certain behavior patterns are sui generis to the production, distribution, and consumption of material goods and services. These patterns can be represented by reference points identified from such societal characteristics as varieties of industry (sectors of the economy), occupations (jobs performed), and consumer groupings (such as households). Other societal characteristics become evident at subsequent stages of our increasing understanding of the role of production, distribution, and consumption of material goods and services in society. As in the case of those already cited, all these characteristics may allow us to draw nominal distinctions, register ordinal series of variation, or record the interval scales of measurement among their respective sets of properties; for example, with reference to conditions of work, the nature of benefit from work, roles of capital and labor, profit mechanism, income, expenditure, savings, investments, price structure, rates of productivity and profit, capital-output ratio, and so on. All these societal characteristics will also represent different forms of social behavior among the relevant reference points. The different forms of social behavior, however, will each be a particular type of human relations to material goods and services. This type of social behavior falls, by consensus, within the purview of economics as a social science subject.

In the same manner we can identify the classificatory variables referring to the social science subject labelled "politics," "government," or "political science." One such variable represents the societal characteristics of the centralization of the State authority through appropriate bodies and the peripheralization of that authority through the corporate bodies formed by the people. The center–periphery relationships of this kind of authority can be examined, by means of appropriate societal characteristics, for world society and for one or more of its configurations. In all such cases we deal, by consensus, with the political life of the people. The different forms of social behavior registered by this aspect of life are therefore enumerated with reference to international power blocs, different forms of government, the characteristics of "opposition," the nature of law and order, and so on. Thus we are concerned with political social behavior, which is different from but analogous to the economic type.

Similarly we can classify another kind of social behavior that expresses the mental characteristics of individuals. Thus classified, the different forms of such social behavior will allow us to draw nominal distinctions between "normal" and "deviant" behavior; register ordinal series of variation among neurotic, psychotic, paranoid, and corresponding forms of deviant behavior; and record the interval scales of measurement of behavior patterns with respect to intelligence, aptitude, personality, etc. All such variations in behavior patterns will, however, be treated as homologous and as referring to the societal characteristics which, by consensus, fall under the social science subject of psychology.

Certain social science subjects seem to be defined by those societal characteristics that do not refer to particular forms of social behavior. Demography appears to be an appropriate example as its core characteristics refer to the growth, decline, and movement of human populations. The subject yields many different societal characteristics at successive stages of understanding the core characteristics of birth, death, and migration. For example, we become concerned with the sex ratio, age-grades, fertility rates, life expectancy, including those that are sex- and/or age-specific, internal or external migration, rural and urban population, and so on. All these characteristics, which are measured by continuous variables, do not seem to require any consideration of different forms of social behavior.

However, as we have pointed out in the context of income distribution, the characteristics of a continuous variable acquire meaning in terms of the cut-off points in its distribution. The cut-off points formulate the definition of social groups, the behavior patterns of which indicate differences in their demographic characteristics. The growth, decay, and movement of populations are thus understood as high, low, or stationary (meaning "none" in the appropriate context) with reference to different social groups that are characterized in this manner, in whatever context the groups are formed. For example, the Italian population grows faster than the French, Indian Muslims register higher fertility than Hindus, the rate of suicide is higher among Scandinavians than among East Europeans, migration leads to a faster growth of urban than rural population in the Third World, and so on.

We may point out, furthermore, that sex- and/or age-specific life expectancy or other similar characteristics do not indicate a mere biological phenomenon. Various forms of social behavior are implied in that context, too; for example, the higher mortality of Indian females than males until they become older, the higher life expectancy of Americans than Indians, the greater mobility of men than women in the Third World, and so on.

Different forms of social behavior are thus seen to be built into the subject matter of demography, although the characteristics it is concerned with may appear to be biological and, even if regarded as societal, seem to be arid and abstract. It can be seen at the same time that while differing in their forms, the types of social behavior with which demography deals are analogous to those of economics, politics, and psychology.

It follows from the above that we may conceive of other mutually distinct but analogous types of social behavior and delegate each type to a social science subject, provided that: (1) the societal characteristics, to which each type of social behavior is related, fall unequivocally and completely under one, and only one, of these subjects; and (2) the forms of social behavior with which these characteristics are concerned do not refer to any other characteristic falling under the purview of another social science subject. In other words, there is no ambiguity in distinguishing the social science subjects in terms of societal characteristics so long as the following three conditions are satisfied: (1) the distinctive character of each type of social behavior, (2) the homologous character of the forms of social behavior under each type, and (3) the distinctive character of the societal characteristics with which the gamut of behavior patterns under (1) and (2) is concerned.

Viewed in this manner, the immense scope of specialization in each of the social science subjects is thus brought to account, without affecting the mutually distinct but analogous character of all these subjects. When the above three conditions are met, we have the following situation:

1. The measure variables, as explained earlier, are given by the societal characteristics. These are formed of one characteristic each or of a combination of several, but always within the limits of a set of homologous characteristics.

2. The context variables, as follows from the discussion on cut-off points in income distribution, are determined from the forms of social behavior. These variables distinguish social groups and classify the specimens in various ways according to the properties of the measure variables considered to denote homologous behavior patterns. In representing the sets of behavior patterns, therefore, the context variables can occur singly or jointly but always in exclusive reference to the type of social behavior with which the social science subject is concerned.

This situation thus specifies a particular level of analysis and comprehension of the social science subjects, namely the primary one for appraising social reality. At the same time, this arrangement leaves room for specialization in each subject by means of successive *orders of variation* registered by the relevant societal characteristics and behavior patterns, i.e., in accordance with the varied constitution of the corresponding measure and context variables.

We have indicated with reference to economics, politics, psychology, and demography the possibilities of considering the measure and context variables in this manner, that is, at successively higher orders of variation in their characteristics while remaining exclusively within the terms of reference of the respective social science subjects. *We should note, furthermore, that these characteristics of the measure and context variables can be cross-classified with reference to different social science subjects without affecting the exclusive constitution of the respective sets of measure and context variables.* For example, the rate of profit can be examined for the multinational enterprises, the characteristics of the police system can be cross-classified for the United States and the Soviet Union, the nature and extent of neurosis can be categorized under a cross-classification of Indian peasants and British industrial workers, and internal and external world migrations can be cross-classified by social groups of various economic, political, and psychological characteristics.

Up to this stage of specialization and coordination of the social science subjects, we can treat them as analogous. *The relations they represent by cross-classification do not affect the inherent structures of the relations they are acknowledged to respectively represent.* As noted, the subjects can therefore be treated as mutually distinct disciplines for understanding society.

We find, however, that the contemporary appraisal of social reality has gone beyond this level of analysis and comprehension. We come across societal phenomena for which the measure variables and/or the context variables are composed of properties that each refer to the societal characteristics and/or the forms of social behavior of several social science subjects. *These phenomena therefore represent information that does not register any inherent structural distinctions according to differences among the social science subjects: the structure of information in such cases is built explicitly into the system of classification to conform to the represented world of human society.* Consensus on this is neither universal nor irrevocable. Nonetheless, we deal here with those societal characteristics which, as mentioned before, involve the problems of identification, duplication, and conceptualization. The characteristics require not a mere cross-classification of the social science subjects but the *integration of these subjects at the first level of unanalyzed observations.* Thus these characteristics point to higher levels of analysis and comprehension of social reality than we have considered so far. Let us illustrate.

When we examine differential fertility according to income levels, occupational groups, or social strata composed of several attributes, we are concerned with meta-demographic kinds of social behavior to provide us with the context variables to measure differences in fertility behavior. Usually, however, any one of these context variables is categorized independently of the measure variable, and the two are cross-classified. For example, couples (which represent the point of reference for such a study) are enumerated at the time of investigation as belonging to one or another of a series of income levels, and the children produced by the couples located at each of the income levels (classes) are simultaneously enumerated. The couple-children ratio as the measure variable is then placed against the context variable of income levels, which amounts to a cross-classification of the economic and the demographic behavior of the couples.

The example indicates the tendency to integrate different kinds of social behavior when treating the measure variable. The couple-children ratio is distributed according to the particular meta–demographic characteristic of the couples as belonging to different income levels. The procedure of classification, however, does not comprehensively integrate the demographic and other kinds of social behavior at the grassroots level, as we shall explain below. The result is that the data on differential fertility by income levels may be fallacious (see R. Mukherjee 1979: 35–36).

The fallacy in thus examining differential fertility by income levels, occupation groups, composite social strata, etc., arises from the fact that one must account for the fertility behavior of a couple over a number of years during which it may have moved up or down the income levels, changed its affiliation to occupational groups or the composite social strata, and so on. For a precise and unequivocal evaluation of differential fertility by income levels or similar societal characteristics, therefore, *the context variable must refer to each and every child born to the couples examined,* including the income levels to which the couples belonged when their respective children were born. In other words, the evaluation of differential fertility by income levels, occupational groups, composite social strata, etc., requires integration (and not mere cross-classification) of the types of social behavior depicted by the respective social science subjects.

The integration of different kinds of social behavior to depict a phenomenon is clearer than in the above case when we examine the nature of migration within a society (i.e., a particular configuration of the world society) to find a rural–urban dichotomy or continuum. Both in terms of the context and measure variables of this particular phenomenon, the migrants' behavior must express various meanings besides those sui generis to their movement from a rural to an urban environment if it is to represent the same, allied, or different ways of life and thus substantiate the concept of dichotomy or continuum. Accordingly, first, different forms and types of social behavior of the migrants are, to be empirically ascertained as representing their pre- or post-migration characteristics and, next, the nature and extent of the occurrence of either or both sets are to be examined in the current life of the migrants, which is the accounting period for this study.

In case the migrants display—predominantly or exclusively—the post-migration characteristics, the thesis of a rural–urban dichotomy will be supported. Otherwise, the thesis of a rural–urban continuum will be supported by the nature and extent of the simultaneous presence of the two sets of characteristics. Clearly, the validity and relevance of either of the above two theses cannot be established from a mere cross-classification of the way of life of the migrants before and after migration, as illustrated elsewhere (R. Mukherjee 1965a: 15-58). The two sets of characteristics must be integrated with respect to the migrants, who are the points of reference for the study, in order to characterize both the context and measure variables of the classification required for the purpose.

With respect to another phenomenon, viz. occupational mobility, we find that the integration of different kinds of social behavior is unequivocally underlined. In this case we are no longer concerned with the first-level variations in behavior among social groups according to the jobs they perform. At that level the jobs are consolidated into homologous and analogous clusters (classes) in exclusive reference to the contextual relationships of humans with material goods and services. But the concept of occupational mobility introduces a hierarchical scale for rating the jobs as high or low on meta-economic considerations such as subjective distinctions in status, objective distinctions in power potentials, etc. The study of occupational mobility is thus concerned with the integration of different social science subjects at the grassroots level by combining, in a manner similar to R.A. Fisher's treatment of "confounded variables" (1949: 107-160), the types of social behavior they are each acknowledged to deal with (e.g., economic, psychological, political, and so on).

This course of integration is manifested, on the one hand, by the measure variable of differentially rated sets of jobs and, on the other, by the context variable of derived social groups (e.g., the "social classes" in the Weberian schema) which are identified with reference to the measure variable. Moreover, as we find from different researcher's study of occupational mobility, the two variables may require construction and coordination in a more and more intricate manner at successively higher levels of our analysis and comprehension of the aspect of social reality examined. The nature and extent of relationship between the measure and context variables can vary under different social conditions, of which an indication is given by the fact that Soviet school children in the 1920s reversed the ranking order of the occupational groups in the United States prestige scale by placing the farmers at the top of the scale and bankers at the bottom (Braverman 1974: 436).

Such an integration of different kinds of social behavior is built into those phenomena commonly labelled "social." The family, for instance, is regarded as the primordial social institution, of which the marriage and kinship characteristics are usually considered as the determinants for classifying family units and arranging the clusters of units in successive orders of variation. We have thus formulated the categories of monogamous and various forms of polygamous families which can also be classified as nuclear and various forms of extended families. The family categories are, of course, cross-classified with other kinds of social behavior in a manner similar to that we have noted with respect to different social science subjects. We, thus, obtain the classification of peasant families vis-a-vis the landlord or industrial worker families, rural or urban families, American or Indian families, and so on. Unless, however, we consider the family as an autonomous institution floating in an ever-changing social universe (which some social anthropologists and sociologists tend to do), we must bear in mind that by their formation and operation the family units present various kinds of social behavior that are not intrinsic to different forms of marriage and kinship configurations.

The family units will not be distinguished as the specimens to be classified unless, along with the marriage and kinship characteristics they display, we take note of other societal characteristics (and the corresponding types of social behavior) in order to identify them. Thus, the common procedure to identify families as forming coresident and commensal kingroups brings in the demographic type of behavior related to habitation and the economic type in forming a consumption unit. The family units are identified in various other ways in accordance with the successive levels of our analysis and comprehension of the contextual reality. These variations indicate different types of social behavior considered in one combination or another: for example, economic behavior with reference to subsistence production in a precapitalist society and household labor formation with reference to nascent capitalist development (Fernand Braudel Center 1979), the demographic behavior in the context of population growth, decay, and movement as conceptualized through such schema as the development cycle in domestic groups (Goody 1958), the cultural-historical and/or the psychological behavior in terms of familial orientations of individuals (Desai 1964; R. Mukherjee 1977a) and so on.

The variable functions of the family are characterized by the types of social behavior that refer to distinct and acknowledged social science subjects. The variable structures of family units, as exemplified above, imply several such variations. We find, moreover, that the categorization of patriarchal (or patripotestal) and matriarchal (or matripotestal) families refers to the integrated role of sacred and secular authority with respect to marriage and kinship characteristics. And this role of familial authority is linked with the economic and political power in the given society through customary or codified laws. Similarly, the recently developed categorization of "patrifocal" and "matrifocal" families refers to the psychological behavior of individuals under distinct cultural conditions (Kunstadter 1963; Safa 1965).

These examples relating to the structure and function of the family tell us that it is at the integrated level of variation in many types of social behavior (and not merely in different forms as related to marriage and kinship characteristics) that the family exists as an entity, registers cross-cultural variations, and changes over time.

Similarly, the stratification of Indian society by the caste structure is regarded as a social phenomenon and is schematized so as to represent different forms of social behavior among the caste units according to the measure variables of a purity–pollution scale. The binary concept of purity and pollution is regarded as based on religious cum ethical properties and practices: their contexts, however, refer to societal characteristics and types of social behavior that fall under several social science subjects. Moreover, the caste system does not represent merely the imputed religious cum ethical behavior. Its continued viability from the distant past to the present can be explained only by the synchronization of purity–pollution stratification with the economic and political structures of Indian society, even though the scenario of synchronization has changed repeatedly (R. Mukherjee 1974: 140-212, 313-335; Kothari 1970; P. Mukherjee 1974:1-14). This is attested by the customary and codified laws in India from the days of the Epics and the Puranas to the *arthasastra* and the *manusmrti* (P. Mukherjee 1978) and later under British rule (R. Mukherjee 1957; 1974:316, 323-333), and by the recently formulated concept of the "dominant caste" (Srinivas, 1966)—the usefulness of which we shall discuss when we examine the limitations of typological classification in Chapter 2.

Education, as noted, is usually regarded as a distinctive social phenomenon because its professed aim is to fulfill the quest for knowledge. Its first-level variations can be conceived in terms of the measure variables of educational standards and specializations in schools, colleges, and universities, and the corresponding context variables of different forms of behavior among the students and teachers belonging to different curricula. Education, however, has always been subsumed under the dominant economic, political, and ethnic behavior patterns, from the days of the obligatorily sacred to the present prevalent secular curriculum of study. Moreover, the contemporary revolts of students and teachers against this dominance—which in 1968 led them to label a category of teachers in West Germany as the "pedantic fools"— clearly manifest the relationship of education to economic and political types of social behavior which are to be synchronized systematically with reference to their respective forms.

The cultural behavior patterns have never been solely social. They have their roots in the material basis of society. They therefore have a component of material culture along with that of spiritual culture; in between the two is the component of aesthetic culture—literature, music, fine arts, etc.—commonly regarded as representing culture. Culture is thus subclassified, and we speak, accordingly, of different forms of behavior among, say, the artisans and the artists, the scientists and the technicians, the Christians and the pagans, and so on. Yet the British categorization of "county" (gentry) and "country" (yeomen), or Vilfredo Pareto's categorization of the Elite and the Mass in terms of his specified attributes of Mr. (reasoning) and Ms. (instincts, sentiments, etc.), imply two or more distinctive types of behavior which are integrated at the grassroots level in order to produce the respective categories. An indication of this is given by the contemporary distinction drawn between the "traditional" and the "modern" elites. This is explicit when Weber speaks of "The Protestant Ethic and the rise of capitalism" or Emile Durkheim of "anomie," and we apply these concepts to world society. We then move far beyond a direct relation between the apposite measure and context variables of any spiritual culture per se. A great many different types of social behavior, referring to multifarious aspects of social reality, are included in these formulations.

From these examples we find that with respect to the societal phenomena we may restrict ourselves to the first-level variations in social behavior. In that case we shall be concerned with particular sets of societal characteristics and the corresponding forms of social behavior, the former yielding the measure variables and the latter the context variables allowing us to identify appropriate social groups with respect to one or another facet of the social reality under examination. We may consider the societal characteristics and the forms of social behavior in successive orders of variations, but they will be located on the level that permits appraising only one or another particular facet of social reality. And since the societal characteristics depicting respective facets of reality can be categorized as economic, demographic, and so on, at the first level of variations in social behavior, we may conceive of the societal phenomena also as economic, demographic, and so on. None of them, however, can be characterized exclusively as social.

So far the phenomena are structured to depict distinctive facets of the social reality. We may cross-classify these facets by analogous arrangements of the matters pertaining to different social science subjects on the same primary level of our analysis and comprehension of the social reality with which the respective facets are concerned. There will not be a qualitative distinction in our understanding of society as a product and a process because, by following the behaviorist tradition, we shall merely take into account simultaneously more than one kind of analogous (not homologous) behavior pattern. As aptly formulated, "the *level of abstraction* within a taxonomy refers to a particular level of inclusiveness" (Rosch et al. 1976: 383). This level of inclusiveness will remain the same for the unilateral and the multilateral classification of the types of social behavior which are acknowledged to fall under respective social science disciplines or, more specifically, subjects.

Behavioral research, thus, truly maintains an *interdisciplinary* perspective, but such a perspective cannot deal satisfactorily with the derived societal phenomena which are structured by the integration of different types of social behavior at the grassroots level. We must, therefore, attend to higher-level variations in social behavior which, as illustrated, are *transdisciplinary*, in cases where we insist on labelling the social science subjects as disciplines, or *unidisciplinary*, if we regard social science as the discipline and its component subjects as specializations.

At these higher levels, as we have shown, the acknowledged social science disciplines will integrate and interact in various possible ways, while the respective types of social behavior which represent the disciplines can be examined as constituted of diverse forms of social behavior emerging from numerous societal characteristics. The integration of the disciplines means, however, that the societal phenomena involved would lose their relevance as exclusively economic, political, psychological, demographic, and so on. On the other hand, these societal phenomena point to the fact that when we raise our sights to the higher levels of analysis and comprehension of social reality (viz., beyond the primary level), we begin to understand how different configurations of world society exist as distinctive entities at a point in time, but change within or beyond the respective configurations over a period of time. For, as mentioned, these phenomena present information that can be built explicitly into the system so as to conform to the represented world of human society. *This class of information does not refer to the structure of a particular set of relations that depicts a schematized facet of the represented world by means of the social science subjects cited as examples.*

Now, if we recall that the distinction drawn between the concepts of "social" and "societal" rests upon the former denoting the conditions for holding a society together (while changing it) and the latter expressing the manifestations of various aspects of a society, we come nearer to an appreciation of what is social, out of all that is societal, from the above discussion. For we notice, first, that our comprehension of what is social out of all that is societal cannot be merely residual, because none of the societal phenomena can be directly labelled as social if they have been characterized as economic, etc., at the first level of variations in social behavior. Secondly, at the higher levels of variation in social behavior, the social phenomena are identified with reference to their overall coverage. And, thirdly, by integrating different types of social behavior in order to structure the information depicted by the phenomena labelled social, we convey a systemic relation between the overall coverage (what might be called the omnibus antecedence) of these phenomena and their residual connotation that emerges after a consideration of the societal phenomena examined at the first level of variations in social behavior. *Within the overall coverage, that is with reference to its omnibus antecedence, the residual information conveyed by these phenomena is structured to show the relations of the represented world of human society.*

In other words, the *social* phenomena convey the relations which are *intrinsic* to the society. By contrast, the other societal phenomena that can be affiliated with the acknowledged social science subjects (like economics, politics, psychology, demography, etc.) are structured so as to represent the relations of the schematically distinguished aspects of the representing world, i.e., as *extrinsic* to the society as a product and a process. In the latter case, the sets of information use relations which have no *inherent* structures: different social science subjects are structured so as to obtain a first approximation of the social reality. A more and more precise and comprehensive approximation of social reality, therefore, requires an integrated view of the societal phenomena. Sociology is acknowledged as meeting this demand, and social research, therefore, is commonly regarded as the specialized concern of the discipline of sociology, as mentioned earlier.

"Social," as emerging from the "societal," thus acquires a specificity of its own which, as we shall see, is amenable to the examination of its properties under successively higher orders of variation, as in the case of other social science subjects. It follows, however, from our discussion that this specificity is revealed beyond the primary level of our analysis and comprehension of social reality. *From the societal to the social is thus the axis on which the operation of social research is to be conceived today.* The scope of social research needs to be clearly defined, accordingly, following from a precise understanding of the role of sociology vis-a-vis other social science subjects, all of which emerge from the undifferentiated pool of knowledge originally placed under the label of "The humanities."

5. SOCIAL RESEARCH

At one time, the attempts to understand the social reality and the ways and means to induce change in one or another configuration of world society were within the orbit of humanistic studies. The antecedents to these studies were various formulations of social philosophy, which were guided by ethical prescriptions. Auguste Comte's (1848: 120, 440) elucidation of his Positive Philosophy (namely, spiritual reorganization) illustrates this perspective: "The grand object of human existence is the constant improvement of the natural Order that surrounds us: of our material condition first; subsequently of our physical, intellectual, and moral nature. And the highest of these objects is moral progress, whether in the individual, in the family, or in society." Similar ethical principles provided the base for understanding and changing human society in other parts of the world.

Irrespective of religious differences, the ethical or moral question in different configurations of world society was not interpreted very differently. The perspective of humanism had to be similar for the survival and security of humankind within and between the societies. This provided the norm for humanistic studies. The subjects falling under this category were, therefore, held together on a unified value-base, while, in increasing numbers, they were differentiated from one another with the accumulation of knowledge on society. The momentum of accumulated knowledge, however, in due course reached a stage at which these subjects could no longer be guided explicitly by ethical norms nor still be called the "moral sciences." *The need arose for "sciencing" society on its own merits (i.e., objectively), and the label "social sciences" or "social science" came into vogue.*

The concern with values, however, remained ingrained in the appraisal of social reality and the inducing of social change—*values defined, contextually, in an objective manner and for empirical consideration as the nature and extent of a person's desire to retain or obtain certain life resources and detestation of certain other resources.* For a while it may have appeared that only from a *value-free* perspective could society be understood objectively. Increasingly, however, it became clear that society represents a virtually infinite but enumerable field of variation in the items of information. Selection of information, therefore, is inherent to the understanding of society, while any selection must be governed by one's value preference. Nothing is perceived, no observation is made without a purpose—implied or explicated, conscious or unconscious. Even those who profess to gather knowledge for the sake of knowledge cannot but collect only those items of information on society which draw their attention according to their likes and dislikes.

Hence, while the orientation to research shifted from an ethically normative to an objective (assumed to be value-free) basis, the understanding of society and the inducement of social change rested, as before, on value premises. These premises, of course, cannot be exclusively individual. If fully randomized, the individuals' values would fail to hold people together, for what one desired, another would detest. Purely personal values would thus act against holding society together as a product and changing it as a process. Therefore, as we have discussed with reference to interpersonal and social action, the value premises must attain a group-character while operating as a variable in society. *It follows that these premises can be empirically ascertained because the description of society and the explanation of social change will refer to the relation of two variables, viz. the items of information (i) and the value premises (v), as in the formulation:* $i_j v_k$.

However, valuation in social science has usually been held constant by assuming a universally applicable value-load, such as by depicting the society as being (or becoming) rational, harmonious, wholesome, progressive, and so on. Overall qualities of this sort are assumed to be intrinsically related, such that, for example, without rationality society cannot be harmonious and, thus, wholesome and, therefore, progressive. The positivistic orientation to social research, as conveyed by qualifying characteristics like the ones above, was thus based on such a value-load that it meant, in fact, the continuation of the subjectively normative orientation to understanding and changing society, although this norm might not be formulated from an ethical standpoint.

In effect, this form of value acceptance allows for specialization in the social science subjects in a value-free manner because the value-base for understanding and changing society is held constant. All social science subjects, including sociology, could therefore be conceived as mutually exclusive but analogous disciplines. This shift in understanding and changing society and, correspondingly, in the specialization of the social science subjects is attested by their continually revised and ever-expanding curricula in any reputable university, especially in the twentieth century. The journals in the respective subjects furnish the same evidence.

In the course of specializing, however, the scope of training and research in any one social science subject has spread beyond its term of reference and been integrated with other subjects. Interdisciplinary research has, therefore, been strongly advocated since the 1950s, *which testifies to the conceptual and operational limitations of considering the social science subjects as separate disciplines.* The knowledge accumulated through specialization in these subjects is also pointing toward the fallacy of accepting a set of universal values. For example, enforced labels like "rational," "harmonious," "wholesome," "progressive," etc., are seen to have different meanings for different individuals, groups, and social systems (for details see R. Mukherjee 1975a: 13-25).

As explained, all such meaningful differences can be empirically charted with reference to relevant action–behavior–relationship syndromes. The immanent course of social behavior is thus brought to account in order to define objectively the basis for specialization of the social science subjects. *Hence, we shall examine in the following pages the manner in which the contemporary accumulation of knowledge on social reality and social change is persuading us to move toward another point of integration of the subject matters on society that is placed on a level higher than the one on which the ethically normative humanistic studies or the deductive-positivistic orientation to social research is located.*

Thus we find that economics, which has always stood in the forefront of all social science "disciplines," is a highly specialized subject today. We also find, however, that it is moving away from its avowed concept of the rational relation of individual human beings to material goods and services. That concept rests on a constant, the so-called "rational behavior" of individuals, which echoes the Protestant Ethic by assuming that a particular type of action is desirable for all human beings. More and more, the concept of rationality as an innate and invariable quality of human beings is found untenable in contemporary research in the field of economics. Many economists are, therefore, veering toward the concept of relations among human beings with respect to material goods and services.

The shift has to do with the *variable* of "social behavior" and defines rationality as the faculty optimizing the relation between ends and means under varied societal conditions. These conditions have been found to be largely noneconomic in character. The controversy over this shift, as between L. Robbins

(1932: 4-6) and Paul Sweezy (1946: 3-8), is now dated. We notice, moreover, that the portrayal of *The Stages of Economic Growth* by W.W. Rostow (1962), which places the concept of "rational behavior" in a modern perspective, makes use of the "traditional society" as an undifferentiated mass; and V.V. Mshvenieradze's critique of this study (1964: 34-35) points out that the moment a traditional–modern distinction is drawn, the portrayal of the contextual reality becomes illogical if it is restricted to a dichotomy and does not take note of the variable axis of social behavior.

Political science has been ranked closely behind economics among the social science subjects. However, before it was labelled as such, the subject of politics referred predominantly (or even exclusively) to rarefied realpolitik and focussed its attention on the maneuverings of the centralized power blocs. Assumptions of rational behavior were the underpinnings of this subject, too. It was, however, found inadequate for appraising the political behavior of humans precisely and comprehensively. Shifting from this stance, therefore, contemporary research in political science does not deal with government per se. A consolidated view of the multidirectional flow of power in society and the relationships among people as the cause and consequence of that flow are matters that concern political science. Our attention is drawn, accordingly, to the integration of various types of social behavior and societal characteristics with the social polity.

Political science, therefore, deals today with such topics as national, ethnic, and social movements with reference to the consolidation of (or their alienation from) a state in existence, the formation of a new state, and the international situation. The politicizing of the people, with respect to the life they wish to lead and with reference to the nation-state and international relations, plays the key role in this research. It is reflected in the "consociation" model of nation-building (Daaldar 1973: 14-31), the consideration of "late peripheral nationalism against the State" (Linz 1973: 32-116), the "matter of nation-choosing by the individual" (Deutsch 1963: 10), and so on. The course of specialization in this subject and its integration with other social science subjects are expressed eventually through the discussions on dependency and mutual aid among the nation-states, the North-South dialogue, etc.

Psychology as a subject by itself was concerned, at the beginning, almost exclusively with individuals. This direction of specialization was distinguished under headings like experimental psychology, clinical or analytical psychology, etc. Correspondingly, social psychology became a specialization which has now became endemic within the subject. The role of individual-oriented psychology, however, has not been undermined in the process. Instead, the particular strain of specialization it is concerned with is now seen to feed research in social psychology which, in its turn, has extended its term of reference beyond an exclusive consideration of the mental faculties of individuals in society. We notice in this context that at the root of such specializations a distinction used to be drawn between the "normal" (rational) and "deviant" (irrational) forms of social behavior. That distinction is disappearing as psychological research becomes more and more concerned with the variability in the mental behavior of individuals in the context of their affiliation with social structural categories and social systems.

This shift in the orientation to psychological research is attested by the contemporary themes for study by psychologists, such as that on stereotypes which involves meta-psychological types of behavior related to status groups, class, ethnicity, nationality, etc. Obviously, a study of these behavior patterns does not draw a distinction between the normal and the deviant. The integration of psychology with other social science subjects is also expressed by combined labels, like psychohistory, psychosocial identity, and so on, which, again, need not draw on the normal–deviant distinction. Moreover, when one examines a social phenomenon like violence, its germination in the psychology of individuals is not ignored, but its manifestation is studied through the interaction of many facets of human life. Gandhi's concept of nonviolence, which has now spread all over the world, acquires a meaning on the premises of a two-sector division of the world economy, viz. the sector of abundance which, according to him, is given by agriculture, husbandry, etc., and the sector of scarcity in minerals, etc., which, for their acquistion, politically motivates individuals to resort to violence (Kumarappa 1951). Violence in America is hypothesized in light of interactions among the demographic, economic, political, cultural, and related behavior patterns of individuals categorized into relevant social groups (Carstairs 1970: 751-764).

Similarly we find that demographic research has gone a long way beyond the perimeter set by the actuaries in preparing life-tables and allied activities, a point noted by L.I. Dublin and A.J. Lotka (1936: iii-iv) while presenting *A Study of the Life Tables*. Investigations into the growth, decay, and movement of population have extended so far in recent years that headings like economic, political, and social demography, and even historical demography have come into use. These composite headings are not efficient because they lead to the already mentioned problems of identification, duplication, and conceptualization of the social science subjects. Nonetheless, they denote the tendency of demography to integrate with other social science subjects at the grassroots level. The labels like economic, political, and social demography do not signify a mere cross-classification of two or more subject matters on society. The measure and context variables of demographic research under such composite headings are constructed with reference to diverse types of societal characteristics and social behavior, which, as we have illustrated, yield different kinds of societal characteristics and social behavior.

Such integration of the social science subjects on the variable axis of social behavior is clearly manifest when we review contemporary research in ecology, which is a rather recent introduction into the family of social science subjects. Barring a few economists and other social scientists who discussed the subject, ecology—which was originally considered as a biological subject—began to be regarded as a specialization in human geography. This we learn from the curricula of many universities in the first half of the twentieth century. And we find that the human geographers examined the relation of human beings with their environment. As based upon the primary level of variations in ecological variables for measurement in the context of the social groups identified accordingly, these scientists studied the seafaring people, the nomads, the sedentary folk, the hill people, the plains people, and so on. With the accumulation of knowledge on ecology and human society, however, the labels like human ecology, social ecology, etc., came into use in the same manner and with the same implications as we have indicated with respect to demographic research.

We notice, moreover, the same trend of extension of research in ecology as we have noted for the other established social science subjects, and which tend to integrate diverse manifestations in society. For instance, we now evaluate such contentions as the "limits to growth" (as posed by the Club of Rome), the unbounded human potential in the light of contemporary scientific and technological developments (as emphatically posed by the Soviet Union), and the imperatives of endogenous development in the Third World by means of the internalization of science and technology through ethnoscience and ethnotechnology (as specifically posed in China, Japan, and India). The investigations deal with the "living organisms' habits, modes of life, and relations to their surroundings," which form the subject matter of ecology, but now the investigation is geared to the integration of multifarious societal characteristics and social behavior. Also, the nature of such integration lies beyond the confines of ecology as the subject used to be and still is generally conceived. The measure and context variables for this course of investigation must evolve from an integration of the ecological, economic, political, cultural, ideational, etc., manifestations in society (e.g., R. Mukherjee 1977b: 11-23; Singh 1977: 131-146; Tsurumi 1977: 147-173).

This tendency to integrate the social science subjects and diverse types of social behavior for a comprehensive understanding of social reality is noticeable even with respect to those subjects which were originally formulated for that very purpose by combining the appropriate subjects. Political economy is a clear example in this respect, for contemporary research on this subject also is involved with those matters that are neither political nor economic according to their generally acknowledged terms of reference.

The relations of power among human beings with respect to material goods and services are ostensibly the matters for investigation in political economy. "Class" and "state" are thus two important entities for examination with respect to their respective structural, functional, and processual interactions. As noted, however, to understand the dynamics of class, one must not only examine the concept of "class by itself," which has historically been determined as in the realm of economics, but also that of "class for itself," which dialectically emerges from the cauldron of political, psychological, and other relevant characteristics of the people concerned.

Correspondingly, to understand the dynamics of the state, one must examine not only the operation of the state *in being* (viz. the nation-state, as it is designated in the UN system) but also the state *in becoming* (viz. possible avenues for separating from another state power and the consolidation of other newly formed or already existing state powers by means of current processes of nation- and state-formation). The latter phenomenon draws our attention to appraising a state power precisely and comprehensively, just as "class for itself" is the key issue for appreciating the role of class in society.

The alienation and consolidation of state powers, however, are engineered by the unequal exchange of material and non-material amenities in the life of the people in the light of the structural division of world society by class, ethnicity, religion, nationality, nation-state affiliation, and so on (R. Mukherjee 1979: 140-206). We are, therefore, concerned with several significant nuances in the phenomena of nation-building (or formation) and state-formation (or - consolidation).

A nation is obviously a supraclass entity, as it comprises complementary and contradictory classes. A class, however, plays the role of catalyst in nation-formation by means of its hegemony in establishing and operating a national market, and aspires to control, or wield, the immanent state power. A state, correspondingly, may proclaim that it is to serve the interest of all people under its control but, basically, serves the interest of a particular class. These two formulations are debatable; nevertheless, they are found to be the crux of research in political economy today.

From this perspective we notice that "class by itself" is a matter of deduction from the relations of production and property arising out of a particular mode of production and the state of development of the productive forces. It can, therefore, be regarded as *manifest*. "Class for itself," on the other hand, is a matter of inference with reference to what is regarded as the expression of class consciousness. It is thus in a *latent* condition until the class struggle attains its logical conclusion. Contrariwise, "nation by itself" (i.e., an identified or identifiable nation-state) is in a latent state because it is always a matter of inference whether a national struggle will emerge in a state and lead to the formation of new uninational states or the consolidation of a multinational state. And, "nation for itself" is manifest through the observable movements of the people in expressing national consciousness. The latent class consciousness, therefore, may be confounded with the manifest national consciousness and create confusion in the appraisal of interrelations between class and state.

In order to remove such confusions, we are required to examine world society in any and all its configurations, in terms of not only its economics and politics, but also its history, psychology, demography, culture, and so on. All these latter societal aspects and the corresponding manifestations of social behavior may not denote the *sufficient* conditions to characterize the interactions among class, nation, and state; they denote, however, the *relevant* and *necessary* conditions. Present-day research in political economy, therefore, consider matters far beyond the terms of reference in politics and economics.

For example, in the light of integration of the social science subjects and the corresponding behavior patterns of the bourgeoisie and the working class in the United States vis-a-vis the Indian bourgeoisie and masses, A. Emmanuel (1972) has illustrated the issue of unequal exchange. S. Amin (1978) has interpreted the historical and material foundations of Arab nationalism. F. Froebel and his colleagues (1980) have posed a new perspective to the international division of labor. G. Arrighi (1978) has examined the efficiency of V.I. Lenin's theory on imperialism in the context of different viewpoints. Andre Gundar Frank (1970, 1972, 1975) has posed the problem of the identification of the bourgeoisie in the Third World as national, comprador, or lumpen by means of their behavior patterns in the context of "development of underdevelopment" which embraces all aspects of human life. And, by introducing the context of history and sociology in *The Modern World-System* (1974), Immanuel Wallerstein (1979: 66-84) has proposed a solution to the perennial debate on the absolute or relative pauperisation of the working class as relative within a nation-state but absolute in the world perspective.

Specialization in social science is thus seen to lead to the formulation of new subjects and the corresponding examination of social behavior, but the course of specialization leads also to the integration of various social science subjects and diverse kinds of social behavior at higher levels of analysis and comprehension of social reality. In the course of this development, the subjects are freed from monopolistic control under previously isolated sets of scholars and made accountable to all social scientists within the ever-widening scope of social research.

As noted, besides the established subjects like economics, etc., demography and ecology (which are relatively recent additions to the catalogue of social science subjects) have moved a long way beyond the perimeters set by the actuaries and human geographers, while political economy is concerned with matters beyond politics and economics. Similarly, religion and ethics are no longer the exclusive prerogatives of theologians, while law, the judiciary, and even medicine have been brought within the scope of social research. All these subjects are acknowledged as integrating various types of social behavior and diverse societal characteristics, as attested by the topical consideration of social medicine, socialist versus bourgeois legal system, "development with justice in the Third World," and so on.

In the course of this development in social science, subjects that had once flourished as distinctive disciplines are becoming redundant. The present status and role of social anthropology is a good example. Emerging with the development of capitalism in Western Europe and the consequent opening up of the world, which was eventually brought under a few colonial powers, the anthropologists remained *outsiders* to the "primitive," "tribal," "preliterate," and similarly characterized societies they studied, however much twentieth century anthropologists attempted and claimed to identify themselves with the people designated as such. The sociologists, on the other hand, have always been *insiders* to their own and other "civilized" societies they have studied.

Both disciplines dealt with the same societal phenomena concerning the ascribed and achieved human groupings for survival, procreation, securing the continuity of human life, and prospering over the course of time. Marriage, family, kinship, caste and any other ascribed grouping, involuntary and voluntary associations, the economic, political, and religious life of the people, and so on, became the nodal points of reference for both of the disciplines. The differential treatment of the subject matter, however, was considered appropriate to the two different types of society as if the two configurations were discrete entities bearing respectively the marks of so-called rational and irrational behavior. Only a few researchers attempted to synthesize the findings between *societus* and *civitus:* a distinction and interrelation drawn by Lewis Henry Morgan (1964: 13-14) and supported even by A.R. Radcliffe-Brown (1922: 40-41), who rejected Morgan's evolutionary principles.

That distinction is now rapidly disappearing. What used to be regarded as a conceptual distinction between the two disciplines is now viewed by some as methodologically useful in studying, say, the preliterate and the literate societies; others find the so-called anthropological and sociological methods to be applicable to all societies. Moreover, the preconceived distinction in levels of variation in social behavior is now empirically revealed as simply degrees of variation. The *primitive – civilized* dichotomy has therefore been replaced by the *traditional – modern* schema.

Yet that schema too is fallacious (see R. Mukherjee 1979: 94-100). Along with the rapid change taking place in all world societies in the second half of the twentieth century, sufficient knowledge has accumulated to conceptualize the societal variations as neither *unique* to nor *discrete* in any configuration of society but as *continuous* in the course of human social development. The growing dysfunctionality of the distinction between social anthropology and sociology is therefore best shown by this conceptual unity of the two disciplines despite their appropriate methodological specializations. These two social science "disciplines" can thus be equated with each other.

Another manifestation of contemporary developments in social science is that not only are subjects now accepted as "scientific" and not "humanistic" (which was once debatable), but this acknowledgement is providing also an essential dimension for appraising any aspects of social reality. The example in this respect is history, which is now seldom regarded as a mere chronicle of events over time. An explanatory label for a historical study like *A People's History of England* (Morton 1951), as against the chronicle of events labelled "The History of England," has become less necessary to convey its social science perspective. We must, however, note the inclusion of various social behavior through such a qualification as *A People's History.*

Conceived in this manner, history as a social science subject cannot but provide a time dimension to one or another aspect of society; otherwise the subject would have no substance to deal with. This is obvious from such combined labels as "economic history" and "political history." And when the label "social history" is applied the integration over time of the social science subjects and all kinds of social behavior is clearly established.

We also notice that this process of integrating the social science subjects in the time dimension is underscored by contemporary historians. E. H. Carr, for example, defines history as "an unending dialogue between the present and the past" (Carr 1964: 30). This growing integration is also made explicit by the contemporary topics of historical research which transcend the categorical distinctions of the already-mentioned joint labels: as for example, *The Agrarian System of Mughal Indian, 1556-1707* (Habib 1963); *The World We have Lost* (Laslett 1965); *The Modern World-System* (Wallerstein 1974); *Roll, Jordon, Roll: The World the Slaves Made* (Genovese 1974); *Some Central Problems Concerning the Proto-industrialization Thesis and Pre-colonial South Asia* (Perlin 1981); and so on.

Developments in social science thus move toward an ever more precise and comprehensive manifestation of the dual processes of specialization and integration of its subject matter *within, between,* and *over* the acknowledged discipline boundaries, and along the variable axis of social behavior. This perspective provides the substance for contemporary social research. However, some clarification on the integration of the social science subjects is needed both in and beyond the context of their developing specializations. It needs also a clear understanding of the value base to integrate the subjects efficiently.

Specialization obviously takes place within the respective social science subjects that deal with the relations of the schematically distinguished aspects of society. Correspondingly, the course of integration is commonly viewed as a cross-classification of these apportioned aspects of human society under subject demarcations, i.e., between the social science subjects. To this extent, however, our understanding of human society remains incomplete, as a mere compilation of its parts and not of the integrated whole. The represented relations denote various manifestations of society but not the characteristics that determine it, as a product, at a given point in time and that change it, as a process, over a period of time. In other words, the represented relations are *extrinsic* to the representing whole and, therefore, our understanding of human society is also extrinsic to its reality. It becomes *intrinsic* when the represented relations are structured to directly represent the real world by disregarding the acknowledged boundaries of the respective social science subjects.

We find an analogy in this respect with the problem faced by natural science in the nineteenth century, on which Friedrich Engels commented (1939: 19):

> It is however precisely the polar antagonisms put forward as irreconcilable and insoluble, the forcibly fixed lines of demarcation and distinctions between classes, which have given modern theoretical natural science its restricted and metaphysical character. The recognition that these antagonisms and distinctions are in fact to be found in nature, but only with relative validity, and that on the other hand their

imagined rigidity and absoluteness have been introduced into nature only by our minds—this recognition is the kernel of the dialectical conception of nature.

Disregarding the acknowledged boundaries of respective social science subjects is thus necessary when these subjects are integrated, and not merely by breaking the mutually demarcated walls between them, which is the motif of the Behavioral School and of interdisciplinary research. The necessity is now to integrate them by also breaking through the ceilings imposed upon the respective subjects in accordance with their mutually distinguished terms of reference for understanding one or another aspect of society. The walls and ceilings, however, cannot be constructed without a floor. *Any conceptual framework to represent social science in this manner requires, therefore, a floor for the unification of the social science subjects on a single basis, their specialization with respect to that base, and a higher floor above the ceilings of specialization in order to integrate the subjects at a higher level of comprehending social reality.*

In other words, the integration of the social science subjects must not be merely operational (such as by advocating interdisciplinary research) in order to achieve a working arrangement. It must be *systemic* to represent a set of connected parts in the organized whole, namely, the society, which is always in a state of dynamic equilibrium because it is both a product at a point in time and a process over a period of time. We return, therefore, to our discussion on the types of social behavior that distinguish the social science subjects and on the integration of these types at higher levels of variation in social behavior.

As noted, the social science subjects other than sociology are now regarded as dealing explicitly with one or another facet of observable (or enumerable) social actions which lead to the deduction of (or inference about) a particular set of social behavior patterns and the interpretation of a specific network of social relationships. *In this perspective, sociology (i.e., the science of society) integrates all the societal facets because, as noted, it is concerned with the basic characteristics of the world, and not with one or another schematically distinguished aspects of that world.* It therefore deals, however broadly, with the appropriate action–behavior–relationship syndromes in order to analyze and comprehend human groups and their institutions in the formation and operation of all configurations of world society, and *how, why,* and *what will be* the changes within and among these configurations. In accordance with the acknowledged division of labor in the realm of social science, sociology thus provides the floor for specialization in different aspects of social reality by means of the respective social science subjects.

On its own, sociology also specializes with reference to its already-mentioned nodal points which represent the medium by which to express the basic and ultimate issues of the survival, procreation, security, and prosperity of human society. It, therefore, lays emphasis on the corresponding range of action–behavior–relationship syndromes. This we find from the history of sociology, the syllabi on the subject in the universities, and the journals in sociology. *We find, however, from the contemporary trends in sociology that while continuing with its specialization, it is also providing the platform (i.e., the upper-level floor) on which all social science subjects can be integrated to depict the comprehensive social reality in its historical sequence, current state, and probable future manifestation.* The themes for the plenary sessions of the World Congress of Sociology in the 1970s and 1980s, in particular, attest to this role of sociology at the present time.

The social science subjects are thus moving toward another unitary point at a higher level of understanding human society than that provided by the ethical norms of humanistic studies or the enforcement of any other universal norm. The implication is that, on the one hand, social research continues to cater to sociology as a specialized social science subject and is, thus, equated with it in our ordinary understanding, as we have noted at the beginning of this chapter. On the other hand, the coverage of social research is enlarged by the widened scope of sociology so as to integrate all specializations in social science. The omnibus antecedence and the residual connotation of sociology thus coincide with the contemporary perspective of social research.

The envisaged unitary point for social research, however, is not clearly defined as yet. *The imposed value-based and assumed value-free social research have both become outmoded, but neither has been replaced by an objective value-base.* What has emerged instead is the acceptance of one or another value-load for understanding and changing society. The value-acceptors have built mutually exclusive houses to represent social science, using our analogy of the floor, walls, and ceilings of specialization and integration of the subject matters on society. As an extreme example, one speaks of bourgeois versus socialist social science, and even of a social science of the Third World.

The upshot is that the propagation of *alternatives* has become popular since the second half of the 1970s. Treated disparately, the alternatives can generate more heat from polemics than shed light on an efficient appraisal of the social reality. Systemization of the alternatives on a unified base is, therefore, a cardinal objective of social research today. This leads us to examine the fundamental characteristics of social behavior for denoting society as a product and a process.

Hindu philosophy (especially of the Sankhya School) posits that nothing is static in the universe, although this illusion is created, in the course of eternal movement shaping reality, when the interacting forces come to a balance at a point in time (see Seal 1958). Modern physics points out that while nothing moves with respect to a frictionless surface, whatever may be its composition, the surface must schematically be stationary at a point in time in order to measure movement (i.e., change) over a period of time. We should, therefore, conceive of the various forms and types of social behavior operating in a society (the surface) as either *complementary or contradictory* to one another. The supremacy of the former kinds of social behavior over the latter holds society in a state of *dynamic equilibrium* at a point in time, and the force of the latter offsetting that of the former effects changes in society over a period of time.

The interactions of these two core-characteristics of social behavior thus provide the dialectic for understanding society as a product and a process. The exploration of this dialectic has been the motif behind the dual processes of specialization and integration of the social science subjects. Irrational behavior is the built-in contradiction to any formulation of rational behavior by Economic Man. *Consensus* and *dissension* represent the basic characteristics of Political Man, and refer to complementary and contradictory social behavior, respectively. *Normal* and *deviant* mental behavior refer to the same dichotomy of complementary and contradictory social behavior, and so it is with the forms and types of social behavior dealt with by other social science subjects.

Correspondingly, we find with respect to the concept of "social development", which integrates all social science subjects, that the value-acceptors stress one or another set of complementary behavior patterns as of prime importance in holding society together as a product, and one or another set of contradictory behavior patterns to denote the prime movers of change (for details, see R. Mukherjee 1979: 83-120). The value-acceptors, thus, deal with various constellations of the information and value variables, which may be denoted by the series: $(i, v)_1$, $(i, v)_2$, . . ., $(i, v)_n$. The series stands for the ways in which the value-acceptors characterize the fundamentals of social reality and the ways and means to change society.

The evaluation of the relative efficiency of the available (and enumerable) alternate explanations of the value-acceptors is, therefore, the crux of contemporary social research. These explanations may be in the form of established theories, variations in the content of these theories, or ad hoc hypotheses. The explanations may refer to a particular phenomenon, a set of homologous or analogous phenomena, or the systemic variations in world society. Coverage by the explanations may be limited to one configuration of world society or few such configurations, or spread over the world at large. However, whatever may be their form, content, and coverage, a *set* of explanations (and not exclusively one or another explanation) draws our attention today in order to ascertain their relative efficiency for appraising the social reality—precisely, objectively and comprehensively.

The objective base for undertaking this task, therefore, cannot be the acceptance of a particular value-load, in whichever manner that load may be defined (i.e., in terms of ethical norms or otherwise). A declaration of the value-free approach, on the other hand, would totally disregard the possibility for formulating an objective base while surreptitiously adhering to a particular value-load. *Our approach, consequently, will have to be the accommodation of all available (and possible) value-loads in a systemic manner,* as demonstrated elsewhere (R. Mukherjee 1975a: 26-87). This will define the unitary point toward which, as mentioned, the social science subjects are moving for higher levels of understanding human society than that provided by the value-free or the value-acceptance approach, for that point will rest upon the truly objective foundation of all value-loads placed on the null base of statistical probability.

From this base any and all explanations in a set will be regarded as *valid and relevant but none as necessary or efficient (and certainly not sufficient)* for appraising the contextual reality and detecting the prime movers of change in that context. *Inductive inference on the relative efficiency of the alternatives can then be made probabilistically, which the deductive-positivistic approach (whether value accepting or seemingly value-free) would totally fail to do* (see R. Mukherjee 1979: 207-229).

Contrary to the general supposition, the *probability (not deterministic) approach to appraising social reality and induce social change synchronizes with the basic principles of Marxism:*

> By examining the whole complex of opposing tendencies, by reducing them to precisely definable conditions of life and productions of the various *classes* of society, by discarding subjectivism and arbitrariness in the choice of various "leading" ideas or in their interpretation, and by disclosing that all ideas and all the various tendencies, without exception, have their *roots* in the condition of the material forces of production, Marxism pointed the way to an all-embracing and comprehensive study of the process of rise, development, and decline of socio-economic formations. (Lenin 1951: 28).

Interestingly, the ancient Hindus were influenced by the inductive-inferential approach to appraising reality:

> Hindu scientific ideas and methodology (e.g. the inductive method or methods of algebraic analysis) have deeply influenced the course of natural philosophy in Asia—in the East as well as the West—in China and Japan, as well as in the Saracen Empire. ... The Hindu Inference is neither merely formal nor merely material, but a combined Formal-Material Deductive-Inductive process..., which must combine formal validity with material truth, inductive generalisation with deductive particularisation. (Seal 1958: iii-iv, 250-51)

And we find that the inductive-inferential orientation to research, which the probability approach of value accommodation demands in the light of alternate explanations for one or more phenomena, is also the felt need of contemporary "exact" sciences that had earlier posited *the* scientific method. Einstein wrote (as quoted in Max Born (1956: 90):

> Concepts which have been proved to be useful in ordering things easily acquire such an authority over us that we forget their human origin and accept them as invariable. Then they become "necessities of thought," "given *a priori*," etc. The path of scientific progress is then, by such errors, barred for a long time. It is therefore no useless game if we are insisting on analysing current notions and pointing out on what conditions their justification and usefulness depends, especially how they have grown from the data of experience. In this way their exaggerated authority is broken. They are removed, if they cannot properly legitimate themselves; corrected, if their correspondence to the given things was too negli-

gently established; replaced by others, if a new system can be developed that we prefer for good reasons.

The natural scientists, like the social scientists, have their differences regarding personal value premises. Einstein wrote to Max Born in 1944: "In our scientific expectation we have grown antipodes. You believe in God playing dice and I in perfect laws in the world of things existing as real objects, which I try to grasp in a wildly speculative way" (quoted by Born 1956: 90). Nonetheless, in so far as the pursuit of research is concerned, Born assumes a similar stance to Einstein's. He stated (1956: vi-vii):

> In 1921 I believed—and I shared this belief with most of my contemporary physicists—that science produced an objective knowledge of the world, which is governed by deterministic laws. ... In 1951 I believed in none of these things. The border between object and subject had been blurred, deterministic laws had been replaced by statistical ones. ... The final criterion of truth is the agreement of a theory with experience, and it is only when all attempts to describe the facts in the frame of accepted ideas fail that new notions are formed, at first cautiously and reluctantly, and then, if they are experimentally confirmed, with increasing confidence. In this way the classical philosophy of science was transformed into the modern one, which culminates in Niels Bohr's Principle of Complementarity.

Thus, whether "sciencing" the physical or the social world, we come to the same conclusion, namely, *the contemporary developments in research require us to adopt the value-accommodation approach and the consequent inductive-inferential orientation.* This requirement, however, poses classification as *a problem in itself.* The appropriate course of investigation requires us to distinguish between the *search* for items of information or data and *research* on the data sets available from a data space which, in its turn, is enumerable from an information space, as noted at the beginning of this chapter.

6   SEARCH AND RESEARCH

We have discussed at the beginning of this chapter how the role of classification is to consolidate our knowledge on the variable properties of a phenomenon by attending simultaneously to (1) a meticulous division of these properties and (2) a systematic collection of the divided properties. The division of the properties is a matter of acquired knowledge and skill in proceeding sequentially from the nominal distinctions drawn with respect to a measure variable, turning the distinctions into an ordinal series of qualitative variation, transforming the series into ordinal numbers, and, finally, reducing the series to an interval scale of quantitative measurement. The collection of the properties is also a matter of acquired knowledge about the context variables, but that knowledge is geared to the limits we impose in order to understand the phenomenon. *We should now examine these limits, because, at a critical point of distinction among them, the need arises to distinguish between the search for and the research on the context variables, and proceeding on this basis a corresponding distinction has to be made with respect to the measure variables.*

The limits we impose can be surmounted sequentially in order to accumulate more and more precise and comprehensive knowledge about the phenomenon. In this sequence, our quest for knowledge is directed to, first, *what* the phenomenon is; second, *how* the phenomenon operates; third *why* the phenomenon occurs; and, fourth, *what will be* the future of the phenomenon as its development emerges through the knowledge accumulated by answering the successive what, how, and why questions.

The first two questions, as we have pointed out, refer to *descriptive* research: the former describing the phenomenon itself, and the latter describing its interrelations with other phenomena. The third refers to *explanatory* research, for it is concerned with an inquiry into the causality of the phenomenon with reference to an established theory or a priori hypothesis as the yardstick to unravel the reasons behind the origin, development, persistence, possible change, and eventual disappearance of the phenomenon. Lastly, the fourth would refer to *diagnostic* research because this probability question can be answered only by a critical evaluation of the relative powers of alternate explanations for the phenomenon with respect to their relevance, necessity, efficiency, and sufficiency for understanding the phenomenon.

Any variable phenomenon, however, cannot be understood without undertaking a course of investigation. In fact classification is inseparable from research, which is defined as "careful search or inquiry..., endeavor to discover new facts, etc., ...course of critical investigation" *(The Concise Oxford Dictionary). Hence, the distinction between search and research is not drawn from the simple fact of undertaking a course of research. It refers to a critical difference among the modes of research, while the respective modes have to do with the limits we impose on understanding a phenomenon in successive orders of comprehension.*

We have, therefore, pointed out that when we undertake descriptive research we search for information to answer the *what* and *how* questions. The information we search for is determined by our value premises: we do not (and cannot) search for any and all information about a phenomenon. As noted, the description of the same phenomenon may vary from researcher to researcher, although the descriptive items of information each belong to one information space defined by space–time coordinates. *The items of information are thus selected, although we may not be consciously aware of, or admit, the selective bases, and assume a value-free stance in research. This selective process provides the contexts for formulating the categories of classification by collecting the divisible properties of the information items.*

For example, the Indians are nominally distinguished from the Westerners as vegetarians. Deviations from this norm are, of course, noted. In general, however, the nominal distinction is drawn in the context of the religious creed and ethical practices of the Indians, especially of those belonging to the higher social strata with whom the Westerners come relatively more frequently in contact. This context yields four categories of classification—vegetarian or nonvegetarian Indians and Westerners—and is supported by the world-wide dissemination of the Gandhian ideology of *ahimsa* or nonviolence, which is a very important tenet of Jainism and under which M.K. Gandhi was socialized. The classification is likely to be validated by the overall (but superficial) information obtained from contemporary India and the West, but that will not substantiate the relevance of vegetarianism as a religious cum ethical phenomenon among the Indians.

A researcher, therefore, may investigate whether the Indians are vegetarians because of their religious cum ethical creed or their secularly enforced practice. A new context will thus be introduced to describe the phenomenon of vegetarianism, by classifying the "vegetarian Indian" category with reference to another context and to the corresponding additional but analogous information items from the same information space.

The second context and the corresponding information items have yielded the following description: (1) the economic base of the Indian masses prohibits them from consuming relatively higher-priced nonvegetarian food items, and (2) their cultural base prompts them through acculturation (viz. Sanskritization) to emulate the upper caste Hindus and profess vegetarianism in order to raise themselves in the social status hierarchy which is controlled in present-day India by the secular power of that group of upper caste Indians. Two more contexts from the economic and cultural base of the Indian masses are thus introduced to further classify the category of "vegetarian Indians."

The value premises of a researcher in the context of Occident–Orient or traditional–modern dichotomies, however, may persuade him to overlook the economic base and equate the cultural base of vegetarianism in India with religious cum ethical prescriptions. This we notice in many studies by Westerners and Westernized "Modern" Indians, while the "native" studies more and more point out the necessity of considering these two value bases under secular value premises (see R. Mukherjee 1976a; 1977c: 43-69ff). The search for information items is thus extended by the latter attempt while referring to the same information space.

We notice in this respect that the secular value premises of a researcher lead to the search for those additional items of information, in both the space and time dimensions, that obviate the context of "traditionalism" in describing the prevailing contemporary vegetarian habits of Indians. Thus, the searched-for items of information indicate that the Kashmiri Brahmins, the Saraswat Brahmins of Maharashtra, the Bengali Brahmins, etc., are traditionally nonvegetarian, like many of the Kshatryiyas, the Rajputs, the Kayasthas, etc., all of whom belong to the upper caste "traditional elite." It is also found that at present many Hindus of all castes and creeds take nonvegetarian food, but surreptitiously in order to retain or enhance their current social status. And it is ascertained that the religious creed and ethical practice of the ancient Hindus did not forbid them from taking animal food; in fact, some Brahmin sages were noted for their preference for beef (Dutt 1931: 65, 191-198, 279, 290).

The items of information thus considered under successive contexts of classification lead to the formulation of an ordinal series of the divisible properties of the phenomenon of vegetarianism with respect to its complement of nonvegetarianism. One can inquire how many Indians are: (1) strictly vegetarian, (2) take duck eggs, (3) accept hen eggs also, (4) consume fish but not meat, (5) eat goat, duck, and other birds, but not chicken nor other varieties of meat, (6) accept chicken, but not beef and pork, and so on. The ordinal series depicting in this manner the extent of vegetarianism can also be turned into a succession of numbers, as indicated; the numerical series can be arranged more precisely and comprehensively. Finally, according to the information on the frequency of consuming vegetarian and nonvegetarian food items, the ordinal series can be turned into an interval scale measuring vegetarianism (and, complementarily, nonvegetarianism) over the space and time dimensions.

Along with such a successively precise and comprehensive division of the properties of the measure variable, the divided properties may be collected for each one of the enumerated contexts of classification; and, as noted, the categories of classification thus formulated can be cross-classified. Therefore, in accumulating knowledge on the "what" and "how" of a phenomenon, all that we shall be concerned with is a systematic division and collection of the relevant information items at each stage of consolidating our knowledge. *Classification remains inherent to the course of investigation, which, with reference to different value premises, deals with a search for information items out of the information space defined by space–time coordinates. In other words, classification does not create any problems for descriptive research.*

The course of dividing and collecting the information items is pursued for explanatory research, but these items are now explicitly predicated by a purposeful search for them with reference to an established theory or an ad hoc hypothesis. The items of information are thus specified as data. *The transition from information to data, however, germinates within descriptive research because in the course of meticulous description of a phenomenon we come to the point of passing the limits of descriptive research to enter the field of explanatory research.* We may illustrate this process with the example of vegetarianism.

We find that the answer to the "what" question is inseparably linked with the "how" question, and this linkage leads to a more and more precise and comprehensive structuring of the measure variable with reference to the nature and extent of vegetarianism and, complementarily, of nonvegetarianism. In the course of this description, a nominal distinction is first drawn between the Indians and the Westerners on the basis of prior knowledge and the related value premises. The "why" question is thus germane to the nominal distinction in terms of the religious creed and ethical practice of the Indians. The question becomes more and more explicit as we search for precise and comprehensive answers to the "what" and "how" questions in the light of the division of the measure variable and the collection of the divided properties of the variable in varied contexts to ascertain the interactions of vegetarianism with the relevant associated phenomena. As a result, while the "how" question is efficiently answered on secular value premises and by the economic and cultural bases, the "why" question is clearly posed in terms of one or another explanatory theory or ad hoc hypothesis, such as the Occident–Orient dichotomy, the traditional–modern scheme, economic viability, elitist ideology vis-a-vis secular practices, and so on.

An explanatory theory or ad hoc hypothesis may also be posed directly. Its treatment, however, cannot bypass the "what" and "how" questions, i.e., the prerequisite for the shift from descriptive to explanatory research. This we have pointed out with reference to Marx's formulation of the Asiatic mode of production, and Marx's and Weber's explanation of the Indian caste system. In the course of answering the "what" and "how" questions, therefore, the "why" question is posed, and it provides the *determining context* for dividing and collecting the relevant measure variable or variables. Thus the data space evolves out of the information space while different theories and hypotheses on the same phenomenon are structured by respective data sets.

The data sets referring to the same phenomenon may contain different kinds of data from their respective data spaces and/or the same kind from one data space but causally or concomitantly related in different ways. For example, Marx explained the origin of the Indian caste system with reference to "the crude form in which the division of labour appears with the Indians" (1942: 30), namely, when "the particular kind of labour—i.e., its craft mastery and consequently property in the instrument of labour—equals property in the conditions of production" (1964: 101-102). Weber, on the other hand, explained the origin of the Indian caste system with reference to "the construction of rational ethical thought and not the production of any economic 'condition' . . . the combination of caste legitimacy with *karma* doctrine, thus with the specific Brahmanical theodicy" (1958: 131).

Marx, however, explained the stability of the caste system in the Indian society with reference to the peculiar social structure provided by the village communities and the consequent ideology which "subjugated man to external circumstances, instead of elevating man [as] the sovereign of circumstances," and thus "transformed a self-developing social state into a never-changing natural destiny" (1853). In this respect, Marx and Weber are seen to refer to the same data space; Weber did not go beyond the same kind of data to explain the stability of the Indian caste system to explain its origin. Instead, he concurred with Marx's formulation of the "never-changing natural destiny" but added the context of "a belief in transmigration" to the doctrine of karma, whereby the latter "was elevated into a cardinal religious obligation, and was fortified by powerful religious sanctions" (1965: 42-43).

We thus find that with respect to the same or different phenomena, and with reference to the descriptive or the explanatory mode of research, dividing

and collecting the properties of the measure variable(s) are the tasks of classifi-
cation. We also find that the manner and the extent of the dual processes of di-
vision and collection are decided by the determining context(s). The motif of
classification is thus established, which is implicit in the descriptive mode of re-
search and explicit in the explanatory mode.

In the next chapters we shall examine this task and motif of classification
more and more specifically and in relevant detail. For the present we may
point out that the stated task and motif of classification have been noted for
pre-Socratic explanations (Stannard 1965). The ancient Hindus followed the
same principles in classifying nature, living beings, and gods (e.g., Seal 1958:
169-201; Mueller 1919; 37-38, 411), and so did the ancient Chinese and other
upholders of ancient civilizations. Similarly we find in the light of our discussion on the value-acceptance approach to appraising social reality that consideration of a determining context for the categorization of a particular set of
measure variables is the prime concern of explanatory research in modern
times. Accordingly, protagonists and antagonists of different explanations of
the same phenomenon indulge in polemics with little substantive result, a point
noted by Sutcliffe (1972: 313) in a seminar on the theory of imperialism.

What is needed, therefore, is diagnostic research, which does not put uni-
lateral emphasis (or de-emphasis) on an established theory or ad hoc hypoth-
esis. As noted, this mode of research would consider all available (and
possible) theories and hypotheses on a phenomenon as alternate explanations.
The explanations will thus constitute, theoretically, an infinite but enumerable
series of available and potentially possible contexts, none of which can assume
the determining stance because all of them would be placed on an equal foot-
ing with reference to the previously characterized *null base. Thus the contexts*
are no longer predetermined, as they were for the descriptive and the explana-
tory modes of research. These two other modes of research, therefore, re-
quired mere search for information or data. But the determination of the most
efficient context out of all those under present and future investigation is now
the crucial matter for research. *The focus of attention in contemporary social*
research thus shifts from the search for information and data to research on
the available (and enumerable) information and data spaces. Let us illustrate.

The economic characteristics of a community of people may be represented by a systematic division of the industry-occupation groupings and their
collection into, say, three categories according to production and property relations, with the mode of production and the state of productive forces remaining the same for all. The three categories may be designated as e_1, e_2, and
e_3. The cultural (often designated as the "social") characteristics of the Indian
people are usually represented by the ethnic-religious-caste hierarchy formed
on the purity–pollution scale. The social groups constituting the hierarchy may
be systematically gathered into, say, three categories as c_1, c_2, and c_3. As noted
earlier, different varieties of consumer behavior are usually found with respect
to either of the two sets of categories, but a mere cross-classification of e_{1-3} and
c_{1-3} cateogires does not reveal which one of the two types of social behavior is

more discriminating and, therefore, has greater power to explain reality.

During an investigation conducted to examine this problem, a process of classification was applied from the bottom of the information space, i.e., by considering together each one of the industry-occupation groups with each one of the ethnic-religious-caste groups and collating the resultant groups successively. The process of classification showed that, as regards consumer behavior, the grouping of the industry-occupation groups into e_1, e_2, and e_3 categories, and of the ethnic-religious-caste groups into c_1, c_2, and c_3 categories, is valid. The consumption pattern of the people, however, did not yield efficiently discriminated social groups with either the industry-occupation *or* the ethnic-religious-caste categories forming the primary set. The empirical data did not produce either of the following two series to indicate that e_{1-3} form the independent variables and c_{1-3} the dependent variables, or vice versa, as in:

$$(e_1c_1, \ e_1c_2, \ e_1c_3, \ e_2c_1, \ e_2c_2, \ e_2c_3, \ e_3c_1, \ e_3c_2, \ e_3c_3) \ \text{or}$$
$$c_1e_1, \ c_1e_2, \ c_1e_3, \ c_2e_1, \ c_2e_2, \ c_2e_3, \ c_3e_1, \ c_3e_2, \ c_3e_3).$$

Instead, the joint consideration of the two types of social behavior yielded such an assemblage of the primarily categorized groups that, symbolically, $o_i r_j$ as a particular industry-occupation (o) cum ethnic-religious-caste group (r) was found to be nearer to $o_i r_m$ than to $o_i r_k$, and, $o_i r_j$ was nearer to $o_n r_j$ than to $o_k r_j$, according to their mutual distances determined by applying the discriminant analysis known as Mahalanobis's D^2 (Mukherjee and Bandyopadhyay 1964: 259-282). It will be noticed that, in the serial ordering of the industry-occupation groups, o_k is nearer to o_i than to o_n, and, correspondingly, r_k is nearer to r_j than to r_m in the serial ordering of the ethnic-religious-caste groups. But when the two kinds of grouping are considered together, the derived social groups, as has been shown, do not follow either of the two serial orders. Evidently, even within such a small universe of variation in terms of place, time, and object, it is not possible to accept the primacy of either the economic or the cultural explanation, although it refers to a simple matter of consumer behavior, easily rendered into a quantitative measure variable.

The example thus points out that instead of unilaterally emphasizing (or de-emphasizing) one explanation to depict the contextual reality, it is necessary to ascertain the relative efficiency of the explanations, i.e., *the relative explanatory powers of the contexts they represent.* Contemporary social research, therefore, goes beyond the search for one or another explanatory context, which we have illustrated with reference to vegetarianism among the Indian people; namely, the search for such an explanatory context is implicit in descriptive research in an information space, and explicit in the case of explanatory research on a data space that has evolved out of the information space. *What is required, instead, is research on the set of context variables available from explanatory research on the phenomenon under examination.*

As we have illustrated, the more we try to answer meticulously the "what" and "how" questions regarding a phenomenon, the more the "why" question is pushed forward and suggests an increasing number of contexts to explain the phenomenon. The relevant information and data spaces thus yield the context variables which, for all practical purposes, reach a *limit of variability. Theoretically, however, they must be conceived as emerging from an infinite but enumerable field of variation.* All these contexts will be examined with reference to the null-base we have described so that they can be researched, precisely and objectively, to find their relative usefulness.

The demand for research into the context variables logically affect the construction of the corresponding measure variables, since the measure variables are no longer given automatically by the context of a description or an explanation, as merely a matter of search for information or data. The measure variables have to be structured, instead, with reference to all the explanatory contexts brought to account (and which may be brought to account in the future) for a program of diagnostic research on a phenomenon. Let us illustrate.

With reference to certain patterns of consumer behavior, the economic context may record more variations than the cultural context. With reference to certain other patterns of consumer behavior, the two contexts may show opposite trends or be unable to differentiate among many patterns of consumer behavior that other contexts can distinguish. We are therefore concerned with the totality of consumer behavior in order to ascertain, precisely and objectively, the relative explanatory power of a set of different contexts. The totality would represent, theoretically, an infinite but enumerable field of variation. The measure variables must, accordingly, be researched with reference to this field of variation.

The measure variables with respect to a set of contexts may also refer to several societal characteristics which must be integrated instead of being cross-classified. For example, the status grouping of occupations yields "social class" categories under the basic assumption that status is highly and positively correlated with the level of material well-being associated with particular sets of occupations. The assumption is occasionally challenged, for example with respect to any distinction drawn between white-collar and blue-collar workers earning the same income. The challenge, however, is usually met by a cross-classification of the economic context of occupational groupings (which is regarded as *equating* the two types of workers) with the cultural context (which is assumed to *differentiate* them).

We find, however, from the total information space that in some configurations of the world society, the white and blue-collar workers are treated as of the same status, while in some others the former group is rated higher than the latter. The situation brings in other contexts to rate the status groups, as mentioned with respect to the United States and the Soviet Union. *It also implies that the measure variables referring to these contexts must mesh together, instead of being merely cross-classified, in order to represent an infinite but enumerable field of variation in the societal characteristics defining the status groups.*

The need for constituting the measure variables in this manner is particu-

larly noticeable with respect to those issues in social research which are given contemporary priority in appraising social reality and which therefore generate lots of polemics. We have mentioned many of these issues that have led to raging controversies, such as the role of the peasantry in social development according to the logic of regarding agriculture as a mode of production or merely as a set of enterprises under the prevailing capitalist mode of production; the revolutionary or the conservative role of the industrial working class in the "developed" societies vis-a-vis the roles of the "nonconformist young intelligentsia" and the "ghetto population... and the 'underprivileged' sections of the labouring classes in backward capitalist countries" (Marcuse 1969: 52-56); the force of religious solidarity versus class contradictions in inducing social transformation, which has become a life-and-death question in contemporary Iran; the formulations of imperialism as against equality among the socialist nation-states, which is the bone of contention between the USSR and China; the nodal point of the "semi-periphery" in the core–periphery axis in explaining societal dynamics in "the modern world-system" (R. Mukherjee 1980: 314-316); the implications of the modern world-system in the context of the "origins of capitalist development" (Brenner 1977: 25-92); and so on.

We must, therefore, regard the reciprocal sets of context and measure variables to have emerged from two infinite but enumerable and interacting fields of variation, in order that our evaluation of the relative explanatory powers of the different contexts is precise, objective, and comprehensive. Consequently, we are involved with research on the relevant information and data spaces in place of merely searching for information or data to substantiate a description or an explanation. As a result, classification must assume a responsibility not warranted earlier. Namely, it is not only concerned with the division and collection of a measure variable but also with the integration of a set of measure variables from the grassroots level up; and it is equally concerned with the same procedure in regard to a set of context variables, while the reciprocal sets of context and measure variables must continually be examined for their interactions.

We shall discuss the method suitable for meeting this responsibility in the next chapter.

Chapter 2
Procedure

1 OVERVIEW

The role of classification, discussed in Chapter 1, is to present in a consolidated manner our knowledge on the characteristics of variation in a population belonging to a specified universe. The characteristics of variation, we have pointed out, must be considered as pertaining to contexts and measures, respectively, and as referring to two mutually distinct but interacting fields of variation (in contexts and measures) in the contemporary perspective of social research. We have also indicated that these characteristics of variation are to be examined with reference to the phenomena which should be labelled *societal* at the primary level of our observation, analysis, and comprehension of social reality, and *social* (by the integration of different kinds of societal characteristics and social behavior) at subsequent levels of our observation, analysis, and comprehension of social reality. And we have pointed out that while moving on the axis from societal to the social, we must systemize the known and knowable information on society, as available and enumerable from the information space and the data spaces referring to alternate explanations of a phenomenon. It follows, therefore, from our examination in Chapter 1 of the concepts of classification, social research, and search and research that the method of classification can be concerned with the following four issues:

1. How we perceive variations in a phenomenon in regard to its constitution and cause, and, consequently, with regard to interactions among (or the integration of) a set of phenomena.

2. How these variations within and between phenomena can be systematically treated under mutually distinguished but interrelated components (aspects) in order that we may formulate an efficient procedure of classification for social research.
3. How the treatment of variations in a phenomenon (and, sequentially, in a set of phenomena) in this manner poses problems which are to be resolved for the formulation of an efficient procedure of classification.
4. How we can evolve an efficient method of classification in consideration of 1—3 above, in the light of the scope and limitations of the prevailing method of classification.

In this chapter we shall deal with these four issues, beginning with an overview of the constant–variable characteristics of any phenomenon: the first issue. The development of social research up to its present stage rests upon this form of dialectical appreciation of the societal phenomena which, eventually, attain a social character.

We thus notice that any phenomenon that is treated as a variable with reference to a system of variation can also be considered as a constant with reference to its internal system(s) of variation. Earth as a planet is a variable in the system of variation represented by a solar system. That system, treated as a constant in this case, is a variable in the universe of solar systems. Correspondingly, earth is a constant with reference to the systems of variation manifested by world phenomena, including those which fall under social research. The societal and the social phenomena, in their turn, are constant with reference to the systems of variation they represent, and are variables with reference to the parts of one or another system to which they belong. For example, in the perspective of religion as a world phenomenon, Christianity, Judaism, Islam, Buddhism, Hinduism, etc., are variables in a system of variation, but any one of these religions may be treated as a constant with respect to its distinctive variation in its network of supernatural ideas, beliefs, and practices with reference to the *core* doctrine.

The systemic relation thus drawn between the *constant* and the *variable* phenomena can be reviewed in a historical perspective. Variations are revealed and eventually classified as knowledge increases on the relevant aspects of reality. Therefore, at any stage of the apprehension of reality, each set of variations is constant in itself; but as knowledge increases on these constant phenomena, they turn into systems of variation. Conceptually, therefore, all that pertains to reality is in a state of variation; and the more we can appraise the nature and intensity of the systems these variations form by their distinctions and interrelations, the better we are able to comprehend reality. *In this endeavor, classification plays a crucial role because it refers to the systematization of knowledge of the phenomena obtained from observation, analysis, and comprehension of the relevant interlocked systems of variations at different levels of exposure to reality.*

It follows that the scope of classification in social research involves a precise, unequivocal, and comprehensive coverage of knowledge on the given phenomena in the light of the state of development of the social science subjects and of sociology in particular. We find in this respect that very little was known about the world societies in the early days of social research and, therefore, most of the societal entities were treated as constant or at most systemized as variables within a limited range of sets of homologous or analogous entities. Seldom were the internal characteristics of these entities examined as variables forming sets of their own.

There were of course departures from this general rule; but an *analytically comprehensive* account of the social situation was lacking for the known societies, except for certain spheres of information usually dealt with by the subjects like economics and politics. Moreover, concept formation and methodology had not reached the stage that seeks for causal explanations of the phenomena through empirical investigations. Glaring exceptions in this regard, with reference to the subjects other than economics and politics, were few: studies of the family and kinship in social anthropology, surveys of the "poor" and "poverty" in sociology, and investigations into the phenomena of "class" and "social class" with the aid of all social science subjects.

Social research, therefore, was predominantly *descriptive,* characterized by answering the first of the four fundamental questions a scientist asks about a phenomenon, viz. "what is it?". The ethnographers, social workers, and social scientists answered this question by presenting the salient features of different configurations of world society and describing the groupings of the people, such as: the family, lineage, and clan; the occupational, political, cultural and magico-religious categories; and so on. *Classification, in this context, was an occasional and incidental aid to presenting some of the collated information coherently.* It had hardly any relevance of its own, except to mark the *beginning* of consolidation of knowledge from descriptive research. Mostly, it drew nominal distinctions among a set of entities, as described in Chapter 1, and occasionally formed an ordinal series within a limited range of qualitative variations.

At the next stage of social research, when some information had been collected about the previously unknown societies, which more or less synchronized with the first stage of research on the relatively known societies, the process of systematization entered into the respective schemes of classification but not necessarily into the classificatory procedure. This distinction between the *schemes* and the *procedure* of classification is of crucial importance for appraising the adequacy and efficiency of classification in contemporary social research, which we shall discuss in the context of the *deductive* (typological) and *inductive* (population) approaches to classification. However, in those days, the social scientists developed schemes of classification by systematically collating the available information on society.

The objective of research was still descriptive, but its coverage had expanded. Its key point was to describe the intrasocietal characteristics as well as to compare different societies with respect to a phenomenon or a set of phenomena. Research was, therefore, geared to answer the second fundamental question one asks about a phenomenon, viz. "how does it happen?". The task involved an analysis of the internal articulations of a phenomenon, and its variations and interrelationships with other phenomena. In this context, classification had (and has) a substantial role to play, but not the crucial one. According to the objective of research, it was still exclusively concerned with the *spontaneously* observable and the *known* variations in the phenomena. And, in most cases, it produced ordinal series of qualitative attributes but more systematically and exhaustively than before.

With the accumulation of knowledge, the perspective of social research began to change from being descriptive to becoming *explanatory*. The social scientists were more and more involved with the "why" question, instead of only the "what" and "how" questions, and began to ask the reasons for what had happened and was happening in world societies. At the beginning, the attempt to explain the social dynamics was more or less an extension of answering the "how" question. Even as late as 1877, for example, Morgan came to the conclusion from his ethnographic researches that: "The growth of property is thus closely connected with the increase of inventions and discoveries, and with the improvement of social institutions which mark the several ethnical periods of human progress" (1964: 445). He did not proceed with the explanation of *why* property was accumulated by a few in society.

Explanatory research based on the "why" question, however, had already begun to draw the attention of social scientists on its own merits. In the course of time it dominated the field of social research. In the already mentioned context of property, for example, the "why" question was central to the writings of Marx in *Capital*, of Rosa Luxemburg on *The Accumulation of Capital* (1951), and of the later Marxist scholars. The same concern with the "why" question is noticed in the researches of all scholars—Marxist or not, and with respect to diverse phenomena.

With the forceful emergence of the "why" question in social research, classification acquired a meaning beyond the inclusive and standardized schemas. The interval scale of quantitative measurement was brought to better use than ever before, and in other ways also the measure variables with respect to a societal phenomenon were respectively treated more meticulously and systematically. Classification, however, remained predominantly concerned with only the *known* variations in the phenomena examined.

Moreover, it was left to the researchers to record in their exclusively individualized manner the interlocking systems of variations they were interested in. In most cases, they cross-classified the properties of their selected phenomena according to their specific requirements, instead of integrating the *ensemble* of properties in the manner we have discussed. *The upshot was that the process of dividing and collecting had entered into the procedure of classification and it had become more precise and unequivocal with respect to individ-*

ual studies, but even with reference to the known variations the attempts of individual researchers were not necessarily comparable.

Lacking in a systematic classification of all the enumerated properties of the phenomena under examination, the individualized efforts of the researchers fell short of being unequivocal and comprehensive. This, as we have noted in Chapter 1, led to lots of enervating polemics. *With respect to classification in social research, the context variables were not treated systematically and comprehensively, affecting the systematic and unequivocal constitution of the measure variables, however meticulous and precise the individual researchers might be in treating the latter variables in their classificatory schemes.*

The need for removing this lacuna is now posed because the explanatory orientation has been instrumental in a further shift in the perspective of social research. Since explanations emerge from the examination of causality in a system of variation, alternate explanations regarding the same phenomenon are proposed by the social scientists. Logically, the examination of the relative efficiency of such alternate explanations thus becomes the subject of research. As a result, social research today is veering toward diagnosis, instead of remaining explanatory, in the light of *probabilistic* evaluation of the *most efficient* explanation at the given state of accumulated knowledge about the phenomenon. That explanation would, on the evidence, appraise the contextual reality the most precisely and comprehensively, and, therefore, the most efficiently predict what is likely to happen to the phenomenon in the immediate future. The remaining two fundamental questions which a scientist asks with respect to any phenomenon have thus attained their inherent importance, viz. "why is it?" and "what will it be?".

With this critical shift in the perspective of social research, which we have briefly pointed out in Chapter 1 and discussed elsewhere in detail (R. Mukherjee 1979), the scope of classification undergoes a qualitative change. Social research, as noted, is henceforth concerned with the continuous process of dividing and collecting the properties of any and all societal phenomena, and correlating all possible variations that have *emerged,* are *emerging,* or can *emerge* from them. In this way the relative efficiency of all available and possible explanations of the social reality can be duly appraised and, on that basis, the immediate future of reality can be diagnosed on a probability basis. The scope of classification widens, accordingly, to categorize in all *available* and *possible* manners the variations inherent to and associated with a phenomenon. A new dimension of *knowable* variations in the phenomena thus enters into the area of classification beside the previously considered dimension of *known* variations.

Needless to say, our knowledge of these variations and the manner of their most effective categorization will not be complete so long as we find it necessary to pursue researches in order to understand the phenomena. Hence, with reference to this never-ending pursuit of social research in sequential progression, classification is to be conceived as a *systemic* consolidation of knowledge about a phenomenon (or a set of phenomena) *before* and *after* further generation of data, analysis of the data, and the consequent deductions made and inferences drawn to appraise reality. This means that classification, which has so far been regarded as consolidating prior knowledge only, must also be amenable to incorporating, unrestrictedly and efficiently, a posteriori knowledge obtained from subsequent analysis. That is, the scope of classification widens to accommodate all possible variations in the store of *obtained* and *obtainable* information at the beginning and end of a course of research.

It is against this flexible but comprehensive scope of classification that we should examine its adequacy and efficiency for pursuing contemporary social research. It will be *adequate,* although referring to some segments of the total information space, if it can unequivocally and systematically categorize all *known* information regarding the phenomenon examined. It will in addition be *efficient,* if it can deal with all *knowable* information with reference to all segments of the information space. Our task, accordingly, is not to outline schemes of classification but to formulate the procedure of classification in such a manner that the present and the potential store of knowledge of the phenomena may be consolidated more and more precisely, unequivocally, and comprehensively.

Doubts are raised, however, regarding the feasibility of evolving a procedure of classification across all social science subjects and all societal characteristics. The concern is with the different ways and means to appraise social reality. As should be clear from Chapter 1, they are planned in accordance with the accepted *levels of comprehension* of the contextual reality, and thus refer to organizing research from various perspectives; the means are conveyed by the adopted *levels of analysis* of the contextual reality, and thus refer to conducting one or another course of research. It follows that the levels of comprehension and analysis of social reality are eventually expressed by different modes of structuring the *units of analysis* which, by definition, are *unities* (i.e., conceptually indivisible) but are seen empirically to be structured by various divisible properties of the societal phenomena (including, schematically, the zero incidence of some phenomena). *Thus the unit of analysis is a constant in the light of a particular level of comprehension and analysis, but is a variable when different levels of comprehension and/or analysis are considered simultaneously;* hence the doubts about the feasibility of evolving a procedure of classification across social science subjects and societal characteristics that would constitute the units of analysis in diverse ways.

The doubts can be resolved by considering the units of analysis on the constant–variable axis of the contexts and measures of classification, bearing in mind that all social science subjects are integrated with reference to the relation between the societal and the social phenomena. We have discussed this process of integration in Chapter 1 with respect to the societal characteristics and the forms and types of social behavior. We may now briefly illustrate the constant–variable relationship of the context and measure variables in structuring the units of analysis.

For example, attitude, which is a frequent subject in social research, could be the unit of analysis in research on "goals in life." In this case, the attitude toward life goals is a constant and, thus, conceptually indivisible. This attitude, however, would be inferred from what the set(s) of persons under examination desire and detest, and what their corresponding actions and reactions are, in the variable contexts of their life conditions. The matters of desire and detestation in these variable contexts would obviously be translated into measure variables of, say, a n-point interval scale, which would be for attitudinal variables. Correspondingly, the actions and reactions of the people in the variable contexts would be translated into measure variables in, say, an ordinal scale, for behavioral variables. Either way, however, these attitudinal and behavioral variables would be selected by the researchers with reference to societal characteristics and their specific properties to be brought into account. These attitudes and behaviors would refer to variable (divisive) properties while the attitude toward the life goals would remain a constant and depict an indivisible property in itself.

Thus, when we consider an attitude toward life goals as the unit of analysis, it becomes the *object of classification* for a research project and, therefore, a constant. The classification, however, is with respect to sets of persons who, by forming mutually distinct social groups, represent one set of context variables that identifies the *units of classification*. The social groups thus formed may not represent persons of all characteristics but only those of specified sex and age, for example, which therefore represent a particular set of context variables to denote the *items of classification*. On the other side, attitudes toward the goal of life can be ascertained by canvassing a battery of relevant attitudes and behavioral practices, which represent another set of context variables directly associated with the corresponding sets of measure variables laid out in an interval or ordinal scale; all the measure variables can be regarded as the *content of classification*.

It follows that just as goals in life as a topic of research can be a constant, the unit of analysis (i.e., an object of classification), it may also provide the context for depicting one of the measure variables for classifying the content of another object of classification, viz. another unit of analysis. For example, if the attitudinal stereotypes of individuals are the topic of research (i.e., the unit of analysis and thus the object of classification), they may refer to the same attitudinal units and items of classification, but the attitude toward life goals may now be part of the content of classification only as one of the battery of attitudinal questions that are translated into respective measure variables for classifying stereotypes. In the same manner we may consider any action or behavior, any social transaction, as a unit of analysis (an object of classification) that is invariant in the given context.

But we may also consider an action or behavior as a context variable, i.e., one of the contexts for identifying the unit or the item of classification or for yielding measure variables for classification. Even dyads or single persons become a variable for a unit or item of classification (i.e., divisible by its qualitative characteristics) from this perspective when they are used to classify the unit or the item of classification. For example, a family unit may be composed of certain persons forming a coresident and commensal kin group as one context for investigating the dynamics of family organization, but consist of a different set of persons (which may include some of the first set) depending on whom the head of the family household regards as family members.

Thus the item, unit, and content aspects of classification are to be regarded as variable: the item and the unit aspects identify the contexts of categorization, from the division into items to their consolidation into units, while the content aspect locates the measure variables with reference to different contexts for measurement. Following this arrangement, the object aspect of classification, which would register the unit of analysis, is usually regarded as a constant (indivisible). When, however, we deal with a set of alternate explanations in contemporary social research, as discussed in Chapter 1, the object aspect of classification also can vary; and this variability may cut across different social science subjects.

These possibilities for considering a societal characteristic or phenomenon on the constant–variable axis of contexts and measures must be systemized in an efficient procedure of classification. We should therefore examine the mutually distinguished but interrelated components into which the variable properties of any phenomena can be placed. A flexible but comprehensive procedure of classification can then be evolved with reference to precise and unequivocal definitions of these components which will denote the aspects of classification of a phenomenon.

2 ASPECTS

For a systematic categorization of variations inherent in and associated with a phenomenon, four aspects of any classificatory schema draw our attention: the *item, unit, content,* and *object* characteristics of the phenomenon. The essential features of the aspects are the following:

1. The *item* characteristics refer to the *indivisible elements,* i.e., those inanimate or animate specimens which are to be classified with reference to a phenomenon. These specimens may be reducible further (e.g., in the case of a social group) or may not be (e.g., in the case of a person). In the present context, however, the specimens are indivisible because they are to express the properties specific to the phenomena.

2. The *unit* characteristics refer to those properties of a phenomenon by which it is distinguished from other phenomena, on the one hand, and according to which it produces a replicated series of the *minimal unities* of classification, on the other. The minimal unities are found at that stage of analytical reduction of the properties of a phenomenon beyond which the phenomenon would cease to be identified as such.

3. The *content* characteristics refer to those properties of a phenomenon which are *not evenly distributed* over all the units and, therefore, will characterize the minimal unities of classification in so far as the latter contain one or more identical properties of the phenomenon at the last stage of dividing these properties.

4. The object characteristic refers to the formation of categories of classification by collating the minimal unities into *successively ordered sets* in the light of those properties of a phenomenon which are regarded as *identical* or *similar* according to the purposes of a program of research.

The *objective* of classification may thus vary according to *why* a particular definition of a phenomenon is adopted for a program of research, while the *object* of classification is concerned with *how* the categories of classification are to be formulated in the context of possible variations in the definition of a phenomenon. The distinction drawn between the objective and object of classification is more noticeable when dealing with such groupings as social class and nation than class and nation-state. It is valid, however, for the classification of all social groups. Hence, the collation of the minimal unities involves a deliberate collection of the ultimately divided properties of a phenomenon according to the procedure of classification concerned with the four aspects listed above.

We shall illustrate these four aspects of classification by referring to some social groups that are frequently mentioned in contemporary social research and that demonstrate some notable societal and social phenomena used to appraise the dynamics of world societies: for example, the distinction between nation-state and nation in the consolidation of, or alienation from, a state power; ethnicity, religion, caste, and tribe in social change and social development as well as in nation-building and state formation; the household and the family as the primordial group in any societal variation; the source of the livelihood of the people in the context of the economic organization of society; and the social class and class structures that are now regarded as playing the key role in social dynamics.

A collection of individual persons (*items* of classification) may identify themselves as citizens of a *nation-state* (*unit of classification*). The state power, which defines their citizenship, exercises its prerogatives in various manners (*content* of classification) which have a significant bearing on the global social system. The state, in its operations, may confine itself exclusively to its citizens, impose its power on other nation-states, or be thus imposed upon. In addition to the processual variations, the content of a nation-state may vary structurally and functionally with reference to the exercise of state power. The state may be a federation of several states, a multinational state, an absolute or constitutional monarchy, and so on. Moreover, all such properties of a nation-state may operate in various combinations. Accordingly, the character of a nation-state is purposively categorized in all sorts of ways (*object* of classification): for example, as monarchic, republican, colonial, bourgeois-democratic, monopoly capitalist, semicolonial, fascist, semifeudal, populist, socialist, communist; and so on.

An *ethnic unit* is identified in terms of a number of persons (*items*) declaring their closest possible oneness in the light of an ethos evolved out of habit and cultural tradition. The nature of the ethos varies from one spontaneously identified ethnic group to another. However, for various reasons, the nature of the ethos may also vary among the ethnic units belonging to the same ethnic group. Accordingly, both possibilities refer to the *content* of ethnicity. The ethnic units, therefore, are to be categorized according to the varying characteristics of the traditional ethos in the context of the known and knowable inter-ethnic and intra-ethnic changes during social development, nation formation, and so on (*object* of classification). Examples of such categorizing are the linguistic-cultural groups of Gujarati, Parsi, Marathi, Punjabi, and Bengali, in the context of the "national integration" of India; black and white, or the Mexicans, Greeks, Italians, Poles, etc., in a similar context in the USA; the East and West Germans in the East and West German republics; the Bengali of West Bengal in India and the Bengali of East Bengal in Bangladesh, or the Indian Punjabi and the Pakistani Punjabi in the context of nation-building and state formation in Bangladesh and Pakistan.

By the self-identity of a number of persons (*items*), a *religious group* (*unit*) is formed to register adherence to a *minimally* cohesive set of supernatural ideas, beliefs, and practices. Thus constituted, the units not only exhibit distinctive ideologies and ethics with respect to the broadly identified religious groups but also are liable to the internal variations manifest in sect membership, ethnicity, nation-state citizenship and other distinctions within a religion. The internal variations are expressed by different interpretations of the core doctrine (a) according to the intrinsic merits of the interpretations or (b) to suit the exigencies of different societies, times and people. For example, the differences among the Christian, Islamic, Buddhist, Hindu, Jewish and other religions are fairly well known, but perhaps not so well known are the distinctive characteristics of the intra-religious units like the *khojas* among the Muslims, the Coptic Christians in Egypt, the Hindus in Fiji, and so on. These variations refer to both cross-cultural and time perspectives and, by their interrelationships cutting across the boundaries of different religions, they offer the possibility for a systemic appraisal of the phenomenon of religion in the global

context as well as for registering trends of change in the phenomenon with reference to the local milieu. Hence, both internal and external variations of the
religious denominations denote the *content* of classification, and the units being categorized accordingly express distinctive differences and interrelations in
the ideological and ethical properties of the world societies at a point in time or
over time periods (*object* of classification).

Caste is known as a Hindu phenomenon, but conceptually and operationally it is extended to other religious groups: for example, conceptually to the
white and the black Christians in the Union of South Africa, and operationally
to the Muslims in the subcontinent of India. In its pristine form among the
Hindus, it is a matter of self-identity by a number of persons (*items*) as members of a group with the specific nomenclature of a *jati*, which is characterized
by endogamy, rules of commensality, and other particular behaviors among a
set of *jatis* according to a purity–pollution standard (*unit*). However, all these
rules, including those referring to connubium, vary among caste units according to the religious sects, ethnicity, and other distinctions in the Hindu and
Muslim societies on the subcontinent of India and elsewhere: for example,
among the Muslim functional and nonfunctional castes in Bengal; among the
Hindus belonging to the *sakta, vaishnava, saiva,* and other sects, or belonging
to the ethnic groups of Kashmiris, Sindhis, Tamil, Assamese, etc., in India;
among the locally evolved Hindu caste units in Guiana, Mauritius, and so on.
As the historians have ascertained, the caste rules and the inter-caste behavior
patterns change due to various exigencies of the local population, and this has
been happening virtually since the time the phenomenon of caste emerged in
Indian culture and civilization. All these variations comprise the *content* of
caste classification. Therefore, the grading and hierarchical grouping (*object*
of classification) of caste units by their content characteristics, in the
place–time–people dimensions of variation in the Indian and allied societies, is
relevant to the study of social change.

A *tribal* unit is usually a matter of statutory distinction drawn by a nation-
state, such as the Scheduled Tribes of India. In that case, the tribes are classified by their meta-tribal characteristics: as hunting, fishing, pastoral,
agricultural tribes; as Negroid, proto-Australoid, Mongolian tribes; as Indian,
Australian, American Indian tribes; as Norwegian, Swedish, or Finnish
Lapps; and so on. But in consideration of the intrinsic characteristics of the
phenomenon "tribal," the statutory tribes also can be classified along with
those which in a nation-state may not have come under such a juridical identification. The "tribal" condition in this context, denotes the early stage of social development of human beings.

The contemporary social scientists seem to accept this evolutionary sequence, but they are generally vague about defining a "tribe." The tendency is
to identify those ethnic groups as tribes which, according to their subjective
judgment—buttressed by some objective characteristics—exhibit "primitive"
features. Nevertheless, some social scientists have posited specific attributes of

a tribe that more or less conform to the definition of this social category as given by the founding fathers of social anthropology and ethnology. For example, Karl Deutsch (1963: 4) defines tribe structurally as "that social and political unit which is above the kingroup and is still small enough to claim common descent although it is large enough to permit intermarriage;" and F. G. Bailey (1960: 265) defines tribe functionally as a set of people who comprise "a relatively large proportion of the total population in the area," have a definite tribal nomenclature, and "still have direct command over resources, . . . their access to the products of the economy. . . not [being] derived mediately through a dependent status on others."

With reference to such descriptions and formulations, we should be concerned with the phenomenon "tribal" in terms of the self-identity of a number of persons (*items*) as members of a group that has a precise nomenclature, usually derived from a belief in their common origin, that enforces endogamy and identifies its constituents as kin and affines, and that represents in the evolution of human societies a preclass (classless) society (*unit*) in terms of the relations of production and property. The classless condition is, however, hardly applicable to any present-day social group which is labeled "tribal." Also, an exclusive identification of this group by kinship relations is not always possible. Hence, the classification of tribes on the basis of their internal characteristics (*content*) refers to their confirmation of, or the nature and extent of their variation from, the given definition of the ideal tribal characteristics. In this way, the phenomenon "tribal" (*object* of classification) can be categorized in the context of social change and social development, as also of nation-building and state formation.

The *household,* the smallest economic cum demographic *unit,* is identified by a number of persons (*items*) living and eating together. The manner of their coresidence and commensality (*content*) may not, however, be the same for all household units. Kin groupings of the households may be one dimension of variation in this phenomenon; the nature of coresidence and commensality may be another; and there may be others, including a combination of the above two. A household may consist of a kin group, commonly identified as a family. It may also consist of more than one family: for example, the kin group of the person who has set up the household and the kin group of his servants comprising a husband and a wife or an uncle and his nephew, and so on. It is equally possible for a household to consist of a family and a nonfamilial unit (a servant, for instance, who has no kin member in the household). A household may be a boarding house, a mess and barracks, a roving band of people, all of which consist of a number of persons who may or may not be related as kin and affines but are living and eating in common. A household may also be conceived of as a unit for investment and generation of income or for inheritance (e.g., of landed property).

The respective sets of household characteristics may cut across one another. For example, the writer found in 1950 that the family among the Acholi in Uganda has a well-demarcated dwelling compound; but in that compound the wives of the polygynous husband have separate huts for the boarding and lodging of themselves and their children, while the husband retains the central hut for his exclusive occupation and eats with his wives in turn. In this case, the household properties are held with reference to the dwelling compound but not the huts of the wives and that of the husband. Parallel instances are occasionally still found today among the landed aristocracies of Pakistan and India, and elsewhere. The German *Grossfamilie* and the household organization in medieval English castles may also be considered in the same context. Moreover, in the contemporary world economy, finding the household becomes a matter of empirical identification in terms of an income-generating, consumption, and investment unit formed over a period (and not a point) in time. The *object* of classification thus defines the unit and content characteristics of a household, which is commonly regarded as an invariant phenomenon.

The *family*, the smallest societal grouping, refers to the self-identity of a number of persons (*items*) as members of a kin group that they regard as their family (*unit*). This *minimal* kin group may also be identified on the basis of personal attributes like coresidence, commensality, etc. In whichever manner a set of families is thus identified, the units vary according to the nature and extent of variation in their kinship composition (*content*). The categorization of family units in terms of the kinship patterns, extensions of these patterns, or the deviations from the core patterns registered in the units denote the operation of the family as an institution over time and space (*object* of classification).

The *source of livelihood* is a common classification in social research, used to denote the economic organization of society and also for explaining the unit formation of some frequently examined phenomena like "social class" in the Weberian sense and "class" in the Marxist conception. The specificity of the phenomenon, however, varies among researchers because not all of them distinguish between its two components: (1) the sector of economic activity to which an income-recipient belongs, and (2) the nature of work performed by gainfully employed individuals. The Statistical Commission of the United Nations has, therefore, sponsored two parallel schemes of classification, labelling the former component as "industry" and the latter as "occupation" (Statistical Office of the United Nations 1968; International Labor Office 1958). In a sense, thus, the source of livelihood as a phenomenon refers to a grouping derived from two primary social groups: (1) the occupational groupings of the people, and (2) the sectors of economic activity to which these occupations belong—the sectors including also those income-recipients who do not record, conventionally, any gainful occupation (e.g., rentier, usurer, prostitute).

Separately, however, occupation and industry can be regarded as two distinct phenomena referring to two kinds of primary groupings in society. As we shall shortly see, this is not so in the case of the phenomena like class, social class, and nation, which refer to derived social groups that are not divisible, unlike the source of livelihood, which can be divided into its two components. The latter phenomenon, therefore, may be regarded as referring to quasi-derived social groups, and the aspects of its classifications may be specified with direct reference to its components.

Accordingly, with reference to the gainfully occupied persons (*items*), *minimally characterizing* the nature of their jobs (*units*) begins the process of occupational classification. The job units refer to a wide variation in job characteristics—usually qualified further by the nature and degree of physical (manual) and mental (nonmanual) labor involved in each job (*content*). Hence, the job units are categorized according to their content characteristics in order to represent one facet of the economic organization (*object* of classification).

Corresponding to the occupational classification of the gainfully occupied persons, the affiliation of *all* income-recipients (*items*) to one or another of the *minimally characterized* economic activities (*unit*) is the basis of their industrial classification. The industry units refer to a wide variety of economic enterprises and establishments, undertakings and services (*content*). Hence, the economic activity units (i.e., the industry units) are categorized in terms of their content characteristics, to represent the other facet of economic organization (*object* of classification).

Class, the predominant concept in the Marxist schema for denoting social change and social development, refers to a derived social group by beginning with the industry-occupation units as the *items* of classification. In order to obtain the *minimal unities* of a class structure, the industry-occupation units are grouped according to their registering the *same* relations of production, as dependent upon the *same* property relations, emerging from the *same* mode of production and the *same* state of development of the productive forces (*units* of classification). These relations of production and property, as well as the modes of production and the state of productive forces, may vary widely and generate various orders of contradiction among some of the units, on account of the nature and degree of exploitation of labor or labor-power—when a conceptual distinction is drawn between labor and labor-power under relevant conditions. The unit characteristics may, on the other hand, help to forge various kinds and degrees of alliance among some units. All such *contradictions* and *complementarities,* which emerge from the exploitation of labor (or labor-power) and lead to the definition of "class for itself" along with that of "class by itself," refer to the *content* of classification. With reference to these contradictions and complementarities, therefore, classes are categorized (*object* of classification) by grouping appropriate class units in order to denote the dynamics of society in the past, at present, and in the immanent future.

The use of the concept of "social class" has the same objective as "class," but refers to another derived social group by following a different pattern of categorization of the primary social groups. The *item* of classification in this case refers not only to the industry-occupation units but also to the religion-caste-ethnic units and sometimes to a rather imprecisely characterized cultural grouping as well. The *units* of classification, then, refer to an *integrated* classification (and not merely the cross-classification) of the item units in order to produce mutually distinct *minimal* status *unities* on the basis of a priori assumptions by the researchers or of self-evaluation by the members of the item units. The *content* of classification refers to the status gaps evaluated by the researchers or by those being studied in order to rank the status units. The *object* of classification is, therefore, the social classes (which are regarded as maintaining the status quo in society or leading to social change) from the construction of a hierarchy of status units according to their ranks. It will be noticed that the object of classification is to identify the social classes, while the objective of classification may vary according to the researchers' or the researchee's manner of identifying the social classes according to their applicable attributes.

The nation as a phenomenon distinct from the nation-state refers to another derived social group. Apparently, it represents a collection of individuals, but these persons are now grouped in terms of (a) the objective attributes of territorial affiliation, common history, community of culture and language(s), and common economic organization, and (b) the subjective psychological sense of identity *beyond* the ascriptive and achieved loyalties derived from the objective attributes and expressed through kinship, caste, religion, ethnicity, class, and social class categories (R. Mukherjee 1979: 140-206). Accordingly, the tribal, caste, religious, ethnic, class, and social class units are the *items* of classification for the phenomenon of a nation. These item units, however, may belong to *one or more* nation-states because of the distinction and interrelation to be drawn between the concepts of "nation for itself" and "nation by itself." The *units* of classification, therefore, refer to territorial consolidation of these item units whether assumed a priori or self-evaluated by the unit members in a manner that may or may not synchronize with the territorial consolidation of the nation-states by the attribute of citizenship. Correspondingly, the *content* of classification refers to the nature and extent of variation in group loyalty such that it allows the upholding, enlarging, or constricting of the existing state boundaries or the formation of new states out of existing states. The *object* of classification, consequently, is the nations and nationalities with respect to variations in the content characteristics of the nation units, while the objective of classification may vary according to the definition of nation and nationalities.

The phenomena we have discussed for purposes of illustrating the four aspects of classification cover the field of social research with respect to both the omnibus antecedence and the specific relevance of the social phenomena. Other societal phenomena can, of course, be considered in a similar manner because (*a*) the definition of each aspect of classification is unequivocal, and (*b*) a sequential relation is indicated among the four aspects in classifying any phenomenon with reference to all its properties. The *item* is the *medium of ex-*

pression of the *properties* of a phenomenon. The *unit* formed by the items denotes the *minimal structure* in which to locate the *uniform* properties of a phenomenon and thus record its *peripheral* characteristics to distinguish it from other phenomena with which it may be associated. The *content,* which is all *intrinsically variable*—structural, functional, and processual—properties of a phenomenon, will lead to the categorization of the *minimal sets* of units exhibiting *identical* properties. Lastly, the *object* forms *successively bigger sets of units,* according to the objective of the particular research project, by grouping those sets of units which register *similar sets* of intrinsic properties of the phenomenon. The associated and the inherent properties of a phenomenon, therefore, are clearly specified by the four aspects of classification: from the last stage of dividing its properties to the last stage of collecting them all together under the label given to the phenomenon.

This coverage of the scope of classification should be readily understood from Table 2.1 which has been prepared with reference to the phenomena we have discussed. A careful examination of the table will also reveal the interrelationships among the phenomena, because the relevant phenomena will be seen to cut across, systematically, their respective aspects of classification. Illustratively, Table 2.1 presents the *frame of reference* for considering classification per se. It provides clues enabling us to systematize our knowledge on (a) the respective sets of variation which the phenomena severally present, and (b) the relevantly interlocked systems of variation at different levels of the social reality, which some phenomena display by their integration at the stage of item and/or unit characterization of a derived (viz. social) phenomenon.

Table 2.1.
Frame of Reference for Classification

Phenomenon	Aspects of Classification			
	Item	Unit	Content	Object
(1)	(2)	(3)	(4)	(5)

1. *Primary Social Groups*

Phenomenon	Item	Unit	Content	Object
Nation-state (= nation by itself)	Persons	Self-identification as citizens	Varying exercise of state power	Character of state power
Ethnicity	Persons	Self-identification by closest possible unity in an ethos based on habit and cultural tradition	Inter-ethnic and Intra-ethnic variations in the traditional ethos of spontaneously identified ethnic groups	Nature and extent of intrinsic and induced variations within and between ethnic groups

Religion	Persons	Self-identification with a minimally cohesive set of supernatural ideas, beliefs, and practices	Variations within and between the core ideologies and ethics of religious groups identified spontaneously	Distinctive and systemized sets of people with shared supernatural ideologies and ethics.
Caste *(jati)*	Persons	Self-identification with a precisely labelled group characterized by endogamy and other behavior on a purity–pollution scale	Inter-ethnic and intra-ethnic, inter-community, temporal, and other variations in the behavior pattern of all caste units forming an analogous series	Grading and hierarchical groupings of caste units in a specified milieu or on a universal basis, but varying over time
Tribe	Persons	Self-identification with a precisely labelled group characterized by endogamy, kinship, and preclass economy	Conformity to, or the nature and extent of variation from, the ideal kinship integration in a preclass society	Categorization of groups indicating survival of the tribal state or detribalization by suprakinship integration and emergence of class relations
Household	Persons	Self-identification with a group characterized by coresidence and commensality, and/or other attributes	Nature and extent of variations in the constituent properties of a household	Categorization of household units by their content characteristics
Family	Persons	Self-identification with a minimal kin group or identification by some other traits	Qualitative and quantitative variations in kinship composition	Categorization of family structures according to information on formation and extension of, and deviation from, kinship patterns

2. Quasi-Derived Social Groups

Source of livelihood

Occupation (UN label)	Gainfully occupied persons	Self-identification as being in a minimally characterized job or identification based on an a priori classificatory schema	Order of variations in job characteristics by (a) the nature work performed, (b) the extent of physical and mental labor involved in each job	Categorization of job units according to their content characteristics

Industry (UN label)	Income-recipients	Affiliation with the minimally characterized economic activity	Nature of economic enterprise and establishment, undertaking, or service	Categorization of the economic activity units by their content characteristics

3. Derived Social Groups

Class "by itself"	Industry-occupation units	Categorization of item units under minimally similar relations of production and property, emerging from the same mode of production and the same state of productive forces	Nature and extent of exploitation of labor/labor-power of one unit by another, or a corresponding alliance between units, as revealed through the relations of production and property among all units formed	Categorization of classes according to the nature and degree of their units' contradictory/complementary relations as determined by their content characteristics
Class "for itself"	Class units (= "unit" of class "by itself")	Categorization of classes (= "object" of class "by itself")	Attitudinal and behavioral traits to indicate, ignore, or resist the generation of class consciousness	Categorization of classes in terms of the nature and extent of class consciousness
Social Class	Industry-occupation, caste-religion-ethnic, and cultural units	Minimal status units assumed a priori from item units or from self-evaluation by unit members	Researcher's or the unit members' evaluation of status gaps of different magnitudes among the status units	Categorization of social classes according to content characteristics of status units
Nation "for itself"	Tribal, caste, religious, ethnic, class, and social class units of one or more nation-states	Territorial consolidation (or aspiration) of the item units assumed a priori or self-evaluated by the unit members	Nature and extent of group loyalty to uphold, enlarge, or constrict the existing state boundaries or attempt to form new states out of existing ones	Categorization of nations and nationalities in terms of the content characteristics of the nation units

Next, therefore, we shall examine this frame of reference in order to evolve an efficient procedure of classification in the light of the problems the framework poses in the course of systematizing the aspects of classification.

3 Problem

The systemic relations established by the aspects of classification in dividing and collecting the properties of a phenomenon can also be extended across the phenomena, provided there is a least common denominator for all these phenomena. In the case of social research, that least common denominator is an individual person. He/or she may directly represent the item characteristic for classification or do it in a group, both of which possibilities are illustrated in Table 2.1. We should also bear in mind that although the item characteristics in a process of societal classification may be inanimate specimens of a particular variety, these specimens must be characteristics of persons individually or in groups. This we have pointed out in Chapter 1 in connection with the categorization of income as a measure variable. Directly or indirectly, human beings represent the least common denominator of all societal phenomena. Let us, therefore, examine how the integration of individuals in multifarious ways registers a systemic relation among the societal phenomena, between the societal and the social phenomena, and among the social phenomena.

Since without group formation human individuals cannot survive and find the means to express their potentialities, their groups must be based on specific rights and duties of group constituents and between groups. Primary groups are thus formed and lead to the emergence of more and more complex groups that refer to successively integrated networks of relationships and the corresponding behavior patterns that hold the individuals together. However, some individuals' or groups' potential for expression may be thwarted for the benefit of some other individuals or groups because the reciprocal relations and the operation of rights and duties may lead to unequal exchange among them. Contradictions that thus develop in the social space lead to the disappearance or recasting of some operating groups and the emergence of new groups. This is how human society moves over time and space; and, therefore, in the course of these historical and dialectical manoeuvres, the phenomena for social research should be regarded as homologous or analogous, i.e., they have a common or parallel origin and development.

Accordingly, the inherent properties of the societal phenomena, considered under the content and object aspects of classification, are homologous or analogous. Their associated properties, expressed by the unit aspects of classification, are also homologous or analogous because these not only distinguish the phenomena by their peripheral characteristics but also maintain their association on the same basis. In addition, links of successively higher orders and levels of behavior patterns within and among the *societal* phenomena (as described in Chapter 1) are forged by the related characteristics of the item aspect of classification; these links denote the omnibus antecedence as well as specific relevance of the *social* phenomena, because while providing the base for the sequential development of the item–unit–content–object aspects of classification, the items for the classification of different phenomena refer directly or indirectly to individual persons and to particular forms of social groups formed by these persons.

As we see from Table 2.1, the items for the classification of the phenomena related to the primary social groups are individual persons who combine or separate in various ways with reference to different phenomena. The individuals $(i_1, \ldots, i_5)$ may form a family as against the individuals $(i_6, \ldots, i_9)$ who form another family, and the two families may form two households or only one. However, out of these individuals, i_1 and i_6 may belong to an occupational group constituted of individuals from various family units, i_2 and i_7 to another, and so on, while $(i_4, \ldots, i_8 \ldots)$ may refer to a group of persons (with individuals from other family units) who are not gainfully employed, but i_4 may be a rentier and i_8 unemployed. With reference to other phenomena related to primary social groups, i_1 and i_6 may be affiliated with different sectors of the economy under the UN label of "industry," $(i_1, \ldots, i_9)$ may belong to the same tribe or caste, $(i_1, \ldots, i_k)$ to one religion, $(i_1, \ldots, i_n)$ to an ethnic group, and $(i_1, \ldots, i_t)$ to a nation-state. Thus, with the individual persons representing—directly or indirectly—the indivisible items of classification, a first-order link is forged for the classification of those phenomena which are related to the primary social groups.

This link will persist for the classification of all societal phenomena because whatever kind of social groups they are, all social groups can be regarded as constituted of a number of individuals: the least common denominator. As we see, however, from Table 2.1, the indivisible items of classification for the phenomena related to the derived social groups are not individual persons. The items may be the units of classification of the relevant phenomena concerned with primary social groups, as it is in the case of social class and "class by itself". The items of classification may also refer, concurrently or exclusively, to the units of classification of those phenomena which are concerned with derived social groups. It can be seen from Table 2.1 that the *item* of classification in the case of "class for itself" is the *unit* of classification regarding "class by itself," and the *unit* of classification in the case of the former is the *object* of classification for the latter. It can also be seen that the *item* of classification in the case of "nation for itself" refers to the *units* of classification for "class by itself" and social class along with those for the tribe, caste, religion, and ethnicity. Thus, links of higher orders and levels are forged for the classification of phenomena related to the primary and derived social groups.

Such links may be forged in other ways also, for example, when two or more phenomena, related to the primary and/or derived social groups, are brought under one course of classification. This, it will be noticed, refers to an *operational* coordination of more than one societal phenomena and not a *conceptual* combination of several phenomena as found in the classification of class, social class, and nation. Nevertheless, distinctively appropriate and useful concepts are brought to bear upon the classification of such *compound* phenomena.

A simple case of this kind, frequently found in social research, is the phenomenon of "family occupation" which is applicable when more than one gainfully occupied person is found in a family: the family occupation is derived from that occupation which out of all occupations recorded for the family yields the largest income or entails the largest quantum of labor or registers its preeminence by some other attribute. In this case, the *item* of classification refers to all persons *and* those with gainful occupations; the *unit* of classification refers to all family members *and* those among them who are gainfully employed; the *content* of classification refers to the properties used to determine the one predominant family occupation out of all occupations in the family; and the *object* of classification categorizes the compounded units according to their content characteristics.

Cases of this kind denote the initial stage for producing links of successively higher orders and levels in the classification of phenomena related operationally to derived social groups. The family occupation may also need to be derived when there is only one gainfully occupied person in the family but he or she is engaged in more than one occupation. In that case, the content and the object of classification have to be determined in the way already noted, but a joint consideration of the phenomena of family *and* occupation in the context of the item and the unit of classification would be only theoretically relevant for standardizing the process of classification.

That, however, would not be the case when, for instance, a classification is devised to cover the phenomenon of detribalization, the germ of which has been noted under the content and object characteristics of the tribe in Table 2.1, which thus illustrates the analogous properties of classification of the societal phenomena related to the primary and derived social groups. Several schema for social change may be examined in the context of a detribalization process, as we have discussed elsewhere (R. Mukherjee 1979: 140-206): tribes – confederation of tribes – nation; tribes – castes – nation; tribes – ethnic groups (with class formation and extension beyond kinship boundaries) – nation; and so on. Accordingly, the second or higher level links with respect to all four aspects of classification are established among the relevant societal phenomena considered together for the process of classification.

Now, as we have discussed in Chapter 1, all societal phenomena are relevant to social reality and require classification by forging links among them. For example, the *relative* necessity, efficiency, and sufficiency of the phenomena of class and social class for understanding social reality is one of the central issues of contemporary social research. Another is the phenomena of nation-building and state formation in the context of changes in the nation-states with respect to religion, ethnicity, class, social class, etc., which may (a) consolidate the existing state further, (b) lead to the splitting up of previous nation-states and the formation of new states and nations, or (c) establish the consociation or confederacy of a number of nation-states. These and other immanent and emergent social phenomena in the dynamic perspective of the world societies are mutually distinct but not exclusive. *This is why value con-*

siderations in social research are so easily diffused instead of being polarized. Indeed, because of their homologous and analogous relationships, all the societal phenomena have become relevant to explaining and diagnosing social reality by adopting the "value accommodation" approach to social research, as we have explained elsewhere (R. Mukherjee 1976b; 1979: 216-229.) Accordingly, the phenomena must not only forge links of successive orders and levels with respect to their item and unit aspects of classification but also with respect to their content and object characteristics. Of the latter, we see a glimpse in Table 2.1 with reference to "class by itself" and "class for itself."

The necessity and further possibility of forging links among the societal phenomena and with respect to the content and object aspects of classification can be discerned from the illustrative phenomena we have already discussed and then cited in Table 2.1. We conceive the characteristics of the tribe in this particular context. We may also reiterate the potential of this linkage between the content and the object aspects of classification for overcoming the separation between some of those phenomena that are often regarded conceptually to be unique or exclusive.

The controversy about the family and the household in terms of their analogous (but not homologous) content characteristics has led to the conceptualization of the "development cycle in domestic groups" (Goody 1958). The familial character may also cut across the characteristics of economic organization (e.g., industry) as in India with the "houses" of Tata, Birla, etc., and in Japan and many other nation-states with their industrial and financial "families." Moreover, the familial characteristics may be relevant to an "anti-social" organization like the Mafia in Italy and the United States.

The caste properties register variation not only ethnically but also with reference to class and social class distinctions. Ethnic variation in religion is important because of the influence of habit and cultural tradition on the specific supernatural ideology and ethics, while social class variation in the practice of a religion cannot be ignored. Class variation in nation-states is undoubtedly important for indicating variation in the nature of state power; correspondingly, class contradictions may play the role of catalysts in the formation of a new nation and a new state. Distinctions by ethnicity and religion also cannot be ignored in the same context, as, for example, regarding the formation of the Republic of India and Pakistan on the Indian subcontinent, first, and that of Bangladesh later.

The problems of classification thus emerge from conceiving the four aspects of classification in such a manner that they maintain a systemic relation both in the intra-phenomenon and inter-phenomena contexts, while themselves being mutually distinct.

For this conceptual framework the most important point to note is that all the four aspects of classification are variables. This is generally accepted for the content aspect of classification, as it is obvious; but even in this case the variable properties may not be treated meticulously and systematically. Less obvious and usually less systematized are the variations in the object aspect of classification, while the unit aspect is commonly held as constant and the item aspect as self-evident from the unit aspect. This follows from the tendency to regard the minimal unities of a phenomenon *as pertaining to its definition and not its classification*. But with the substantial accumulation of knowledge about variations in societal phenomena, the assumption that the units of classification are automatically identified by the definition of a phenomenon is no longer tenable.

Indeed, the definitional properties of the phenomena are in the process of change. We have now moved up from a definitive understanding of the peripheral characteristics of the phenomena at a preliminary level of their analysis to the next level of *indeterminacy*, and have not yet reached the level of dialectical resolution of the issues involved so as to define the phenomena precisely, unequivocally, and comprehensively. This has complicated the scope of classification in social research since the unit aspect also contains variable data, and they are known and knowable as we can see from Table 2.1.

With reference to the primary social groups, variations in unit characterization appear to be of marginal or no importance because individuals identify themselves with units of family, household, occupation, industry, caste, religion, ethnicity, nation-state, and so on. But, as we find on Table 2.1, self-identity is not the only means of distinguishing the units of classification for the phenomena related to the primary social groups.

Moreover, even where self-identity plays a role, it may have to be qualified in order to characterize the units of classification. A person may claim to belong to one family but the attributes of coresidence and commensality (irrespective of the less employed but no less relevant attributes of ownership of family property, performance of familial rites, family integration, etc.) may put him or her in another family or characterize the person as a "non-familial unit" (R. Mukherjee 1977a: 1-6). A household is a self-identified coresident and commensal unit, but the controversy has not been resolved as to whether a boarding house is a household or if each one of its members forms a household (cf. Government of India multipurpose national sample surveys). More ticklish is the controversy on whether or not an income-generating unit—which is not a consumption unit at all points in time (and which may be an investment unit but not a unit for inheritance)—is a household. In spite of self-identification and being gainfully employed, controversy persists on whether a moneylender or a landowner letting out his land for sharecropping should be regarded as having an occupation or should be put under the "industry" classification of income recipients without a gainful occupation.

To illustrate further the present state of indeterminacy in social science, "What is a tribe?" is a perennial question for the social anthropologists. In spite of an almost unanimous acceptance among the social scientists that caste in India refers to the *jati* and not the *varna* stratification of society (see R. Mukherjee 1957: 61-80), the process of self-identification as a member of caste units creates problems and leads to the spontaneous formation of subcastes, sub-subcastes, and so on. The definition of a religious unit as a set of people sharing "self-identification with a minimally cohesive set of supernatural ideas, beliefs, and practices," or of an ethnic unit as "self-identification through the closest possible unity in an ethos," implies known and knowable variations in the unit characterization of the phenomena of religion and ethnicity. Finally, out of the examples cited, only for the phenomenon of the nation-state does the unit characterization appear to be constant; but there are variations in this case too, for example, with respect to those persons who hold dual citizenship in different nation-states.

We notice from these examples that the item characteristics of the phenomena related to the primary social groups are also liable to variation; they need not be self-evident and constant. Would all persons be classified as forming family units or would some of them be denoted as nonfamilial units? The distinction was found important for appraising the dynamics of family organization in West Bengal over twenty years ago (R. Mukherjee 1977a). Similar variations have been cited or are implied for other phenomena, including the nation-state. For example, all Hindus as persons may not affiliate themselves with a caste classification; some would categorically oppose the system, and on "traditional" grounds, too: we tend to forget that there are many heterodox doctrines within the Hindu view of life. As regards the nation-state classification, there are many people all over the globe who are not citizens of any nation-state.

Moreover, regarding the phenomena related to the derived social groups, their item aspect of classification varies according to its reference to the unit characteristics of the phenomena related to the primary social groups. In addition, if the item aspect refers to the unit aspect of some derived social groups, as it does in the case of the "nation for itself" with reference to class and social class, the item aspect varies according to the variable conceptualization of the units used for the classification of the phenomena related to the derived social groups.

This problem would seem to be irrelevant in cases where a phenomenon is defined precisely. But, first, all the definitional characteristics of a phenomenon may not be equally emphasized by the researchers according to their orientation and purpose; and, secondly, the definition itself may need elaboration or revision in the light of the continual accumulation of knowledge on world society and changes in different configurations of world society over time and space.

For example, the concept of "class by itself" in the Marxist schema appears to leave no room for equivocal identification of the class units, but subtle distinctions in interpreting the similarity or difference in the state of the productive forces and even in the modes of production have been noticed for the classification of class structures. More easily noticeable perhaps is that while the class units are to be identified from a joint consideration of the production and the property relations with which the industry-occupation units are involved, differential emphases are paid to the inherent characteristics of the two relational aspects and sometimes one of the two may be ignored altogether. For example, should the sharecroppers be distinguished from the agricultural wage-laborers in terms of the relations of production or both be classed together in terms of property relations as "dispossessed peasantry" (see R. Mukherjee 1957: 46-58)? All these variations in the definitional characteristics of "class by itself" have a crucial bearing on the evolution of an efficient understanding of an agrarian society (see R. Mukherjee 1981).

Furthermore, when some scholars, like Herbert Marcuse, introduce the possibility of emergence and/or resolution of class contradictions through the intervention of "nonconformist young intelligentsia," the "ghetto population," the "underprivileged sections of the labouring classes in backward capitalist countries" (Marcuse 1969: 52-56), the *minimal* unit characterization for the classification of classes becomes far more widely variable than is usually envisaged. These possibilities have generated polemics among the Marxists and obviously concern the known and knowable variations in the unit aspect of classification of the phenomenon of class. A resolution of these variations will no doubt systemize our knowledge of social dynamics at a higher level than that which we have reached today. Therefore, at the present state of our knowledge about the phenomenon of class, its unit aspect will have to be regarded as variable and not unequivocally constant.

The unit aspect of classification of the phenomena of social class and of the nation is obviously variable on conceptual grounds, for in both cases the aspect refers to status units and territorial units "assumed a priori" as can be seen from Table 2.1. The operational significance of this kind of variation is well known. Whether white-collar and blue-collar workers earning the same income represent different status units is still moot in social class classification. Similarly, preliminary investigations into the growing alienation of the people from state power in Sikkim and the Darjeeling District of West Bengal pointed to the need for distinguishing the ethnic-territorial unit of the local Nepalis according to whether they hold citizenship in India or Nepal (R. Mukherjee 1979: 175).

Moreover, even though these kinds of units may be evaluated by the members of item units, as also seen on Table 2.1, the process of self-evaluation can be neither unanimously the same for all the evaluators nor absolutely unequivocal for some of them, at any rate. This was reported with respect to the "social grading of occupations" in Great Britain (Moser and Hall 1954: 29-50). Similarly it was noticed in the context of their demanding autonomy for the hill people in the Darjeeling District of West Bengal that of the autochthonous ethnic unit of the Lepchas an appreciable number (but not all) called themselves Nepalis.

However, the variations thus involved in the unit characterization of the two phenomena of social class and nation by the researchers and the researched will surely provide clues to the knowable information about them, as we have noted in the case of class as a phenomenon. For the same reason, in the immediate or the immanent perspective of *all* societal phenomena, the unit aspect of classification must be regarded as variable while the item aspect also cannot be regarded as self-evidently constant. Hence, the point to underline is that variability in each one of the four aspects of classification has a specificity of its own, regardless of the selectivity of researchers in examining some particular characteristics of a phenomenon in just one aspect.

This point is implicit to the construction of Table 2.1 because it records (1) the distinctive peripheral characteristics of the phenomena imparting specificity to their respective item and unit aspects of classification, (2) the distinguishing characteristics inherent to the phenomena which impart specificity to the content aspect of classification, and (3) the stated objectives for categorizing variations that impart specificity to the object aspects of classification of the respective phenomena. Nevertheless, regarding the unit–content–object aspects of classification, their specificities may appear to be obliterated for some phenomena such as for caste and social class, out of the examples cited.

That may be due to a seemingly similar set of characteristics put under the unit–content–object aspects of classification of a phenomenon. For example, the behavior patterns on a purity–pollution scale identify the caste units, give content to these units, and allow them to be categorized on the same basis under the object aspect of classification. But the caste units can be distinguished in a particular manner by one set of their constituent content, regardless of the total possibility of variations in the contextual behavior patterns which fall under the content aspect of caste classification. Also, the hierarchical grading and grouping of the caste units in terms of their content characteristics can be made in various ways, regardless of how one or another set of researchers and researched would like to construct the caste hierarchy.

Similarly, it may appear with respect to social class classification that the central objective of status evaluation of the items concerned removes the distinctions among the unit–content–object aspects of classification. But we have pointed out that there are various possibilities of identifying the status units by the researchers and the researched, regardless of the totality of characteristics denoting the status gaps which fall under the content aspect of social class classification. Also the status hierarchy for categorizing the social classes under the object aspect of classification may be construed in various ways, all evaluated on their specific merits, regardless of the what–how–why of the identification of status units and the evaluation of status gaps among the units.

Moreover, in the context of caste, social class, and similar social groups, we enter into a distinctive field of variation because the status gaps, inter-caste differences, etc., may be of variable magnitudes and direction with respect to the status units, caste units, and similar units employed *one at a time* as the point of reference in grading all the units in a series. *It is generally found from field studies that the inter-unit gaps are more subjectively variable with respect to those units which the unit constituents regard as near one another than those which they consider to be far apart.* It is also found that the constituents of units 5 and 6, for example, may contest their relative positions as higher or lower in the grading of, say, 10 units, and the same may be observed among the units 1–3, 7–9, and so on. This means that the subjectively appraised units of classification may not be *equispaced* and their hierarchical ordering may not be *unilinear.* As referring to the content and object aspects of classification, these issues therefore pose additional problems which we shall discuss later in this chapter in connection with the suitability of graph theory and set theory for classification in social research.

For the present, we may conclude that *with respect to classification as a system by itself, its four aspects should be conceived as independent, parallel, and, at the same time, interconnected subsystems.* Operationally this means that the aspects of classification are to be regarded as *mutually distinct but analogous:* distinct, because they vary independently with respect to the specific nature of variable characteristics of the phenomenon they cover; and analogous, because with respect to a phenomenon they draw a sequential relationship among the item–unit–content–object characteristics.

In the inter-phenomenal context, also, the mutually distinct but analogous character of the four aspects of classification holds because the societal phenomena are homologous or analogous. Moreover, their interrelationships may now cut across the aspects such that, for example, the item characteristics of one phenomenon may be related to the unit characteristics of another phenomenon, the unit characteristics of the second phenomenon may be related to the content or object characteristics of a third phenomenon, and so on, as one can see in Table 2.1. *Hence, the problems of classification emerge from the conceptualization of its four aspects to represent flexible but comprehensive, and mutually distinct but analogous, systems of variation both in the intra-phenomenon and inter-phenomena contexts.*

These problems may now be enumerated as follows:

1. While classification means the systematization of knowledge about phenomena obtained from observation, analysis, and comprehension of the relevant interlocked systems of variation at different levels of discovered reality, *the procedural identification of the four aspects of classification should be clearly distinguished with respect to all phenomena.* On the one hand, these four aspects denote a sequential relationship of the item-unit-content-object characteristics of a phenomenon, and, on the other, each aspect should be regarded as variable on its own account. Hence, with reference to classification per se, each one of its four aspects is to be regarded as a system of variation and treated accordingly.

2. In order to systematize the variations in each aspect of classification, *the phenomenal characteristics with which each aspect is involved are to be*

treated distinctly at the last stage of dividing them, on the one hand, and as consolidated successively up to the last stage of collecting them, on the other. If the aspects are thus systematized, the selectivity of researchers in preparing their schemes of classification, by stressing some aspect characteristics considered relevant, will not impose any constraint, for comparable purposes, on the total field of variation. *Instead, by following this procedure, it is possible to assess precisely and unequivocally the relative efficiency of different schemes of classification for the same phenomenon.*

3. Besides those variable characteristics of a phenomenon which are known in the current state of knowledge, some knowable variations are suggested by the critical researchers or by incipient indications of such variations sometimes available from rigorous and intensive research. Hence, *the process of systematization in the four aspects of classification should be so designed in the course of dividing and collecting the respective sets of characteristics of a phenomenon that it will not only be amenable to the known variations in the existing state of knowledge about the phenomenon but also to the knowable variations that may be suggested or rudimentarily noticed in any one of the sequentially related four aspects.*

4. Since the societal phenomena are homologous or analogous, their characteristics exhibited in the four aspects of classification are also analogous both from the intra-phenomenon and inter-phenomena perspectives. Accordingly, the analogous nature of the mutually distinct systems of variation represented by the four aspects of classification enables us to comprehend the known and the knowable variations of all interlocked systems of variation within one theoretically conceived social space. However, in this social space, the analogous nature of the phenomena perceived at different levels of discovery of reality may draw sequential relations between different aspects of classification in the inter-phenomena context; for example, the unit aspect of one phenomenon may be related to the item, content, or object aspect of another. *Hence, to be adequate and efficient, the procedure of classification should be such that, on the one hand, it systematically and meticulously divides all aspect properties of all societal phenomena in order to maintain uniformity from the last stage of the dividing process on, and, on the other, it systematically and successively collects all these properties in a manner that does not impose any constraint on comparing the collated sets of properties.*

The problems of classification we have thus enumerated follow from our discussion in Chapter 1 on the context and measure variables from the perspective of contemporary social research. We had noted that for explanatory research the context for classification is provided by the explanation itself, and for descriptive research by what the researcher wishes to describe. In both cases, therefore, the object of classification is fixed and, thus, the context variable is turned into a constant. Accordingly, against the given context a measure variable employed to depict a phenomenon (and, therefore, placed under the content aspect of classification) is categorized in the manner and to the extent necessary for the explanation or description. The unit characterization of the phenomenon and the corresponding item characteristics are also given by the explanatory or descriptive purpose (i.e., by the invariant object aspect of classification). The item and unit aspects of classification are, therefore, also turned into constants. Hence, the frame of reference for depicting the four aspects of classification is redundant: the division and collection of the properties of a phenomenon do not make classification a problem in itself.

For diagnostic research, on the other hand, which contemporary social research demands, the procedure of classification for descriptive or explanatory research becomes inadequate and inefficient. Diagnostic research requires (*a*) the simultaneous examination of a set of explanations of a phenomenon, (*b*) the assumption of possible variations in the definitional properties of the phenomenon, and (*c*) the accommodation of additional explanations which may be posited along with the continual accumulation of knowledge about the phenomenon. The object, unit, and item characteristics of a phenomenon therefore cannot be regarded as constants. Instead, all these three characteristics and, consequently, the content characteristics of a phenomenon also, must be regarded as theoretically representing mutually distinct but analogous fields of variations. And, since classification is now concerned with the known and the knowable properties of a phenomenon, all the four aspects of classification must refer to infinite but enumerable fields of variation in these characteristics.

We should therefore examine, next, whether the prevailing typological approach to classification can satisfactorily resolve the problems we have enumerated with reference to the framework of classification that is theoretically valid for all modes of research but becomes particularly relevant and necessary for the diagnostic mode of research demanded today.

4 TYPOLOGICAL APPROACH

We have mentioned that in the days of descriptive research schemes of classification were evolved on the basis of types deduced from what were regarded as the essential features of the phenomena examined. The item and the unit aspects of classification were more or less regarded as invariant at that stage of social science knowledge, and the types were evolved from spontaneous observation of some variations in the content and the object aspects of classification. Eventually, the typologies were standardized by the schemes of classification sponsored by authoritative scientific bodies (e.g., The Royal Anthropological Institute of Great Britain and Ireland 1954; Murdock, et al. 1950, the census authorities of the "developed" societies, like Great Britain, France, the United States). So long as the basic information for concept formation and definition of the societal phenomena was not substantial, there was hardly any alternative to typing the variations observed in the content and object aspects of classification, and standardizing these variations by the schemes of typological classification. The point, however, has been rather ignored that this procedure cannot be efficient, or even adequate, in the present state of social science knowledge and with the qualitative change in the objective of social research, the critical relevance of both of which has been noted in the preceding pages.

The basic principle of the typological approach is to observe variations in a phenomenon from the top downwards, as it were, of the information space constituted by the characteristics of the phenomenon. Then, the observed variations (the measure variables) are categorized into types, a set of which may be arranged to form a nominal or ordinal series according to the character of the object of classification. By reversing this deductive process of classification, the population approach enumerates variations in the phenomenon upwards from the bottom, so to speak, of the information space constituted by the characteristics of the phenomenon. Following the inductive process, the population approach categorizes the variations with reference to the frame of reference we have outlined and in the manner which would resolve the problems of classification posed by that framework.

The population approach, as noted, may not be applicable until sufficient information has been generated to support its adoption, and unless the demand for it is created by the need for the diagnostic mode of investigation from the contemporary perspective of social research. However, even though the first condition is met and the second is felt, the typological approach to classification still dominates the current course of social research. We must, therefore, examine the lacunae in our understanding of the inherent scope and limitations of the typological approach by answering the following three questions:

1. Can the typological approach evolve a comprehensive series of *types* to denote the known variations in a single phenomenon in an unequivocal and systematic manner?

2. Can this approach formulate an unequivocal and systematically comprehensive series of types when a *set* of homologous and/or analogous societal phenomena are integrated in order to derive another societal or a social phenomenon, even while referring to the known variations only in these phenomena?

3. Can this approach deal effectively with the *knowable* variations in a phenomenon or a set of phenomena?

The typological approach seems to answer the first question in the affirmative. As pointed out in Chapter 1, the sponaneously observed variations in a phenomenon can be systematized into an unequivocal series of types to denote nominal or ordinal distinctions, and even the interval scale of quantitative variations. The formulation of the series, however, varies from researcher to researcher according to their views on the object of classification, the decisive emphasis they respectively place on some classificatory attributes as against others, and their differential identification of the units and items of classification. Even with respect to the known variations associated with only one phenomenon, therefore, the typological approach fails to yield an unequivocal and comprehensive series of types, and thus fails to systematically consolidate our accumulated knoweldge of the phenomenon. We may illustrate this lacuna in typological classification with reference to (a) the secondary and derived phenomena of class and social class, and (b) the primary and primordial phenomenon of family. We have already described the essential characteristics of these phenomena.

Status evaluation in society, which is the essence of social class classification, is primarily based on a hierarchical arrangement of the sources of livelihood of the people. As we have mentioned, these have been exhaustively listed by the UN agencies under digit codes to denote industry and occupation, and the lists are periodically revised and enlarged without affecting their systematic structure (e.g., International Labor Office 1949, 1958). Few social scientists, however, make use of these typologies to evolve their social class classifications, and, thus, their spontaneously evolved schemes suffer from a basic limitation on their comparability.

Moreover, those who employ these typologies impose other constraints because of their subjectively variable consideration of other relevant properties defining the *social classes*. Caste-religious-ethnic, cultural-educational, and other differences are considered by some researchers in evolving their respective schemes, but not in a systematic manner that leaves room for all possible variations with reference to these properties. As a result, we encounter a perennial controversy over various categories of social class classification such as the identity or distinction between while-collar and blue-collar workers earning equal incomes who may be further distinguished as white or black, or as native-born Americans or various kinds of immigrants, like the Mexicans, Italians, Greeks, Japanese, etc., in the United States.

We shall not discuss the analytical issues thus involved in status grading, which with reference to any set of entities (e.g., occupations or castes) is not equispaced or unilinear. As noted, multilinear principles are generated from the variable points of reference in any process of status grading by self-evaluation of the individuals to be graded in a scale; and the issue grows to serious proportions when societies with sharply different value preferences are brought under a uniform classification of the social classes. We have mentioned in this context H. Braverman's citation of Jerome Davis's study of the Soviet school children in the mid-'twenties: "In rating a list of occupations adapted from one of the common U.S. 'prestige' scales, these children reversed the order of rank found in the use of the scale in the United States, putting farmers first and bankers last" (Braverman 1974: 436).

However, while these issues can be more aptly discussed with reference to the *problems of analysis* in social research, we should note here that the lack of systematization of the entities to be considered for social class classification may extend so far that in a particular configuration of world society the source of livelihood may not be regarded as one of the properties of this process of classification. Instead, the scheme of classification may be formulated exclusively on the basis of a characteristic peculiar to a society. For example, in India the social classes are sometimes categorized in exclusive reference to the caste—tribe structure of the society. In the USSR, on the other hand, the concept of social class has been popular with the social scientists since the 1970s (e.g., Ossipov and Kolbanovsky 1974), but referring almost exclusively to the occupations of the individuals. The relative efficiency of all these schemes of social class classification therefore cannot be duly evaluated for consolidating the contextual knowledge precisely and comprehensively.

The classification of *classes* according to the Marxist scheme appears to be less subjective, as it is invariably based on the industry-occupation groups. But, as we have noted, the derivative properties of "class" refer to the relations of production as dependent upon the property relations emerging from the modes of production and the state of the productive forces. Moreover, these properties are assessed not only in the context of the nation-state but also in the world context of center-periphery relationships. As a result, the possibilities of known variations alone are enormous, but these are seldom considered systematically and unequivocally by the researchers in evolving their typology of classes. This interferes with a precise and comprehensive appraisal of the relative efficiency of the schemes of classification. Mere polemics prevail over the usefulness of equating or differentiating many categories, such as the sharecroppers and the agricultural wage-laborers, on the one hand, and the supervisory farmers and the rentiers, on the other, in an agrarian society; the Third World bourgeoisie as lumpen, comprador, or national; the bourgeoisie of the West as monopolistic-hegemonistic and/or multinational; the mercantile and industrial categorization of the bourgeoisie in the history of Western Europe; and even the categories of Soviet "bourgeoisie" and Soviet "proletariat" (Bettelheim 1978).

The social scientists involved in macroanalysis, particularly with reference to the secondary social groups, are, however, more and more aware of the limitations of the standard typological classifications or their ad hoc revisions. They are, therefore, discussing the relative relevance of the known attributes of the secondary and tertiary social groups (like nations and not nation-states), and searching for the crucial attributes denoting the respective phenomena. This may eventually lead them to adopt the population approach to classification which we shall discuss below. However, most of those interested in the study of the primary social groups do not seem to be conceptually and analytically concerned with the classificatory problems. This we have noted with respect to the UN sponsored industry-occupation classification of social groups. We also find that as late as in the 1970s, a critique of the typological classification of family structures sent for comment to fifty experts evoked responses from only three; and of these, one ridiculed the attempt, another expressed doubts about the feasibility of evolving a generalized procedure for universal classification, and the third, by advocating an abstract method of using graph theory, forfeited the inherent characteristics of family as a social group (R. Mukherjee 1972). Clearly, what Talcott Parsons wrote more than two decades ago is still valid today (Parsons 1954: 177):

> On the sociological side, family studies have overwhelmingly been oriented to problems of individual adjustment rather than comparative structural perspective; while from the anthropological side, a barrier has grown out of the fact that a major structural aspect of a large-scale society cannot be observed in a single program of field research. To a considerable extent the material must come from the kind of common sense and general experience which have been widely held to be of dubious scientific standing.

Yet the limitations of the typological classification of family with respect to its spontaneously observable properties have been obvious for a long time from both micro- and macrostudies. For example, according to the scheme of classification sponsored by the Royal Anthropological Institute of Great Britain and Ireland (1954: 70), a simple (nuclear) family consists of "a father and a mother and their children;" that is, it is involved with all the three kinds of intra-family relations which may be labelled and symbolized as conjugal (c) between husband and wife, parental-filial (p) between parents and children, and inter-sibling (s) between brother(s) and/or sister(s). But Murdock and his colleagues refer to the variations ($c + p$) and ($c + p + s$) only, explicitly reject the variations c, p, and ($p + s$) as irrelevant to what is a family, and do not mention the variation s in that context (Murdock et al. 1950: 86). W.F. Ogburn and M.F. Nimkoff, on the other hand, insist on the possible variations c, p, ($c + p$), ($p + s$), and ($c + p + s$) as characterizing the nuclear family, without mentioning the variation s in that context (1955: 459). And C. Kirkpatrick takes into account all possible variations in these three intra-family relations in order to classify a family unit under the nuclear category (1953: 15).

Possibly because the composition of the nuclear family is not complicated, its rigorous study automatically leads to a population-style classification instead of merely upholding the typology; and that this course of classification is necessary in order to explicate the family organization has been substantiated (R. Mukherjee 1977a: 31-36, 51, 92, 151-152). However, the obvious fallacy behind the typology of "simple–compound–complex" families has more or less gone unnoticed, although it is implicit in many well known family studies. By characterizing the nuclear family as *simple* and defining its properties as given above, the Royal Anthropological Institute of Great Britain and Ireland has described (1954: 71) the *compound* family as consisting of plurally married consorts and their children or "a group formed by the remarriage of a widow or widower having children by a former marriage." In addition, a *composite* family type has been suggested to account for the simultaneous presence of polygyny and polyandry in a family, while relegating the exclusive presence of one of these two forms of marriage to the *compound* family (Chattopadhyay 1961: 82-83). But the three family types cannot unequivocally account for those families which comprise only never-married persons exhibiting step-relations among them, for example, a family of step-brothers only (R. Mukherjee 1977a: 27-28). Would this family be typed as *simple* or *compound*?

Moreover, the *compound* or *complex* type does not take into account the incidence of those families which record (*a*) varied combinations of monogamous, polygynous, and polyandrous marriages, (*b*) no children born to the ever-married couples, or (*c*) no step-children belonging to them (see Ariga 1956: 199-207, 215-222; Majumdar 1955: 36ff; R. Mukherjee 1977a: 27-28; Prince Peter 1963; Zensho 1956: 222-230). The questions arise in this context: (1) should a family of a remarried widow and/or widower who have no children and none by former marriages be categorized as a *simple* family?; (2) would the same categorization apply to the families comprising first and subsequent marriages of monogamous couples with no children or with children only from the current marriages?; and (3) what would be the typology for the families with both monogamous and polygamous couples which have either no children or only those emerging from the current monogamous marriage?

Evidently, the typology's problem is derived from an unsystematic and equivocal consideration of three kinds of familial properties that are part of the content of classification: (1) forms of marriage, (2) incidence of children from former marriages in case of remarriage, and (3) occurrence of step-relationships. If these properties were systematically and unequivocally taken into account in all their possible detail, typology would have turned into the population approach. The transformation, however, may not always be so easy, as can be seen with the nuclear and the simple–compound–complex typologies, while such unsystematic classification of the known properties of families is more likely to dissipate and diminish knowledge than to consolidate it properly. We may illustrate this possibility with reference to the subjective variations inherent in the selectively compartmentalized typology of the nuclear–joint–extended families.

With reference to the definition of the nuclear family as consisting of a father and a mother and their children, a *joint* family is formed "when two or more lineally related kinsfolk of the same sex, their spouses and offspring, occupy a single homestead and are jointly subject to the same authority or single head;" and an *extended* family is "the dispersed form corresponding to a joint family" (Royal Anthropological Institute 1954: 72). Putting aside the controversial attribute of centralized familial authority, these definitions can identify only two joint family types, precisely labelled as patrilineal-patrivirilocal and matrilineal-matriutrolocal (Barnes 1960: 850-866): patrivirilocal because the evermarried females in the former and matriutrolocal because the ever-married males in the latter type will live in the family of oriention of their respective consorts. However, deviations do occur from the two joint family types by the incorporation of one or a few family members who do not fit the stipulated pattern; for example, the presence in a patrilineal-patrivirilocal joint family of the widowed daughter (with her children) of the male head, or the presence in a matrilineal-matriutrolocal joint family of the brother (with his wife and children) of the female head.

The families deviating from a joint family pattern in these or other ways may not be infrequent in a society, although (a) the nature of deviation may be ignored to fit the "deviant" families into the joint family pattern or (b) the typologist may formulate an amorphous type in which to classify them, like the "intermediate type of family" which comprises "a simple family with some remnants of the earlier large group" (Chattopadhyay 1961: 82). In West Bengal in 1960–61, 29% of the families containing lineal and/or affinal relations were found to have deviated from the patrilineal-patrivirilocal pattern which is regarded as the norm of family organization in that society. The characteristics of these deviant families could be taken into account only by the population approach, which led to the conclusion that the joint family system is persisting in this society but only by drastically cutting down the collateral ramifications of the family unit (R. Mukherjee 1977a: 36-58).

The failure of typology to consolidate knowledge even on the basis of known information alone affects our understanding of the dynamics of family organization in many other ways. A few more joint family types, out of the typologists' residual category of "extended families," have been formulated in the light of observed variations in the residence and the lineage affiliation of the two sexes in the family units, for example, the *matripatrilocal, avunculocal,* and *natolocal* joint families (Murdock *et al.* 1950: 88ff). Attempts are thus made to form a series of mutually distinct and analogous joint family types. The process, however, cannot but be segmental in view of such an approach which starts from the top of the social space to detect patterns of kinship composition. The series formed in this way does not precisely, unequivocally, and comprehensively account for all analogous variations in the kinship composition of the extended families in a way which can systematize our knowledge on variations in family organization.

For example, in the natolocal (*taravad*) family organization of the Nayars and other ethnic groups in south India, the family tree extends matrilineally but (a) the ever-married brothers are enjoined to stay in the family without their wives and children, and (b) husbands are enjoined not to stay in the family of their wives. It is found, however, these days that the heads of some *taravad* have brought their consorts to live with them. If this were the only possible variation from the traditional *taravad* organization, it could perhaps be categorized as another family type. But, resulting from a social institution in abeyance, various patterns of joint family organization may be discerned in that society. This is noticed in cases where the matrilineal-matriutrolocal, matripatrilocal, natolocal, or avunculocal patterns are in the process of replacement, but not necessarily by the patrilineal-patrivirilocal or the nuclear family exclusively (e.g., Dube 1969: 443; Gough and Schneider 1962: 545-576, 631-652; Roy Burman 1967).

These studies imply that without adopting the population approach the emerging or emergent patterns of intra-family relations cannot be clearly categorized. For this purpose, (a) the extended family patterns need to form a comprehensive but flexible series; (b) the possibilities of different pattern formations in intra-family relations should be conceived of as *infinite but enumerable;* and (c) the course of categorization must proceed inductively from the bottom, as it were, of the total field of variation constituted by (a) and (b), instead of only some possibilities being deduced as mutually distinct and analogous joint family types. Since the typologists do not qualitatively alter the procedure of classification in this manner, their attempts to explain the aforementioned situations become fallacious or inadequate (R. Mukherjee 1972: 439-42).

This state of affairs with the typological classification of a single phenomenon brings us to the second question we have posed: the adequacy of the typological approach for classifying the known variation in a *set* of phenomena. We have noted that variations are currently occurring in the natolocal kinship organization of the family among several ethnic groups in south India (e.g., *taravad* among the Nayars). Theoretically, the variations can lead to the nuclear, matrilineal-matriutrolocal, patrilineal-patrivirilocal, bilateral-bilocal, etc., family organization, or a reversion to the status quo ante. Therefore, unless one conceives of the family as the primordial social institution floating freely in an everchanging social universe, we must examine the integration of the familial types (and the kinship forms) of social behavior with other kinds (e.g., economic, psychological, demographic, political) in order to ascertain the probabilistic course of change (or no change) in the natolocal family organization.

We find in this respect that detailed information is available for each family household of the Chetlat Islanders, for whom the natolocal *taravad* is reported to be the norm. A scheme of classification evolved from the bottom of this block of information shows that 50% of the family households strictly retain their natolocal organization, 38% register a variation toward a matrilineal-matriutrolocal structure, but only 2% toward patrilineal-patrivirilocal organization, while 10% of the family households are nuclear (R. Mukherjee 1972: 441). Thus the *null consideration of all possible kinship patterns* of the family units *does not substantiate either of the two hypotheses—neither an irrevocable transition from the matrilineal to the patrilineal family organization nor to the nuclear.*

Moreover, this process of classification suggests that the percentage incidence of different kinship patterns in family units may be different for other communities in which *taravad* is also reported to be the norm. For example, it is seen from the data supplied by L. Dube on the Kalpeni Islanders that 77% of the family households retain the natolocal organization, 19% register the matrilineal-matriutrolocal variation, 1% the patrilineal-patrivirilocal form, while for 3% the family organization is nuclear (1969: 44). *Hence, any cross-classification or integration of the kinship forms of social behavior with the psychological, demographic, or other kinds of behavior follows a systematic division and collection of the measuring variables from the bottom of the information block on the kinship behavior,* i.e., with reference to the null point of all theoretically possible variations in kinship relations in the family units. Any other way of dividing and collecting these measure variables, which may be spontaneously observable and deducible from the top of the same block of information, would be fallacious, or at any rate, inadequate.

Thus, while any dysfunctional relationship between the family and the household is irrelevant to the dynamics of family organization in these societies, although that has been conjectured (Roy Burman 1967: 110-111), the patrifocal–matrifocal typology of Kunstadter (1963) and Safa (1965) also may be of little relevance in the present context. The Kalpeni Islanders are Muslims, and the ethics of Islam support the patrifocal type; but 96% of the family households in Kalpeni are natolocal or veering toward being matrilineal-matriutrolocal. On the other hand, a cross-classification or integration of the kinship and the economic behavior of these people, with respect to property relations within and between the family households, may point toward the retention of the norm of natolocal organization or toward variation in the direction of matrilineal-matriutrolocal organization, out of several possibilities. This is suggested by Dube's investigations which need pursuing systematically because many kinds of social behavior must play a role in changing the natolocal family organization of the people concerned.

It follows that if we wish to take note of only a few of these variables for a course of analysis (such as kinship, demographic, psychological, and economic behavior), we should, first, systemically divide and collect the societal characteristics and the forms of behavior pertaining to each type of behavior with reference to the null consideration of all possibilities within each kind. Afterwards, we should integrate these variations in all possible ways so as to ascertain how and why the family organization changes in diverse directions but with unequal magnitudes. Just any sort of cross-classification of two or more social science subjects will not serve our purpose, for, owing to the information generated by the primary research information on various aspects of the Chetlat, Kalpeni, and other similar societies, the issue before us is not of any single explanation but of the *relative efficiency* of different explanations in appraising the contextual reality.

The failure of the typological approach in deciphering the systems of variation is clearly manifest in the typology of "dominant caste," which denotes an unsystematic cross-classification of different kinds of social behavior. With a view to explaining social change in modern India, this type has been formulated by combining some characteristics of economic, demographic, political, and cultural behavior; namely, the ownership of "a sizeable amount of the arable land locally available," relative numerical strength in the locality, "a high position in the local hierarchy," Western education, "jobs in the administration," and "urban sources of income" (Srinivas 1966: 10-11). Evidently, the six characteristics refer to spontaneous observations on Indian society and to an imprecise characterization of the already mentioned kinds of social behavior. Moreover, the typology utilizes an unsystematic division and collection even of the selected properties as present or absent separately or in combination. Indeed, unless the six imprecisely defined attributes are simultaneously present to denote the "dominant caste," the probability for which is very low indeed, the typology yields 63 ($= 2^6-1$) mutually distinct but analogous categories. It is, consequently, left to the judgment of each individual researchers to identify which one of the castes in a locality is the dominant caste. Moreover, as we have discussed elsewhere, while the typology tends to categorize two social groups as the haves and the have-nots with respect to material goods and services (R. Mukherjee 1979: 49-54), the ambiguity inherent in the typology does not allow us to evaluate the relative power of the concept of "dominant caste" vis-a-vis the analogous concepts for appraising social change in modern India, such as class conflict or consensus.

This illustration of the failure of typology to account even for known variations leads us to consider also the knowable variations in a phenomenon or set of phenomena, which form the substance of the third question we have posed with respect to the adequacy and efficiency of the typological approach to classification. As noted, the move from the known to the knowable variations is indicated for the classification of the derived social groups frequently mentioned in contemporary social research: for example, when Marcuse points to the schisms in the categories of the petty bourgeoisie and the proletariat in his formulation of the "nonconformist young intelligentsia," the "underprivileged sections of the labouring classes," and the "ghetto population" as the catalysts of a qualitative transformation of the Western and the Third World (Marcuse 1969: 52-56); when the concept of secondary feudalism or semi-feudalism, mooted by a "dependency model" calls for precise categorization of the relevant societies; when nation-building—a not-yet-known but knowable process—requires appropriate categorization of the relevant attributes in order to denote the phenomenon of "nation" (R. Mukherjee 1979: 140-206); and when the world–system forces are postulated to fix the core–periphery relationship among the nation-states, on the one hand, and lead to the transformation of some of the peripheral nation-states into semiperiphery, on the other (Wallerstein 1974).

The issue of knowable variations is probably more clearly manifest when we examine the primary social groups. This was implied in Chapter 1 in the context of our examples of the formation of nominally distinguished, ordinally arranged, and, ultimately, quantitatively graduated interval-scale series of measure variables for consolidating our knowledge on the societal phenomena more and more precisely, unequivocally, and comprehensively. Quite explicitly, we may now raise the issue with regard to the primary group of the family. This important area of knowable information was mentioned more than two decades ago, but we have not yet been able to consolidate our knowledge in this context because of the inherent limitation of the typological approach. A.R. Radcliffe-Brown wrote (1959: 51–52):

> The existence of the elementary family creates three special kinds of social relationships, that between parent and child, that between the children of the same parents (siblings), and that between husband and wife as parents of the same child or children. A person is born or adopted into a family in which he or she is son or daughter and brother or sister. When a man marries and has children he now belongs to a second elementary family, in which he is husband and father. This interlocking of elementary families creates a network of what I shall call, for lack of any better term, genealogical relations, spreading out indefinitely.
>
> The three relationships that exist within the elementary family constitute what I call the first order. Relationships of the second order are those which depend on the connection of two elementary families through a common member, and are such as father's father, mother's brother, wife's sister, and so on. In the third order are such as brother's son and mother's brother's wife. Thus we can trace, if we have genealogical information, relationships of the fourth, fifth or *nth* order.

The point, however, is not only to collect genealogical information but also to illustrate how our knowledge about the "network of genealogical relations," that is, on the *kinship distances* among the family members, can be consolidated. This opens up an important dimension of classification because it can reveal the varying nature and degree of integration in families as they incorporate intra-family relations ever more remote and diverse. For example, with reference to any family member located at the lowest generation level, three families may represent the patrilineal-patrivirilocal pattern of lineal and affinal relations up to the second ancestral generation; but at that generation level the relationship may extend out to the first and second degrees of collaterality for two respective families while for the third it may not reach at all (e.g., the extension of collateral relationship in the three families may extend out to father's father's father's brother's son in one, to father's father's brother in another, and only up to father's father in the third). Information of this kind is of decisive importance to family studies to ascertain, for example, whether the join family organization in a society is being nuclearized or is maintaining its viability by reducing its collateral ramifications (Nimkoff 1959: 34; R. Mukherjee 1977a: 36-49, 166-186).

Moreover, the *intensity* of the rights and duties implicit in a classificatory relationship may vary significantly according to the kinship distance between the relevant parties. In virtually all societies the prescribed behavior pattern between uncle-aunt and nephew-niece is increasingly relaxed the more degrees apart they are; for example, when the "uncle" is father's father's brother's son, father's father's father's brother's son's son, and so on, instead of being directly related to the "nephew" as the sibling of the nephew's father. Indeed, different kinds of lineal and affinal relations are sometimes lumped together beyond a certain degree of collateral distance between the persons in the dyadic relationships. For example, in English and American societies the terms "uncle" and "aunt" refer to all kinds of male and female avuncular relationships, but the remotely related uncles and aunts are addressed as "cousins" (Parsons 1954: 183). Here the inter-generational difference in behavior patterns is removed after a certain degree of collateral distance: the exact cut-off point in this context, therefore, deserves categorization in order to consolidate our knowledge on the family and kinship in different societies.

However, the broad indication of kinship distances in families refers to their total generational extensions and, occasionally, the maximum degree of collateral expansion in any generation level. Typologically, it refers to Murdock's "fraternal joint family," Chattopadhyay's "vertically extended" and "laterally joint" family types, etc. (Murdock 1949: 33; Chattopadhyay 1961: 79–80). But these typological attempts are inadequate and ambiguous because they do not measure the contour and content of generational and collateral expansions of the families.

For example, with reference to the patrilineal-patrivirilocal pattern of intra-family relations, K.P. Chattopadhyay illustrates the vertically extended family as comprising "a man, his wife, his married sons and their children and, also, the unmarried sons and daughters of the man and his wife;" and the laterally joint family as comprising "several brothers, each with his wife and children living together" (ibid.). Murdock's "fraternal joint family" thus can be equated with Chattopadhyay's "laterally joint" family.

But what about the families, which may be found in large numbers in a society, that do not fall under these types (R. Mukherjee 1977a)? Thus, should a family constituted of a man, his wife, his sons, sons' wives and unmarried children, *and* his brother's son be categorized as (1) "vertically extended" because, in the main, it is the man's family of procreation which constitutes the unit, or (2) "laterally joint" because the man's brother's son is present in the unit (although the collateral link formed by the man's brother and his wife is missing), or (3) "vertically extended—laterally joint" as a residual category because the unit does not strictly fit into either of the two family types?

Clearly, the deductive process of classification—which the typological approach must pursue to produce its types by focussing our attention from, as it were, the top downward into the information space comprising a societal characteristic—prohibits our undertaking the classification of the *knowable*. In order to remove this constraint with reference to the example cited, we must, first, ascertain all possible kinship distances among the family members in every family examined; that is, we must focus our attention on the total population in the relevant information space. Secondly, we must proceed with the categorization of families in terms of the kinship distances considered as the indivisible attributes of classification; that is, we must adopt the inductive process of classification from the bottom of the relevant information space upwards, as it were.

This requirement of the inductive process of classification in general and the population approach in particular is indicated for all the phenomena cited in Table 2.1, and can be illustrated with respect to other phenomena. Thus, to consider what is usually regarded as a relatively static phenomenon, the ideal tribal condition is conceptually invariant but the variations from this ideal state are the substance of classification of the tribal phenomenon. Accordingly, what has happened, what is happening, and what is likely to happen in the near future, with reference to suprakinship organization and the emergence and proliferation of class relations, are not matters of spontaneous observation from the top, as it were, of the information space. These variations refer to prior knowledge as well as to subsequent knowledge gained from the generation of relevant data, their analysis, and the deductions made and inferences drawn from successive stages of research. Hence, as we have noted under the scope of classification, if classification is to systematize knowledge about the particular phenomenon, and therefore must be able to categorize all possible variations in that context, the categories should be allowed to emerge unrestrictedly from the prior and subsequent knowledge. *Procedurally, therefore, classification must be oriented inductively to the population of the relevant characteristics and not deductively to only some segments of the population which are spontaneously observed or detected.*

We may similarly consider the classification of those phenomena which are far less "static" than the tribal situation. Each of them is comprised of a wide range of known and knowable properties that require categorization in a systematic manner both before and after the successive stages of research in order that our knowledge of them can be consolidated precisely, unequivocally, and comprehensively. It is the population of the variable characteristics and, furthermore, of all interlocked systems of variation that therefore is the basis for the categories of classification. It would be inadequate and inefficient if that base was provided only by some spontaneously observed or detected segments of the population that can produce some types as categories of classification.

Ignoring these urgently topical considerations, however, some social scientists consider that the revision and elaboration of the standardized typologies will be commensurate with our continual flow of knowledge about societal phenomena and, therefore, classification per se need not draw the attention of social scientists. Indeed, some of them, and particularly those who were concerned with microstudies but were bold enough to generalize to one or another configuration of world society (or to world society as a whole) from their restricted knowledge, have sneered at such attempts (e.g., Pocock 1963; Barnes 1972: 435).

Nevertheless, because of the obvious inadequacy of the master typologies in explicating so many different situations, many social scientists engaged in explanatory research today evolve their own typologies in the light of the standardized schemes and with reference to their respective programs of research. While not clearly distinguishing the four aspects of classification, they also occasionally consider variations in the item and the unit aspects of classification. This we have noted while discussing the problems of classification. Moreover, the most rigorous ones among them may be imbued with the theoretical concern that a consistent extension of precise and purposeful typologies, emerging from more and more empirical examination of the societal phenomena, will eventually take into account all possible variations in the phenomena. But the attempt of these neotypologists cannot remove the inherent constraint of the typological approach which produces *selectively compartmental* categories of classification instead of evolving the categories *unrestrictedly*. Moreover, the sphere of *knowable* information for purposes of classification and systemization of knowledge is beyond it purview.

The inherent limitations of the typological approach, in spite of these attempts to remove them, may therefore be enumerated as follows:

1. Since the "types" can be evolved when the variations in the phenomena are examined from the top, as it were, only those variations are classified which are spontaneously observed or detected.
2. Since the distinctions and the sequential relation among the four aspects of classification are not relevant to the typological approach, it cannot classify the properties of a phenomenon systematically and comprehensively.
3. Since the interrelationships among the types evolved with reference to more than one phenomena are matters of spontaneous observation or ex postfacto deduction or inference, a systematic and comprehensive classification of all societal and social phenomena is beyond the purview of the typological approach.

Typology could resolve these limitations if: (1) the content and the object aspects of classification did not receive the engrossed attention of the typologists; (2) all the four aspects of classification were regarded as mutually distinct but analogous systems of variation with respect to each and all societal phenomena; and (3) the distinctively variable characteristics under each aspect of classification, with reference to each and all societal phenomena, were systematically accounted for in the process of dividing and collecting them. In order to fulfill these conditions, however, it would be necessary to explore the information space containing all the properties of all the phenomena from the bottom, as it were, and not from the top. Clearly, this would forfeit the raison d'etre of the typological approach.

Typology, therefore, cannot but be subjectively selective and therefore useful only in a restricted way to research: it cannot take account of classification per se. Indeed, if in conformity with the expectations of the neotypologists, typology could ever take into account all possible variations of the phenomena examined, and in the systematic manner required to solve the problems of classification, it would be equated, in theory, with the population approach to classification. And that could only occur through the inefficient time-consuming and costly procedure of (1) *reallocation* of the contextual and measurable properties of the types under the systems of aspect variation, and (2) *reassessment,* on that basis, of the precision, lack of ambiguity, and comprehensibility of the types for representing the information space of all properties of the phenomena. We need not, therefore, discuss this possible but inefficient equation between the typological and the population approaches to classification.

The population approach, however, is not yet established in social research, although it is now increasingly appreciated for research in physical anthropology, palaeontology, and prehistoric archaeology—all of which have a bearing on social research (see Dobzhansky 1962; Garn 1962; Hiernaux 1962, 1965; R. Mukherjee 1965b; Swartz 1965). In the case of social research it has also been suggested in some instances, for example, for ethnic unit classification (Ember 1964; Fuchs 1964; R. Mukherjee 1964). Next, therefore, we shall examine how this approach may be applied to classification in social research.

5 POPULATION APPROACH

We should first recapitulate the following points discussed in this and the earlier chapter regarding *(a)* classification per se, *(b)* the role of classification in the contemporary perspective of social research, and *(c)* the limitations of the typological approach to classification:

1. Classification must deal with the mutually distinct but analogous fields of variation in the context and measure variables. It should deal with these two kinds of variables with respect to a phenomenon in such a manner that they can be conceived as emerging, theoretically, from infinite but enumerable fields of variation and interacting in all possible ways from the last stage of dividing the properties of a measure variable to the successive groupings of these properties with reference to any context.

2. The measure variable must not be regarded in the narrow sense of quantified data but, at the same time, we must not lose sight of the sequence from qualitative (nominal and ordinal) to the quantitative distinctions of an interval scale of unit distances. Concurrently, the contexts for categorizing the measure variable into classes should not be regarded as constant. They represent the systemic variables for depicting the item, unit, and object aspects of classification, while the measure variable belongs to the content aspect of classification.

3. The aspects of classification are to be regarded as mutually distinct, analogous, and, at the same time, freely interacting among themselves with

reference to the classification of all societal and social phenomena. Hence, the problems that emerge in thus evolving the framework of classification must be resolved by the approach adopted in any process of classification.

4. From this perspective, the typological approach consolidates, in a certain measure, the comparative *extent* of variation into a nominal or ordinal scale, but not systematically, unambiguously, and comprehensively in view of the total scope of qualititive variations involved in the phenomenon or set of phenomena under examination. It does not lead a process of classification to measure the comparative *quantity* of variation on an interval scale of unit distances. Moreover, it fails to enter into the knowable fields of variation in the contexts and measures of the phenomenon or phenomena under examination.

5. Therefore, although the typological approach to classification is strongly supported by those social scientists who take the view that quantification in social science would jeopardize the intrinsic nature of the subject matter, it cannot meet the requirements of an efficient procedure of classification from the contemporary perspective of social research, as outlined in the preceding pages.

It is against this background that we should examine the usefulness of the population approach to classification. Bearing in mind the negative appraisal of the typological approach, we should demolish, first, a false notion regarding the population approach. From *quality,* that notion swings to the other extreme of *quantity,* as we have remarked in Chapter 1 in connection with the distinctive roles of classification and analysis.

Quantification facilitates the adoption of the population approach to classification because *(a)* the data on the interval scale of unit distance emerge from a null point, accumulating from zero incidence on up, and *(b)* the items of enumeration previously qualified by the qualitative attributes of a phenomenon are now characterized by sets of quantitative traits. The properties of a measure variable can, therefore, be divided and collected unrestrictedly, as is required in an efficient procedure of classification. The corresponding qualitative data, by contrast, will not be equally unambiguous, flexible, and comprehensive.

This we find from a simple example of transforming of quality into quantity, with which the development of physical anthropology is closely associated. The qualitative assessment of individuals' height as tall, medium, and short is liable to variation according to the researchers' subjective judgment. A person whom a Bengali may regard as tall may be categorized as medium or even short by a Yankee. If, on the other hand, height is measured on an uniform scale of inches or centimeters starting from the zero point of measurement, we shall be able to deal with all possible variations in the height of individuals, not just those observed and irrespective of our subjective judgment on them.

It follows that, starting from the null point, two series of quantitative data can be divided and collected unrestrictedly, and one of them may seem to provide the context for the other in terms of the relations between them. For example, the incomes earned by individuals may be highly correlated with their intelligence quotients, and the latter may be regarded as the context for the former. As we have shown in Chapter 1, however, the cut-off points in categorizing both of these quantitative series of variation for purposes of classification refers to characteristics beyond those of the respective variables. Additional characteristics of nominal or ordinal distinctions may be indispensable in order to classify the regressional relations among a set of variables, as we find in the case of the application of path analysis to a topic like developmental relations in social stratification and political participation (Nie, Powell, and Prewitt 1969).

Thus the more clearly we can translate a variable from quality to quantity, the more precise, flexible, and comprehensive it will be for its categorization whether exclusively or as integrated with similar variables. Quantification, however, does not automatically resolve the problems of classification, and that is for two main reasons:

1. While the quantitative data now compose the measure variable(s), they have to be categorized according to the qualitative attributes of the societal phenomena brought under classification, in order to decide on the cut-off points in the series of variation.

2. While presenting a generalized picture of the field of variation, a quantitative series of data may comprise such variations as require qualitative distinctions and these distinctions (as well as their interrelationships) may be of crucial importance to social research.

These two qualifications refer to the context variables, which we have found in Chapter 1 to be indispensable for the formulation of categories of classification, and which show that any analytical technique (e.g., cluster analysis, small-space analysis, multiple classification analysis) cannot usurp the distinctive role of classification in research. As discussed in this chapter, furthermore, the two points refer to the context variables related not only to the object of classification but also to the unit and item characteristics of the phenomena brought forward for classification. We must, therefore, consider the quantified social science data also with respect to the frame of reference we have evolved and, consequently, with reference to the problems of classification the framework poses. *Quantification must not be regarded as resolving the problems of classification, as is often asserted, sometimes forcefully so.*

This we may illustrate with reference to the socially important series of quantitative data such as: *(a)* income as a measure of the economic viability of individuals and of the social groups constituted by them, and *(b)* the ownership of land (or its control under any legal stipulation) as a measure of economic power (or lack of power) in an agrarian society. Obviously, both income and land are quantitative measures when given specific denominations (e.g., in acres and rupees in India), but the measures can be made uniform on the world scale under, say, hectare and US dollar equivalents.

We may accept the quantitative measure of v as denoting the nature of the income hierarchy in the population regardless of Pareto's contention that the value of v, in his formula $y = ax^{-v}$, as below or above 1.5 would indicate the probable occurrence of revolution or civil war in a society (Davis 1941a: 394), where y stands for the number of people having the income x or greater. Pareto, however, had postulated that an income hierarchy would not exist for low incomes and, therefore, his stipulation was that "the origin of measurement is at a sufficiently high income level" (Davis 1941b: 23). But the formula has been found applicable to the income distribution of all the households in the samples of villages in the districts of Birbhum and Bogra in the British Province of Bengal in 1937 and 1941–42, to the income distribution of 13,645 randomly selected rural households in the same province in 1946, and to the entire income distribution in the sample of 108 communes out of 274 in Hokkaido in Japan (R. Mukherjee 1957: 3–4; Hayakawa 1951: 174–183). The variate v, therefore, fully conforms to the population approach to classification; but it acquires a meaning for social research provided *(a)* it is categorized with reference to appropriate social groups, and *(b)* the quantitative data it consolidates do not conceal such qualitative distinctions as are necessary to appraise reality precisely and unequivocally.

Thus, the classification of social groups in order to categorize variations in the nature of income hierarchy requires a qualitative appreciation of the relevant phenomena; for example, could it be utilized with reference to tribe, caste, religion, ethnicity, nation-state, class, social class, nation, and so on, or any combination of such phenomena? Otherwise, what would the categorized values of v signify beyond the obvious fact that income hierarchies are present in more or less acute forms in a set of social groups?

It may be pointed out, of course, that the less acute the income hierarchy, the more equality there is within a social group. But such a tautological statement would merely describe the statics of the social groups by answering the question "what is the situation?" Also, the time-series data on the value of v for these groups will not take us beyond answering only that *what* question, although the answer will now be framed in dynamic perspective (e.g., Davis 1941a: 403). The other three fundamental questions of "how and why it is so," and "what will it be" in the future, will remain in the realm of conjecture and speculation.

For example, the already mentioned samples of Bogra, Birbhum, pre-Partition Bengal, and Japan, and others from the United States during 1914–19 yielded the values of v as 1.6244, 1.4839, 1.8055, 1.4077, and 1.56 ± 0.12, respectively (R. Mukherjee 1957: 4). The standard deviation of the mean value for the United States suggests that all these cross-cultural values of v are of the same order. What discovery, then, have we made beyond the obvious information that in the first half of the twentieth century income hierarchies were present in colonial Bengal, industrializing Japan, and the highly industrialized United States? Should we now conjecture, in order to answer the how and why questions, that the *same* process of a monetized economy operated in "poor" Bengal, "prospering" Japan, and the "prosperous" United States? Should we also, speculate on the what will be of the people in these three societies on that basis?

Instead, in order to proceed further on the basis of the precise information obtained from the values of ν, we may examine the curves of income concentration obtained from the data giving the ν-values, although, initially the additional information also will merely answer the question "what is it?" Almost simultaneously, H.O. Lorenz and C. Gini suggested the use of curves of income concentration and, for a distribution of income following Pareto's formula, Davis (1941b: 32-34) proposed the construction of the curve according to the formula $q_x = 1 - (1-P_x)^{1/\delta}$ where p_x stands for the percentage of income recipients possessing x or more, q_x for the percentage of the total income possessed by this percentage of income recipients, and $\delta = \nu/(\nu-1)$. In a similar manner, curves of concentration of land owned or otherwise possessed, or of any other corresponding quantitative attribute, such as the consumption of cereals or protein in a social group, can be constructed.

The curves of concentration of income, like the formulation of the curves of concentration of land or any other similarly quantitative manoeuvre, will provide us with a generalized picture of inequality in the given field of variation and a measure of the nature of inequality as more or less acute. For example, the values of $1/\delta$ for the already mentioned samples of Bogra, Birbhum, and Bengal were found to be 0.3863, 0.3261 and 0.4461, respectively (R. Mukherjee 1957: 5). We may further calculate a concentration ratio $\rho = 1/(2\nu-1)$ which will vary between 0 and 1 while δ varies from 1 to ∞ (Davis 1941b: 34). Subject to a systematic categorization of the relevant social groups to locate such values, as for the values of ν, these quantitative data, therefore, will efficiently consolidate our knowledge with reference to the question "what is it?" But would that knowledge be adequate?

Much is hidden behind the curves (schematically shown in Figure 2.1), data for which social research must provide in order to answer the three other fundamental questions we have mentioned. A curve is obviously composed of a series of linear segments which are connected at various angles. The illustrative curve is made of 6 segments which form 5 angles directly (as shown by the continuous lines and angles in the Figure) and 10 angles indirectly (as shown by the extensions of the 6 segments by dotted lines and the angles they form). Because these segments form a curve, some of them must be dyadically allied to each other, but in distinctive sets. This is indicated by angles close to 180° formed by the segments within a set, e.g., segments 1 and 2, 3 and 4, and 5 and 6 in Figure 2.1. Also, because these segments form a curve, some of them are placed in sharply contradictory positions. This will be indicated by those segments that form nearly 90° angles between them, e.g., 1 and 5, 1 and 6, 2 and 5, and 2 and 6 in Figure 2.1. And the remaining dyadic arrangements will be in between the extreme positions taken by the distinctive sets of segments: in the illustrative case by segments 1 and 2 at one extreme, and 5 and 6 at the other. The segments in this middle position will form angles which are neither close to 180° nor to 90°, e.g., 1 and 3, 1 and 4, 2 and 3, 2 and 4, 3 and 5, 3 and 6, 4 and 5, and 4 and 6 in Figure 2.1.

Figure 2.1

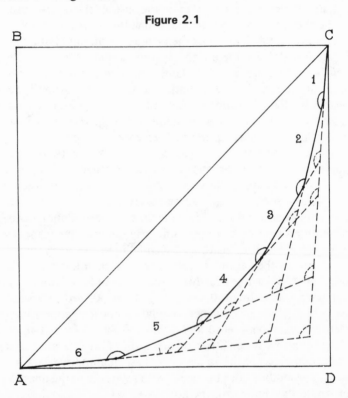

The reduction of the curve into a series of linear segments in this manner is the first step toward eliciting what the curve contains. The segments represent complementary and contradictory sets of items of enumeration and the other set(s) of corresponding items which are placed in between those at the top and bottom of the curve. The characteristics of the sets, however, will not be revealed unless the information that the sets convey the most appropriately are duly classified in order to consolidate our knowledge about the variations in income (or any other quantified societal characteristic) which the curve depicts in a precise and comprehensive but abstract manner.

The linear segments, forming one or another set, can be deciphered more and more unequivocally and systematically, as we have discussed in Chapter 1 with reference to small-space analysis. The categorical cut-off points in that context will be determined by the manner of identifying the segments in terms of their constituent items. This means that each set of items of enumeration must express a mutually distinct but analogous group character with reference to each constituted segment. The nature of group formation of course varies according to the qualifying traits of the items denoting the group character. The segments may, therefore, represent the income class units or the units of classification of any other social phenomenon, while the items of classification will be given by the property p_x of the curve and the content of classification by the property q_x of the curve. Hence, the best possible characterization of the segments and their consequently precise identification will establish the most appropriate unit characteristic for eliciting the hidden meaning of the curve. And it follows that the best manner of consolidating the segments (units) into mutually distinct but analogous sets (classes) will be the object of classification.

We may thus organize the data in which the context and measure variables are integrated by certain maneuvers, as pointed out in Chapter 1, according to the framework of classification we have outlined. The result will obviously be an efficient consolidation of prior and subsequent knowledge with respect to the *what-how-why-what* paradigm, the fundamental questions for understanding reality. It should, however, be realized that to attain this goal (*a*) classification must precede and follow analysis in a systemic manner, (*b*) the efficiency of the quantified measure variable will not be duly appreciated without the qualitative contexts, and (*c*) the context and measure variables must be treated under the four aspects of classification in such a way as to satisfactorily resolve the already mentioned classificatory problems.

We may also bear in mind that only the quantitative variates can be transformed into curves of one shape or another, and that a particular shape (as in Figure 2.1) can be varied in the details of its delineation in order to bring out cross-cultural or temporal variations in the characteristics it contains. Therefore, from the shape(s) of the derived curves as in Figure 2.1, or from those obtained directly from their distributions, such as *J, U,* the parabola, etc., we shall obtain cues for examining those sets of people and social groups—out of the total population—appropriate for appraising the social reality precisely, systematically, and comprehensively.

Quantification, thus, prepares the ground for the adoption of the population approach to classification in the best possible manner. With or without forming curves as discussed above, it presents the measure variable the most systematically and comprehensively. It does not, however, lead ipso facto to unfolding the procedure for classification in terms of this approach. Instead, the qualitative data of various kinds, representing the properties of the phenomena to be classified, are not only involved in the quantification of these properties but also deserve equal (if not primary) attention in evolving the procedure of classification. Thus the population approach to classification should be conceived not as exclusively quantitative but as progressing from quality to quantity and not vice versa.

This point is implied in the recent sophisticated series of analyses of social mobility and social grading of occupations (Hope 1972; Ridge 1974; Goldthorpe and Hope 1974). Nevertheless, there are instances of direct application of the quantitative techniques for purposes of classification according to the population approach. Whether or not such attempts will eventually succeed in systemizing our knowledge precisely, unequivocally and comprehensively, or persuade researchers to accept the rule of transforming quality to quantity, is still a moot question. However, such attempts illustrate prima facie the failure to take note of the inherently qualitative character of the societal phenomena. For example, M.D. Maclachlan, who would definitely reverse the preeminence of quality over quantity by using graph theory, noted with reference to classification of family structure (1972: 435–436):

> The calculus involves nothing more than a genealogical interpretation of the theory of graphs, a powerful, flexible, and well-developed formal system concerned with the mathematics of points and lines. A conventional genealogical chart is a perfectly good mathematical graph as it stands. It contains points (male, female, living, and deceased) connected by lines of descent, marriage, and siblingship, so that in a genealogical group there is a kintype or chain connecting every pair of points. The number of lines in a chain equals the genealogical distance between the two points, a primary relationship containing one line, a secondary relationship two, and so on. The number of linking relatives in a chain equals the number of lines minus one....
>
> Thus the question of nuclearization can be answered in two ways. It may be that the componential structure of a population's households is becoming more or less genealogically complex, or it may be that complexity within the componential structures is increasing or declining...
>
> ...My work thus leads me to believe that the development of a general theory of kinship will require us to move much further away from immediate empirical concerns than we have gone so far.

Now, as M.F. Nimkoff pointed out a long time ago, "family changes may be matters of degrees as well as of kind" (1959: 34), and it is the change in kind that is of crucial relevance in appraising family organization in the context of the patterns formed by the intra-family relations. Various kinds (along with the degrees) of lineal and affinal relations form different patterns of family organization. Deviations from the high density probabilities of any one of these patterns are noted for a given configuration of world society and its members; the cutting-off of the ramifications of lineal and affinal relations at some critical limit leads to the qualitative transformation of an extended family into a nuclear one (viz. when all kinds of lineal and affinal relations have disappeared from the unit). In this process, just two people with a lineal or an affinal relationship (e.g., a person and his/her son's son or a person and his/her brother's wife) can form an extended family, so that the distinctive relationship between the two relatives is relevant to the classification of the family as a social phenomenon.

Needless to say, all these variations can be located in a "genealogical inter-pretation of the theory of graphs" provided the existing and the missing points, lines, and chains are qualitatively characterized. Otherwise, even after a systematic classification of the categories to locate the variations in family organization (e.g., in a set of mutually distinct but analogous ethnic groups), the picture drawn by the quantitative variates proposed by Maclachlan with reference to the points, lines, and chains would be as generalized as those we have discussed with reference to income hierarchy, curves of concentration of income, land, and so on. Clearly, Maclachlan's "componential structures" may become "less genealogically complex" or the "complexity within the com-ponential structures" may decline, and yet the process may not substantiate the nuclearization of a set of joint families. The issue is *not* of a *graded* reduc-tion in such complexities, but of a *critical limit* in their reduction which may or may not be reached regardless of any graded reduction registered. Only with reference to such a qualitatively determined limit can one deduce or infer whether or not a transformation from the joint to the nuclear family has taken place or is in the offing.

This point we have deduced with reference to empirical data (R. Mukher-jee 1977a: 38–49). We shall discuss the inferential problems with which the is-sue is involved in Chapter 4. *For the present, we may point out to all crusaders for quantification in social research that quantification is an essential but sub-sequent step after qualitative appreciation of the societal and social phenom-ena in the course of our accumulation of knowledge about them. Just any kind of quantification may not be useful, while a valid quantitative technique must not be rendered futile by our claiming for it more than it can deliver.* In this context, Maclachlan's viewpoint that we should "move much farther away from empirical concerns than we have gone so far" is ominous. We may recall what W.F.R. Weldon, K. Pearson, and C.B. Davenport (1901: 1, 5) said of the then new journal, *Biometrika:*

> [It is to] serve as a means not only of collecting under one title biological data of a kind not systematically collected or published in any other periodical, but also of spreading a knowledge of such statistical theory as may be requisite for their scien-tific treatment.... [However], *the danger will no doubt arise in this new branch of science that—exactly as in some branches of physics—mathematics may tend to di-verge too widely from nature* [emphasis added].

For classification in social research, therefore, proceeding from quality to quantity is irreversible, given the present state of our knowledge about societal phenomena. Accordingly, under each aspect of classification, we should con-ceive of sets of properties of a phenomenon in such a manner that all relevant societal phenomena that are homologous or analogous can be utilized sepa-rately and jointly in the formation of the sets. This process must be amenable, without any ambiguity, to dividing and collecting the properties of each and all of the phenomena in a systematic and comprehensive manner, such that, the aspects of classification being mutually distinct but analogous with respect to the homologous and analogous phenomena, it becomes possible to evolve flexible but precise categories of classification in the light of all possible (i.e., known and knowable) variations regarding the phenomena.

The sets will also circumvent the problem we have noted earlier with respect to grading and hierarchically ordering the units of classification of some phenomena (like caste and social class). As mentioned, the relevant units may not be equally spaced in their grading according to the scale on the basis of which the content of classification is conceived. Also, with reference to the object of classification, the hierarchical ordering of the units may be multilinear as the point of reference for grading is shifted from one unit to another. But we have mentioned that such variations are particularly noticeable for those units which are regarded by their constituents to be near one another. The existence of mutually distinct but analogous *sets of units* is thus implied in terms of systemic relations among the properties of the phenomenon under consideration. Our task is to evolve the appropriate sets that, in terms of the properties of the phenomenon, will yield categories of classification in unilinear and perhaps also equispaced manner, but without involving any constraint on the classificatory process. This will lead to conceptual clarity and operational efficiency in classification.

To perform this task systematically, the "formal system concerned with the mathematics of points and lines" would be an aid to constituting the sets appropriately, *provided the qualitative basis of the sets is not lost sight of.* Given the present state of our knowledge about societal phenomena, graph theory may thus be of great utility, but we must bear in mind that all theories (set theory, graph theory, or any other) help us to build models which are like the scaffolding erected to build a house. The scaffolding cannot replace the building, while the design of the house should be prepared only with the best possible integration of the current state of knowledge. Any theory, therefore, may not provide the "master calculus" to analyze a phenomenon. Instead of regarding the theories as *exclusive alternatives,* we should regard them as *complementary* and use them in the sequence appropriate to our state of knowledge about the phenomena. This consideration will lead us to a more effective understanding of reality.

Hence, in order to categorize societal phenomena, we need to identify, first, the operating social groups or sets of individuals, that is, the specimens, in whichever manner these are identified. Secondly, in order to further increase the efficiency of the sets for classificatory purposes, we are required to examine their inter-group and intra-group variability and their corresponding patterns of interaction. Set theory is particularly useful for the former, graph theory for the latter. According to whether the relevant data are quantified and quantifiable, or qualitative, we may apply the D^2 statistic of Mahalanobis (R. Mukherjee and Bandyopadhyay 1964) or some analogous tool of analysis (R. Mukherjee 1965a: 74-94, 100-101) in order to identify the operating social groups by examining *inter-group* distance or divergence. We may then apply tools like the fractile graphical analysis of Mahalanobis (1960) or Maclachlan's graph theory in order to obtain a precise picture of *intra-group* variations. The two interacting processes of consolidation of knowledge for appraising social reality are implicit in Lazarsfeld's and Menzel's conceptualization (1961: 422-440) of the relation between individual and collective properties, and Galtung's calibration of the developmental parameters (n.d.: 148-151).

It is necessary to stress in this context that we must never lose sight of cross-fertilization of empirical findings and theoretical constructs. This will always be as relevant as it was in 1901 when Weldon, Pearson, and Davenport made the comment we have quoted. Today, even the mathematical or theoretical statisticians are finding it difficult to develop their field of knowledge without the contact with substantive problems which only empirical research can offer (Birnbaum 1970). And what is found inadequate for the development of statistics would be disastrous for social science if we "move much further away from immediate empirical concerns than we have gone so far." Classification, which is inherent in empirical research, does not thereby forfeit its role. On the contrary, it has gained consideration on its own merits because of the contempory need for research in place of the mere search for information and data, as discussed in Chapter 1.

The *empirical concerns,* however, must be distinguished from *empiricism,* which we have pointed out in Chapter 1, in the context of value considerations in social research, to have no substance at all. We have also pointed out that *objectivity* must be distinguished from *objectivism,* and that data should be regarded as a variable composed of its information and value components (= i_jv_k). Hence, we cannot assume either a value-free or a value-acceptor stance in social research; instead, the evaluation of the relative efficiency of alternative explanations would judge the most effective set on the basis of its accommodation of all available and possible values in the context of the objective information dealt with. Now, in the light of all that we have discussed so far, we should prepare a suitable *matrix for classification* in social research according to the population approach.

We have noted that our knowledge of societal phenomena will always be short of their totality. The social space comprising all their properties will also remain limited to our contemporary comprehension of any given place–time–people variations. Nonetheless, if we an theoretically conceive of the social space as comprising *infinite but enumerable* properties of all societal phenomena, and can examine these properties from the last stage of dividing them into indivisible elements up to the final stage of collecting them under the appropriate labels (as discussed in the context of Table 2.1), then our ever-accumulating knowledge will continuously arrange the known and the knowable variations in the phenomena in a systematic order from the bottom, as it were, of the social space. Accordingly, the formation of the sets of properties of each and all of the phenomena will be more and more clearly distinct and more and more unequivocally amenable to their systematic collection. As a result, the population approach to classification will be more and more efficient, leading classification toward sufficiency.

What is needed, therefore, is to translate the properties of each phenomenon under the respective aspects of classification into their indivisible elements and enumerate them as 1, 2, 3, ... At any stage of our accumulation of knowledge on the phenomenon, these elements will be distinguished as i_1, i_2, i_3,... for the item characteristics; u_1, u_2, u_3,... for the unit characteristics; c_1, c_2, c_3,... for the content characteristics; and 0_1, 0_2, 0_3,... for the object characteristics. Now, since these indivisible elements of the properties of a phenomenon falling under each aspect of classification are mutually distinct but analogous, and since they may not occur (i.e., they occur with zero incidence) with respect to the properties of another phenomenon, all possible variations in collecting them in any manner from the *bottom* of the social space would be as 0, 1, 2, 3, ..., 12, 13, 23, ..., 123, ... Correspondingly, the mutually distinct but analogous properties of two phenomena considered together under each aspect of classification can be laid down schematically as shown in Table 2.2.

In each cell of Table 2.2, distinguished by its position along the rows and under the columns, the variations referring to the properties of the two chosen phenomena are separated by a point for their respective identification. The variations regarding the first phenomenon are shown down the column for each row, and those regarding the second phenomenon are shown across the columns for each row. The cells of the table, thus, represent the points of a matrix chart of all possible combinations of the indivisible elements of the properties of two phenomena under one aspect of classification.

Table 2.2.
Matrix Chart of All Possible Combinations of the Indivisible Elements of the Properties of Two Phenomena under One Aspect of Classification

0.0	0.1	0.2	0.3	...	0.12	0.13	0.23	...	0.123	...
1.0	1.1	1.2	1.3	...	1.12	1.13	1.23	...	1.123	...
2.0	2.1	2.2	2.3	...	2.12	2.13	2.23	...	2.123	...
3.0	3.1	3.2	3.3	...	3.12	3.13	3.23	...	3.123	...
...	...	...	...	...	...	...	...	...	...	...
...	...	...	...	...	...	...	...	...	...	...
12.0	12.1	12.2	12.3	...	12.12	12.13	12.23	...	12.123	...
13.0	13.1	13.2	13.3	...	13.12	13.13	13.23	...	13.123	...
23.0	23.1	23.2	23.3	...	23.12	23.13	23.23	...	23.123	...
...	...	...	...	...	...	...	...	...	...	...
...	...	...	...	...	...	...	...	...	...	...
...	...	...	...	...	...	...	...	...	...	...
123.0	123.1	123.2	123.3	...	123.12	123.13	123.23	...	123.123	...
...	...	...	...	...	...	...	...	...	...	...
...	...	...	...	...	...	...	...	...	...	...
...	...	...	...	...	...	...	...	...	...	...

Now, the top left matrix point 0.0 of Table 2.2 indicates that the indivisible elements of the properties of a third phenomenon in any aspect of classification can be laid down independently as 1, 2, 3, . . . , that is, without reference to the two phenomena considered in the table. Alternatively, the third set of elements can be integrated into the matrix by enumerating its points as 0.0.0, 0.0.1, 0.0.2, . . . , by moving from left to right along the rows of the table, and as 0.0.0, 0.1.0, 0.2.0, . . . , by moving from the top to the bottom of the columns of the table. The expansion of the matrix in this manner incorporates all the points shown for two phenomena in Table 2.2 and, in addition, those for the three phenomena as 1.0.0, 1.0.1, . . . , along the rows and 1.0.0, 2.0.0, . . . , along the columns in the appropriate places of the matrix chart. The last enumerated matrix point at the bottom right of the expanded Table 2.2 would then be 123.123.123.

This possibility of extending Table 2.2 shows that, under each aspect of classification, the indivisible elements of the properties of all societal phenomena can be conceived of as mutually distinct but analogous at the last stage of the dividing process of the classificatory procedure. At the same time, they can be systematically grouped without imposing any constraint on the course of collecting together the characteristics of the societal phenomena.

Along with registering variations in the properties of the societal phenomena under one aspect of classification, Table 2.2 represents the generalized matrix for registering interrelations among the item, unit, content, and object characteristics of classification. Since the aspects of classification are mutually distinct, analogous, and sequentially related for any phenomenon, its unit characteristics can be expressed by any manner of combining the corresponding item characteristics. The unit characteristics also are given by the elements 1, 2, 3 , . . . of the matrix chart shown in Table 2.2; and these are indivisible, like the elements of item characteristics, because their breakup does not uncover the unit aspect of classification. Each one of the unit elements, however, is composed of one out of all possible combinations of the item elements; and, as shown in Table 2.2, the unit elements can combine in all possible ways with respect to the properties of the phenomena considered for their item characteristics. The possibility of forming mutually distinct but analogous units of classification with respect to the known and knowable properties of all societal phenomena is, thus, infinite but enumerable.

The content characteristics of the societal phenomena can be treated similarly by first translating the content properties of each phenomenon into indivisible elements 1, 2, 3, . . . , and then combining these elements of one or of more than one phenomenon in all possible ways, as discussed with reference to Table 2.2. The unit characteristics, therefore, can be qualified by the corresponding content characteristics according to the formulation and expansion of the matrix chart in Table 2.2. In this case, however, instead of combining the properties of more than one phenomenon in all possible ways but under one aspect of classification, we are concerned with the combination of all possible variations in the unit and content aspects of classification of the phenomena considered.

The possibility of formulating the unit cum content characteristics is the same as for separate formulations of mutually distinct but analogous units and contents of classification with respect to the known and knowable properties of all societal phenomena. The unit elements, qualified by their content elements, thus yield another set of indivisible elements 1, 2, 3, . . ., because each element in this set integrates one of the indivisible unit characteristics with one of the indivisible content characteristics. Therefore, all possible ways of combining the indivisible elements of the unit cum content characteristics of the phenomena, according to the formulation and expansion of Table 2.2, provide the necessary scope for registering the mutually distinct but analogous unit cum content characteristics of all known and knowable societal phenomena in an infinite but enumerable field of variation—the social space. The matrix depicting the object aspect of classification is thus defined precisely, unequivocally, and comprehensively.

The result is that any course of categorization under the object characteristics is unambiguous and flexible with reference to any particular objective of classification. At the same time, categorization is precise, unequivocal, and comprehensive with respect to the item–unit–content characteristics of the phenomena from the last stage of dividing their respecting properties to the final stage of collecting them independently and sequentially under the object aspect of classification.

The matrix chart of Table 2.2, generalized in the manner we have discussed, denotes the application of the population approach to classification across the phenomena systematically and unambiguously. We have noted that the interrelationships among the societal and the social phenomena may cut across their respective aspects of classification (e.g., the unit aspect of one phenomenon may refer to the item aspect of another). This, however, will not impose any constraint on the procedure of classification involving all phenomena. The matrices for respective aspects of classification, and those depicting interrelations among the item–unit–content–object aspects, can be combined into one master matrix structured in the same manner as the matrix chart of Table 2.2. The process of classification, therefore, can proceed just as described for a single phenomenon or a combination of several phenomena; but now the object characteristics of the phenomena play a more specific role than before, in order to register how the social phenomena are derived from the societal phenomena.

The problems of classification we have posed can thus be resolved by the population approach, which can be made more and more efficient as we go on systematizing our knowledge about the phenomena by classifying them before and after the course of investigation, analysis, deduction, and inference, by rigorously following the procedure outlined above. According to the population approach, the procedure rests upon the total social space of the indivisible elements of the properties of the phenomena conceived to be examined from the bottom upwards, and not from the top downwards as it is for the prevalent typological approach.

Chapter 3

Application

1 FAMILY: AN EXAMPLE

We have noted that the conceptual and methodological issues involved in the categorization of classes, social classes, nations, and similarly derived social groups are now examined with meticulous care because contemporary social research is especially concerned with the systematization of knowledge about those phenomena which indicate social dynamics. In ever-increasing detail, therefore, researchers list the properties of secondary and tertiary group formations, and attempt to systematize these properties under classificatory schema. The contents of these schema may be arranged according to the procedure of classification we have discussed in the last chapter in order that the population approach to classification may be applied rigorously and thus make the schema efficient.

But we face an initial difficulty in this regard. The systematic search for the properties of the derived social groups leads us to the enumeration of more and more primary groups that, as noted, join in specific combinations to form the derived groups. However, a meticulous search for the properties of the primary social groups is not common because the existing typologies for these groups are generally regarded as satisfactory. With respect to choosing an appropriate primary group, therefore, we may demonstrate the application of the population approach to classification and evaluate its efficiency relative to the typological approach.

Out of the frequently researched primary groups we have mentioned in the preceding pages, the household and the nation-state would be rather too simple cases for illustrative purposes. The tribe ought to be examined from the perspective of detribalization, which, as noted, brings in other primary and derived social groups for consideration. Hence, we also may leave out the tribe as an example. The occupational and industrial classifications need little methodological considerations, owing to their systematic listings by the UN agencies. Their properties for categorization may be examined on conceptual grounds, as we have mentioned, but that should be the task of some specialized researchers. Caste is a parochial phenomenon in the world context, although it does require systematic classification. This, therefore, would be a concern of the social scientists interested specifically in India and Hindu society in particular. Religion is too vast a subject to be considered in a small monograph like this. Some attention has already been given to ethnic unit classification, and to examine it from the population approach may no longer be an unfamiliar task: this has already been indicated by several commentators on R. Naroll's thesis on this topic (Naroll 1964: 283-312).

Therefore, as an example we may choose the family from among the phenomena and social groups discussed in the last chapter. It is appropriate because the typologists have paid considerable attention to this topic of classification since the beginnings of specialization in social anthropology and sociology.

The classification of the family is involved with variations in all the four aspects of classification, although (as noted) these variations have not been handled unambiguously. Even the item aspect of its classification is a variable. If we define family in terms of coresident and commensal kin groups, which is its most commonly accepted definition, some persons would be identified as *nonfamilial* units because they have no kin or affines living with them. If, at the other extreme, we define family in terms of whom a person considers to be his or her family member (i.e., a definition in terms of familial integration), some persons may acknowledge themselves as nonfamilial units. The nonfamilial units may emerge also with reference to other attributes found relevant to defining the family, while this kind of item variation in the classification of families has an important bearing on systematizing our knowledge of this societal phenomenon (See Table 2.2).

For example, in West Bengal during an investigation in 1960-61, 13% of the randomly sampled 4,934 persons were found to be nonfamilial in terms of coresident and commensal kin groups. Of these, a distinction by sex showed that 93% of the female nonfamilial units, as against 43% of the male nonfamilial units, acknowledged themselves to be nonfamilial in terms of familial integration. Most of these women were widows who were isolated as regards their intra-family relations, while most of those men who registered familial integration were married but living away from their family to provide for it (R. Mukherjee 1977a: 29-31, 163).

We may therefore denote individual persons (items of classification) as forming nonfamilial units and as falling under family units with reference to all possible attributes that may be considered at the present state of our knowledge in defining the family (unit characteristics). These attributes in their indivisible forms will be denoted by the series 1, 2, 3, ... Accordingly, the field of variation in the item and the unit characteristics of the family, from the ultimate stage of dividing the relevant properties through the successively consolidated stages of collecting them, will be given by the following series, in which the numerals to the left of the decimal point denote the unit characteristics and on the right the item characteristics: 1.0, 1.1, 2.0, 2.1, 3.0, 3.1, . . . , 12.0, 12.1, 13.0, 13.1, 23.0, 23.1, . . . , 123.0, 123.1, ... The series is simplistic; nevertheless, once we thus note variations in the item characteristics, we leave room for considering any other eventuality in this context in a flexible but comprehensive manner.

The unit characteristics of the family in contemporary social research may vary in many other ways than the two we have pointed out. At one time, the family household (i.e., a coresident and commensal kin group) could have been regarded as the *invariant* peripheral characteristic of this phenomenon. The members of such a household, integrated by kinship bonds, regarded a corresponding household as another family, although the two might have kinship relations between them. The familial integration of the household may have been sustained by the members' common economic organization for production and consumption in preindustrial societies, while it was stabilized by the ideology and ethics symbolized by the family deity, rites and ceremonies, centralized authority, etc. Social research in its earlier phases, especially as conducted by the anthropologists, provides us with ample cross-cultural and temporal data in this respect.

In any case, the generational extension of the family units was limited by the short life-span of individual members. As a result, four-generation families were not numerous and further generational extension of the families was virtually ruled out. The collateral ramifications of the family units could spread ad infinitum, but that would have made the units unwieldy and impracticable for operational purposes. In many societies, therefore, the lawgivers recommended the splitting of family units after a certain degree of collateral spread. Such stipulations in an essentially subsistent agricultural society were recorded by the Hindu lawgivers like Kautilya and Manu (Shamasastry 1951: 181-182; Bühler 1886: 366-367). In any case, whether or not there was any such stipulation, the families split as the need arose.

The family household is still the dominant unit characteristic of the family in virtually all societies. For West Bengal in 1960–61, only 3% of the total households were found to deviate from it (R. Mukherjee 1977a: 210). However, the integrative characteristics of the family households are becoming more and more variable. The ideological integration in the common worship of the family deity, the familial rites and ceremonies, a centralized authority, etc., are on the wane in many societies. Individual ownership rather than family ownership of property is on the ascendance; and the economic bond among the family members is much less noticeable in extended families than before. Even the attributes of coresidence and commensality are not as invariant as previously. An appreciable number of people do not work where they live, and eat at least one main meal at their work place. The movement of people from one place to another has increased and is found to cause variations even in the relative incidence of extended families, as will be seen from Table 3.1.

The social scientists are, therefore, inclined to revise the definitions and characterization of the nuclear and the joint family (e.g., Desai 1956: 3, 147-148; Karve 1953: 10). Some of them would even bypass the concept of household and define family according to the "growth cycle of (the effective minimal) lineage" (e.g., Fortes, 1949: 63). One may detect fallacies and also subjectivity in these attempts; for example, how to detect objectively what is the *effective minimal* lineage? Nevertheless, contemporary research on the family demands that its unit characteristics be regarded as variable, with respect to both known and knowable variations. For example, unless it is left to the esoteric judgment of the researchers, the time variate (t_1, t_2, . . .) is necessary to examine the "growth cycle of lineage", and the individuals of the lineage—with respect to whom the family unit is to be identified—are to be regarded as variables (i_1, i_2, . . .).

Moreover, if in the context of "organized group of ideas, beliefs and conditioned emotional responses shared by a society" (Linton, 1956: 5-6) we concern ouselves with the larger kinship configurations and for cogent reasons identify these kin groups as political, musical, industrial, gangster, and other

Table 3.1.
Percentages (with Standard Errors) of Types of Family Households Formed in West Bengal According to Length of Time Persons Lived Together in 1951

Type of family household	Persons living together		
	16 days or more in December	6 months or more in 12 months	Throughout the year
(1)	(2)	(3)	(4)
Nonfamilial	12.40 ± 1.24	12.53 ± 1.73	13.33 ± 1.93
Nuclear	45.10 ± 3.61	46.58 ± 3.70	47.98 ± 3.89
Patrilineal joint	25.88 ± 2.49	26.09 ± 2.35	25.87 ± 2.61
Other extended	16.62 ± 0.18	14.80 ± 0.11	12.82 ± 0.08
Total	100.00	100.00	100.00
(Sample N)	(739)	(733)	(704)

Source: R. Mukherjee 1977a: 209.

kinds of "families" (e.g., the Kennedy, Nehru, Bach, Tansen, Ford, Birla, and the Mafia families), then we shall have to take note of other attributes than those usually employed to denote the peripheral characteristics of family units. Such an attempt may bear fruit in the process of systematizing our knowledge of the family with respect to where the familial integration ends and the kinship integration begins (or how the two overlap), while clearly registering the interrelationships among several systems of variation, like the political, cultural, economic, etc., on the one hand, and the family and kinship, on the other. We shall examine in Chapter 4 some of these context variables for the classification of family structures.

In any case, even with respect to conventional family research, the unit characteristics of the family cannot be held as constant. Instead, we must consider these characteristics as representing a system of variation existing independently of and, at the same time, registering interrelationships with other analogous systems of variation. Irrespective of the manner in which the item characteristics of the family may vary and in whichever manner we may examine its content and object characteristics, its unit characteristics vary in such a way as to register the peripheral properties of the family vis-a-vis other societal phenomena.

Operationally, it may not be a difficult task to record these variations. We have only to proceed systematically to collect the relevant data, as seen from the specimen Schedule 3.1 which has been prepared in the context of two rather extreme definitions of the family: (1) according to the familial integration of the individuals selected as the points of enquiry; and (2) in terms of the coresident and commensal kin groups these individuals have formed.

The content and the object aspects of family classification are more variable than its item and unit aspects. We have cursorily illustrated in the last chapter how variations in the first two aspects have drawn the engrossed attention of social scientists, yet they have not been able to categorize the known variations unequivocally. Also, because of their adopting the typological approach, they have more or less failed to proceed further to take note of the knowable variations. In the rest of this chapter, therefore, we shall discuss these issues to illustrate how the population approach to classification can be applied to social research and what we may gain by it.

2   Kinship Patterns

Let us begin with the five immediately noticeable intra-family relations: conjugal *(c)* between husband and wife; parental-filial *(p)* between parents and children; inter-sibling *(s)* between the children as brother(s), and/or

Schedule 3.1: Blocks 1.1, 1.2, 2: Field Data.

Please circle appropriate numbers:

Block 1.1 Who are your family members?	Your kinship relation with each of them (X for none)	Does he/she live and eat with you? (No = 0, Yes = 1)	Sex (male = 1) (female = 2)	Marital status (unmarried = 1) (ever married = 2)
(1)	(2)	(3)	(4)	(5)
1 Self	Ego = E	1	1/2	1/2
2 _____	_____	0/1	1/2	1/2
3 _____	_____	0/1	1/2	1/2
_____	_____	0/1	1/2	1/2
_____	_____	0/1	1/2	1/2
Block 1.2 Who else lives and eats with you?				
1 _____	_____	1	1/2	1/2
2 _____	_____	1	1/2	1/2
3 _____	_____	1	1/2	1/2
_____	_____	1	1/2	1/2

Block 2
Family unit characteristics:
Familial integration = Persons listed in Block 1.1 without X in col. 2.
Family household   = Persons in Blocks 1.1 without X in col. 2 nor 0 in col. 3 *plus* persons in
1.2 without X in col. 2.

N.B. Allowing for an X in col. 2 of Block 1 is necessary because a few informants may be guided
by sociocentric, instead of egocentric, kinship relations (Service 1960: 752-754) and report a
servant as a family member by calling him, for example, an "uncle". A few such cases were
noticed during a sample survey of West Bengal during 1960–61 (R. Mukherjee 1977a: 6).
Cols. 4 and 5 provide the link between Schedules 3.1 and 3.2, as we shall find later.

sister(s), lineal *(1)* between blood relatives (or the adopted relatives) who are
not directly related under *p* or *s;* and affinal *(a)* between persons related by
marriage of either or both of them or of their blood relatives. All these relations can be further distinguished: for example, as cohusbands and cowives
under *c* who may be regarded as "brothers" and "sisters," respectively; as father or mother *and* son or daughter under *p;* elder and younger *or* never-
married and ever-married brother(s) and/or sister(s) under *s;* and various kinds
and degrees of relationships under *l* and *a*. However, so long as we restrict ourselves to *c, p,* and *s*—the three relations involved in the nuclear family

typology—the possible variations can be easily enumerated for purposes of dividing and collecting their properties systematically. This we have denoted in the last chapter as any series of indivisible properties 1, 2, 3,..., and their all possible combinations.

Complications arise when we wish to categorize the family units— "extended" in typological terminology—in terms of their constituent lineal and/ or affinal relations. The first complication, related to $c, p,$ and $s,$ is that s has now to be distinguished as B for brother and S for sister, or as Z for son and D for daughter with respect to their parents. Any other set of symbols may be preferred by a researcher; however, these symbols will have to be qualified as never-married (Bu, Su, Zu, Du) and ever-married (Be, Se, Ze, De). This becomes necessary in order to detect patterns in the kinship composition of the extended families, as we shall see presently.

The second complication refers to the fact that the lineal relatives of a person are those who trace blood (or adopted) relation with him or her through his/her parental-filial and/or inter-sibling relationships. One's paternal and maternal relatives are, therefore, the affinal relatives of that person's mother and father, respectively. The same (male) person's children and his sister's are lineally related on the paternal side for the former and the maternal side for the latter. There are also many other ways by which diverse categories of lineal and affinal relations may be located in a family if its composition by kin and affines is a purely random arrangement. The categorization of extended families, therefore, is an impossible task unless distinct patterns of lineal and affinal relations are detected among them; empirical research has shown that such patterns do exist in society. They have thus given rise to labels like "patrilineal" or "matrilineal joint family" in the standardized schema of typological classification. Our objective is to ascertain the basis of such a course of categorization from the bottom, as it were, of the social space under consideration, so that the family units can be collated precisely and unequivocally within the scope of all known and knowable possibilities.

We may note, accordingly, that the lineal relatives of any person denoted as *Ego (E)* will be given by the kinship notation series constructed from any permutation and combination (but not from the individual occurrence only) of the notations F for father, M for mother, B for brother, S for sister, Z for son, and D for daughter (or any other set of preferred symbols). The affinal relatives of E will be, in the first instance, the consorts of his or her siblings, children, and other lineal relatives; beyond that, more distant affines can have virtually an infinite possibility of relationship to E through the first set of Ego's affines and through Ego's consort(s). The first set of affinal relatives will be denoted by adding the notations H for husband or W for wife, as relevant, to the individual notations $B, S, Z,$ or $D,$ and to the kinship notation series formed by the permutations and combinations of the six notations F, M, B, S, Z, D and ending in one of the last four notations. The second set of affinal relatives will be represented by an inclusive notation (K) which will be used for any or all of the permutations and combinations of the eight notations *F, M, B, S, Z, D, H,* and *W* after the first occurance of the notation *H* or *W* in the kinship notation series.

Hence, with or without the simultaneous occurrence of the conjugal, parental-filial, and inter-sibling relationships, the random lineal and affinal relationships which *E* may draw for himself or herself as his/her extended family, and which may accordingly be called a "kindred" family *(K),* following Rivers (1926: 16), will be given by the following formula (0.0) as:

(0.0)

$$K = [(E) (F.../M.../B/S/Z.../D...) (H, W) (K)]$$

where the dots after a notation indicate that it may be repeated *ad lib.,* and at least two notations must be recorded in each notation series (e.g., *FF, ZWMM, FBZDHS*) to denote *l* or *a.*

Now, if the kinship relations in a family are to be found to conform to a consistent pattern, the family members cannot have drawn these relationships in a random manner. The inclusive notation *(K),* therefore, should not be used in any formula denoting a pattern of intra-family relations. Furthermore, the only affinal relations will be consorts of those kin of E who represent the given pattern, provided it allows for the inclusion of these consorts of the blood relatives. Therefore, a necessary condition for registering the consistency of any pattern of intra-family relations will be to allow for the possible occurrence of only specific kin of E, with or without their consorts. It follows that to keep clear the consistency of the patterned configuration, the marital status of the chosen kin and affines of E will have to be specified, which is done by appending the relevant symbol *u* for never-married and *e* for ever-married to the last notation in a series, for example, *Bu, Be, Su, Se, Zu, Ze, Du, De, MBe, FSDu.* (The notations *F, M, H,* and *W* obviously denote an ever-married status.) We may now recall the first complication we mentioned with reference to the categorization of the extended family type.

A kin or affine qualified as ever-married may in certian situations require further specification as married *(m),* widowed *(w),* divorced *(d),* or separated from consort *(s).* In that event, the dichotomous qualification as never- or ever-married may have to be revised by a different grouping of these four attributes of individual marital status. For example, if a divorced or separated (but not a widowed) woman is to be regarded as having as much claim on her father's patrilineal family organization as her unmarried sister, the distinction drawn between Su, Du, and Se, De may be replaced by Susd, Dusd and Smw, Dmw. Such cases, however, are mostly of hypothetical interest. Dependent as they are upon specific usages in a given society at a particular point in time, they can be subsumed under the dichotomous qualification of never- or ever-married. For the present, therefore, we need not take into account this supplementary complication.

The third major complication in categorizing extended families arises from the fact that the notation *E* is a variable for any family because in order to categorize a unit according to any consistent pattern of intra-family relations it registers, we must not impose any restriction on variation. Any member of a family, therefore, may be regarded as *E*, that is, the point of reference for depicting the relationships of kinship and affinity in the family, as we have indicated in Schedule 3.1. But a pattern of intra-family relations may refer to certain kin and affines of any male (Emu, Eme) or a never-married female (Efu), *and* to the corresponding kin and affines of the husband of an ever-married female (Efe). Other forms of variation also may be appropriate in this context. Therefore, in order to register the consistency of any pattern of intra-family relations, another necessary condition will be to specify the notation *E* by its sex and marital status as shown above and in certain other supplemental ways, as will be indicated in due course. Also, to some of the specifications of E, one or more kinship notations may have to be appended in order to denote that all kinship relations with Ego will have to be traced through a particular relative, for example, EmuF and EfuF (= EuF), EmeW, EfeH.

Within the terms of these conditions, various patterns of intra-family relations can be constructed. Obviously, each pattern refers to a particular characteristic foliation of the family tree and could thus be depicted by a specific genealogical chart denoting these characteristics. Hence, so that the validity of the formulae given below can be checked and the discussion on kinship pattern formations followed coherently, the genealogical characteristics of the patterns cited are given in thirteen diagrams in Appendix 3A. For easy reference, the numbering of the diagrams corresponds to the numbering of the respective formula depicting the patterns; e.g., Figure 0.1 corresponds to the formula 0.1. In these diagrams the symbols are $\triangle$ for male and O for female; $\triangle$ and ϕ denote that the individuals referred to are not present in the family; the equality sign between a male and a female denotes the conjugal relation, and the vertical and horizontal lines denote, respectively, the generational and collateral extensions of the family tree.

Now, the simplest patterns would denote the nuclear type which may be labelled: (1) Nuclear-absolute (N_0), as it contains both never- and ever-married children of the spouse(s); and (2) Nuclear-specific (N_1) because, with reference to the more extended type, it contains only the never-married children of the spouse(s). Thus labelled, the two variations in one set of kinship patterns will be denoted by the following formulae (0.1 and 0.2) as:

(0.1)

$$N_0 = [(EuF/M, Eme, Efe) (H, W, Z, D)]$$

(0.2)

$$N_1 = [(EuF/M, Eme, Efe) (H, W, Zu, Du)]$$

where $FH = MH = F,$ $FW = MW = M,$
      $FZ = MZ = B,$ $FD = MD = S.$

The patterned variations in the extended type can be specified correspondingly, so that the categorization of these families as of a particular variety of joint family will emerge freely on the basis of the initial formula 0.0. This can be illustrated with reference to the known patterns and, on that basis, one can make deductions and inferences on the knowable patterns as relevant in a program of research.

Thus, the most frequently found patterns of intra-family relations in the extended structures are such that while patrilineage or matrilineage is consistently maintained, the process does not disrupt or even disturb the family of procreation (Warner 1958: 52n) of each and every evermarried person in the family (i.e., the subunits of consort(s) and their never-married children within the extended families). These situations are typified as the patrilineal-patrivirilocal (P_0) or matrilineal-matriutrolocal (M_0) joint family. Their possible kinship constituents compose the extended structures denoted by the following formulae (1.0 and 2.0):

$$\text{(1.0)}$$

$$P_0 = [(\text{Eu, Eme, EfeH}) \ (F.../B/Z...) \ (M, \ W\!, \ \text{Su, Du})]$$

$$\text{(2.0)}$$

$$M_0 = [(\text{Eu, EmeW, Efe}) \ (M.../S/D...) \ (F\!, \ H, \ \text{Bu, Zu})]$$

The formulae may be applied to any grouping of kin and affines which is regarded as forming a family according to any manner of selecting the parafamilial (peripheral) attributes identifying the family units. The labels of the two patterns connote the family members residence; patrivirilocal and matriutrolocal refer, respectively, to evermarried females' and males' living with their consorts' families. The two formulae, however, can be applied to any set of related data. If the members of a family, however it may be defined and identified, are found to conform to the constituent kinship characteristics stipulated for formula 1.0 or 2.0, we may categorize the family accordingly. In this way we are not restricted to any particular manner of identifying the units of the phenomenon, as we shall also find with respect to other pattern formations of extended families.

The formulae 1.0 and 2.0 thus denote the fullest flowering of patrilineal and matrilineal patterns because, at the current state of our knowledge about variations in the family, they record the most stable forms of its extension in the male or female line. We may, therefore, consider them to represent two limits of variation in pattern formation of intra-family relations.

Between these two limits, intra-family relations may conform to patterned variations in many ways. One may argue that these patterns are not as stable as the above two and so we may consider those extended families which do not strictly register the patrilineal or the matrilineal pattern to *deviate* from one or both of them. (Later, we shall discuss this proposition with reference to the process of pattern formation instead of the fact of patterns formed.) Nevertheless, we should note that relatively stable patterns sharply different from the above two have been found in the world's societies.

For example, the institution of *taravad* has governed (and still governs to a large extent) the social organization of the Nayars and many other ethnic groups in South India and the neighboring islands in the Arabian Sea and the Indian Ocean. In terms of family organization, and especially the formation of coresident and commensal kin groups, this institution is associated with a kinship pattern in which the lineal relationships are drawn through the maternal female ancestors while the ever-married males are scrupulously excluded from their family of procreation and the ever-married females kept from their husbands' families. The distinctive pattern of intra-family relations in these *natolocal* (T_0) families, as Murdock (1949:17) has labelled them, is given by the following formula (3.0).

$$(3.0)$$

$$T_0 = [(EmM, Ef)\ (M.../S/D...)\ (B, Z)]$$

Another pattern of intra-family relations, which has been noticed enough to earn the label *avunculocal* (A) (from Murdock 1949: 17), shows lineal relations drawn consistently through the ever-married male's mother's ever-married brother; while this family is that of procreation for both spouses, to neither of them is it the "family of orientation" (Warner, 1958: 52n). This kinship pattern can be reproduced by the following formula (4.0):

$$(4.0):$$

$$A = [(EuF, Eme, EfeH)\ (M.../\underline{S}/D...)\ (\overline{B}e, \overline{\underline{Z}}e)\ (W, Zu, Du)]$$

where:

1. The notations *Be* and *Ze* are overlined because at least one of them is obligatory for the occurrence of any preceding notation.
2. The notations *S* and *Ze* are underlined because *Ze* cannot occur in a notation series without the previous occurrence of *S* in the series.

Several other kinship patterns are discernible in many societies, although they may be less stable than the natolocal and the avunculocal patterns. In the contemporary world perspective, however, the matrilineal pattern itself also may be as unstable as these, while the stablest has to be the nuclear pattern of spouses with never-married children (N_1). But then there are systematic variations from all pattern formations of the extended families, which include also variations even from the patrilineal pattern. Moreover, over time, these patterns do not necessarily take a unilinear direction of change toward the patrilineal or, eventually, the nuclear pattern. There is also the point that how and why various kinship patterns are formed with respect to family organization in particular societies, and how and why they change over time in kind and degrees, are not always comprehensibly known to us. Researches on the family are, therefore, concerned with the "what, how, why, and what will be?" questions in this context; our task, accordingly, should be to adopt the population approach to classify family structures in terms of all known and knowable variations.

For this purpose we may consider the *kindred (K)* family to represent the *null* situation because any kin or affines of any family member selected as its ego (E) can belong to it. From *K*, and without attributing any evolutionary sequence to it, we may obtain the direct possibility of forming the nuclear family which may be "spouses with never- and/or ever-married children" (N_0) or "spouses with never-married children" (N_1), although consistent reproduction

Figure 3.1.
Axial Relations of Kinship Patterns of Family Units

($K =$ kindred, $N_0 =$ nuclear-absolute,	$N_1 =$ nuclear-specific,
$P_0 =$ patrilineal-patrivirilocal,	$M_0 =$ matrilineal-matriutrolocal,
$P_1 =$ matripatrilocal (transitory),	$M_1 =$ patrimatrilocal (transitory),
$P_2 =$ matripatrilocal (truncated),	$M_2 =$ patrimatrilocal (durable),
$P_3 =$ matripatrilocal (durable),	$A =$ avunculocal,

$T_0 =$ natolocal, $T_1 =$ (variant 1) natolocal toward P_0, $T_2 =$ (variant 2) natolocal toward M_0)

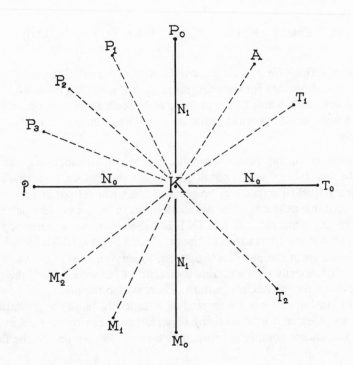

of the families may eventually bring them into conformity to N_1. However, and again without attributing any evolutionary sequence to it, we may obtain various pattern formations for the extended family. We should therefore conceive of a social space at the focal point of which is located the K families with all possible pattern formations of the intra-family relations radiating from it in all directions.

At the top and bottom points of the y-y' axis passing through the focal point 0, we may locate the most consistent of these patterns, that is, the patrilineal-patrivirilocal (P_0) and the matrilineal-matriutrolocal (M_0), respectively. Logically, and also to maintain the link with P_0 and M_0, the nuclear pattern with never-married children only (N_1) will be located on this axis and between both K-P_0 and K-M_0.

It follows from the properties located on the y-y' axis that the x-x' axis will represent those patterns that register exclusively the lineal *or* the affinal relations. The latter possibility is extremely remote because a consistent pattern comprising only affinal reltions is hardly a feasible proposition. It is also unlikely that a pattern will consist of only those lineal relations that are drawn through the male line and where there are no affinal relations, unless there is no concept of incest in the society; the young ones in the family need to be reared by their mothers. The converse (lineal relations only through the female line, without affinal relations), however, is not only feasible but has also been found in the *taravad* organization. The natolocal (T_0) pattern, therefore, should be placed on the x-x' axis at the extreme right-hand point. Logically, the nuclear pattern with spouses and never- or ever-married children (N_0) will be located on this axes in the same manner as N_1 on the y-y' axis.

Now, in the four quadrants formed by the two axes, we may place all possible variations in kinship patterns according to how far each one of them is away from P_0, T_0, and/or M_0 and approaches any one of them. Theoretically, we may not be able to locate all the variants in the two-dimensional schema, so a three- to n-dimensional schema may be required. Operationally, however, we can proceed by locating the known kinship patterns on the two-dimensional schema, keeping a watch on as to whether or not it can also accommodate the knowable patterns suggested from further research on the family.

Thus, starting with P_0, we may face a situation where consistent patrilineal relations refer also to the married female kin, unlike the case of the patrilineal-patrivirilocal joint family, which refers to ever-married females only as affines to the family of orientation of their husbands. As a *transitory* arrangement, the ever-married female kin may stay in their family of orientation with their husbands, but only so long as they do not have any children. Joint families of this sort have been found and are labelled "matripatrilocal" (Murdock 1949: 17). In order to specify the distinct pattern of intra-family relations this variation represents, we need to further qualify the notation E as a kinmember of the family or as an affine in the same context.

The procedure may be suspect because it seems to involve subjective judgment by the researcher or the subjects regarding who among the members of a family should be characterized as its kin or affines. However, if a conceptual distinction between kin and affines is relevant to the family organization in a society, the family members themselves would be able to identify one another accordingly at the time of data collection.

This the writer found during his fieldwork in the Indian subcontinent (including the later nation-state of Bangladesh, formed in 1971), France (among the Breton peasantry), Uganda (among the Acholi), Turkey, and Sweden (among the Lapps). For example, if a man deviates from the prescribed procedure and settles down in his father-in-law's family with his wife and progeny, he and his family of procreation are at once distinguished from and by other family members. Similarly it was noticed by the writer in 1941 that if a married brother and his wife were staying in the matrilineal-matriutrolocal family of the Khasis of Assam (in British India), they were at once identified as "outsiders." On the other hand, if a man customarily resides in his wife's father's residence under a society's prescribed form of matripatrilocal residence, he is identified as an affine in the family. Clearly, when a subjective distinction attains general consensus it also attains objectivity.

Yet certain forms of *preferential* marriage in a society may appear to obscure the procedure of identification. Where, for instance, cross-cousin marriage is practiced, a man's wife may also be his mother's brother's daughter—a blood relation. However, in that man's patrilineally and patrivirilocally extended family, her role would be as a wife and, therefore, as an affine. In this manner, the qualification of each and every ever-married person in a family as a kin or an affine would be clearly specified, and that of their progeny accordingly.

We may, therefore, variously characterize Ego, the point of reference for drawing kinship relations with other family members, as: Eme^k = ever-married male kin, Eme^a = ever-married male affine, Efe^k = ever-married female kin, Efe^a = ever-married female affine, Eu = unmarried child of me^k and fe^a, $E'u$ = unmarried child of me^a and fe^k, or $E''u$ = unmarried child of me^a and fe^a. With respect to $E''u$, we shall not be concerned with the formulation of kinship patterns for nonnuclear structures, for, as noted, a family of affines is at most a remote proposition, if feasible at all. $E''u$, therefore, can conform to the N_0 or N_1 pattern only; however, for the nuclear patterns this form of qualification by kinship or affinity is irrelevant. Hence, with respect to the already mentioned characteristics of Ego, we may formulate various kinds of extended kinship patterns for family units.

Thus, the following formula (1.1) depicts the P_1 variety of matripatrilocal pattern in an extended family:

(1.1)

$$P_1 = [(Eu, Eme^k, Eme^aWF/WB, Efe^kF/B, Efe^aH)$$
$$(F.../B/Z...) (M, S, D) (H, W)]$$

where the notations in the last set of parentheses can refer directly to the reference points with or without any kinship or affinal notation.

Other variations in the matripatrilocal pattern can be considered, which have the common feature that the daughters of P_0 do not leave their paternal families after marriage. More common in earlier times than today, this variation is still found in the subcontinent of India, mostly in wealthy families, as in many other societies.

In Bengal, particularly, it led to two kinship patterns, of which the first—once prevalent among the Brahmins—is now obsolete and so is relevant in historical research only. According to this pattern (P_2), the polygynous husband of "pure lineage" *(kulin)* perennially moved from one father's-in-law family to another, while each of his wives and her children lived in the family of her own father. According to the second pattern (P_3), the husband lives with his wife and unmarried children in his father's-in-law family. P_2 was the result of the institution of *kulin,* P_3 of *gharjamai,* which means literally that the son-in-law lives in his father's-in-law family.

Unlike $P_1,$ P_2 is a *durable matripatrilocal pattern but truncated* because the husbands of the ever-married female kin are not to be reckoned as family members. P_3 is a complete and durable pattern in so far as the matripatrilocal pattern can be a complete and durable one vis-a-vis the patrilineal-patrivirilocal pattern P_0. However, in order to distinguish the two kinship patterns, P_2 and P_3, the never-married persons—who are all kin in the P_0 structure—should be distinguished as either Eu or $E'u$: among them, Eu is prescribed by P_0. As noted, it would not be difficult to distinguish Eu from $E'u$ on both operational and conceptual grounds. Moreover, it is seen from the formulae 1.0 and 2.0 that although for both kinship patterns the unmarried persons as reference points are denoted as $Eu,$ they may be distinguished as Eu for P_0 and E'u for M_0. Thus, the variants P_2 and P_3, which take note of this distinction, justify the label matripatrilocal rather than P_1 by deviating from P_0 toward M_0. This will be seen from the following formulae (1.2 and 1.3).

$$(1.2)$$

$$P_2 = [\ (Eu, \ E'uM, \ Eme^k, \ Efe^k \ F/B, \ Efe^a \ H)$$
$$(F.../B/Z...) \ (M, \ W, \ S, \ D) \ (Zu, \ Du) \ ]$$

$$(1.3)$$

$$P_3 = [\ (Eu, \ E'uM, \ Eme^k, \ Eme^a \ WF/WB, \ Efe^k \ F/B, \ Efe^a \ H)$$
$$(F.../B/Z...) \ (M, \ S, \ D) \ (H, \ W, \ Zu, \ Du) \ ]$$
(The stipulation on notation for P_1 holds good for P_2 and P_3).

With respect to the variants $P_1,$ $P_2,$ and P_3 of $P_0,$ any further genealogical extension through the ever-married female kin will upset any consistent pattern formation. This, however, can be avoided by restricted foliation of the family tree in a manner other than those registered by P_0 and its variants. Thus, the patrilineal extension of the family may cease to operate and lead to a strict adherence to the matrilineal-matriutrolocal (M_0) pattern, or to other patterns that also conform to matrilineage (e.g., natolocal—T_0), or to those in which both patrilineage and matrilineage are taken into account in a distinctive manner (e.g., avunculocal—A).

As noted, we are not concerned with any evolutionary sequence of kinship patterns from any one direction or another (e.g., from the matrilineal-matriutrolocal to the patrilineal-patrivirilocal), but with their systematic operational flexibility in forming various patterns. Further variations, therefore, may be considered.

For example, with reference to the natolocal (T_0) pattern, two variations are at present noticeable among the Nayars and other ethnic groups in South India. According to one of these two, which may be labelled T_1, the men in a *taravad*—sometimes only the de facto head—bring their wives and children to live with them. According to the other, which may be labelled T_2, the women of a *taravad*—sometimes only the de jure head—bring their husbands to live with them. By following the stipulations for P_1—P_3, these two variants of T_0 can be expressed by the following formulae (3.1 and 3.2).

$$(3.1)$$

$$T_1 = [\ (\text{EuF, E'u, Eme}^k\text{M, Efe}^k, \text{Efe}^a\text{H})$$
$$(M\ldots/S/D\ldots) \ (B, \ Z) \ (W, \text{Zu, Du}) \ ]$$

$$(3.2)$$

$$T_2 = [\ (\text{E'u, Eme}^k\text{M, Eme}^a\text{W, Efe}^k) \ (M\ldots/S/D\ldots) \ (B, \ Z) \ (\text{H}) \ ]$$

Obviously, if the variant T_1 is followed consistently and the importation of the brothers' and sons' families of procreation is widely followed in the *taravads,* then not only will these men be established as "fathers" in these families, but the mothers, sisters, and daughters of the wives' will move, correspondingly, from their *taravad* to their husband's and be established there as "wives." As a result, T_0 will turn toward the P_0 pattern. Alternatively, if the variant T_2 is followed consistently and the importation of the husband-father of the mothers-sisters-daughters of the *taravads* becomes widespread, T_0 will turn toward the M_0 pattern. Logically, therefore, and without attributing any evolutionary or inexorable sequence to such changes in the kinship patterns, we may examine patterned variations from the matrilineal-matriutrolocal (M_0) to T_0 or P_0. For this also we have tangible evidence.

On the Indian subcontinent there are several "tribes" for which the norm of family organization is regarded as matrilineal-matriutrolocal (M_0), as with the Khasis in the State of Meghalaya in India. Due to various factors operating on these societies since the 1940s, in particular two variations from the M_0 pattern are becoming more and more noticeable: (1) the ever-married male kin stay in the M_0 family with their consort(s) only until they have their progeny, and (2) the ever-married male kin stay in M_0 family with their consort(s) and unmarried children. The two kinship patterns they form may be labelled "patrimatrilocal," complementary to Murdock's "matripatrilocal," and are denoted by M_1 and M_2, respectively, because they tend to develop away from M_0

toward P_0, M_2 more than M_1, just as P_1, P_2, and P_3 move from P_0 and toward M_0.

Needless to say, as we found for P_3 and P_2 in comparison with P_1, M_2 is less transitory than M_1. Moreover, all these variants may lead to the N_0 or, more likely, to the N_1 pattern, which in many cases they do. Anyhow, we are at present concerned with the M_1 and M_2 patterns on their own merits and not in regard to the course of evolution they may finally undergo, although all the possibilities are accommodated in our schema by locating N_1 on the y—y' and N_0 on the x—x' axis. Hence, by following the stipulations for all the kinship patterns, these two will be given by the following formulae (2.1 and 2.2):

$$(2.1)$$

$$M_1 = [\, (E'u, \, Eme^k M, \, Eme^a W, \, Efe^k, \, Efe^a H)$$
$$(M.../S/D...) \, (F, \, B, \, Z) \, (H, \, W) \,]$$

$$(2.2)$$

$$M_2 = [\, (EuF, \, E'u, \, Eme^k M, \, Eme^a W, \, Efe^k, \, Efe^a H)$$
$$(M.../S/D...) \, (F, \, B, \, Z) \, (H, \, W, \, Zu, \, Du) \,]$$

Figure 3.1 shows how the thirteen kinship patterns we have described can be depicted as radiating from the null point of the *kindred* family *(K)*, which registers no pattern at all. It will also be seen how these known patterns form a systemic pattern of variation among themselves. Therefore, the knowable patterns, which may emerge freely but systematically from the null situation, may be ascertained with reference to more radii in the circle than shown in Figure 3.1.

That this is a feasible proposition will be realized from Tables 3.2 and 3.3, each of which shows in sequence the fourteen kinship patterns, including the inclusive pattern *(K)* which, as explained, does not register any single pattern. Table 3.2 introduces the substantive Table 3.3 through the symbols of kinship patterns and the corresponding numbers of the formulae given in column 1 of Table 3.2 and repeated in column 1 of Table 3.3. The formulae are constructed under the same principles and with the same symbols as noted earlier. We repeat them to assist comprehension of the contents of Table 3.3:

1. The notations in the four sets of parentheses are sequentially arranged.

2. The Ego reference point is given by the notation *E*, which is qualified as: *Eu* = unmarried child of *me^k* and *fe^a*; *E'u* = unmarried child of *me^a* and *fe^k*; *Eme^k* = ever-married male kin; *Eme^a* = ever-married male affine; *Efe^k* = ever-married female kin; and *Efe^a* = ever-married female affine.

3. The notation series is composed of: *F* = father, *M* = mother, *B* = brother, *S* = sister, *Z* = son, *D* = daughter, *H* = husband, *W* = wife, and *K* = any permutation and combination of the eight other notations.

4. Within each set of brackets, dots mean that the notation can be repeated ad lib., each repetition indicating extension of the relationship to all generations; oblique slash (/) and comma (,) mean that the notation can occur only once because the relationship refers to one particular point in generational *and* collateral spread of a family unit.

5. For all patterns the notations in the last set of parentheses (col. 5) can occur directly after the Ego reference point, without any notation attached to E from the previous sets of modifiers (cols. 3 and 4).

6. For the avunculocal (A) pattern, *Be* and *Ze* are overlined because at least one of them must occur after M, S, or D; and S and *Ze* are underlined because *Ze* cannot occur without S preceding it.

Table 3.2.
Family Unit Kinship Composition Patterns

Formula	Symbol	Pattern	Kinship Composition
(1)	(2)	(3)	(4)
0.0	K	Omnibus	Any assortment of kinship constituents
0.1	N_0	Nuclear-absolute	Spouse(s) and/or children, ever-married or not
0.2	N_1	Nuclear-specific	Spouse(s) and/or never-married children only
1.3	P_3	Matripatrilocal: *gharjamai* (durable)	Ever-married male affine and female kin with unmarried children in patrilineal-patrivirilocal family
1.2	P_2	Matripatrilocal: *kulin* (truncated)	Ever-married female kin with unmarried children in patrilineal-patrivirilocal family
1.1	P_1	Matripatrilocal (transitory)	Ever-married male affine and female kin in patrilineal-patrivirilocal family until the birth of their first child
1.0	P_0	Patrilineal-patrivirlocal	Ever-married female affine with children in husband's family of orientation
4.0	A	Avunculocal	Ever-married male, wife and children, with mother's ever-married brother, his wife and never-married children
3.1	T_1	Natolocal (variant 1)	Ever-married male sibling of *taravad* with his wife and never-married children
3.0	T_0	Natolocal: *taravad*	Siblings without spouses but with female siblings' progeny
3.2	T_2	Natolocal (variant 2)	Ever-married female sibling of *taravad* with her husband and children
2.0	M_0	Matrilineal-matriutrolocal	Ever-married male affine with children in wife's family of orientation
2.1	M_1	Patrimatrilocal (transitory)	Ever-married male kin with wife but no child in matrilineal-matriutrolocal family
2.2	M_2	Patrimatrilocal (durable)	Ever-married male kin with wife and children in matrilineal-matriutrolocal family

Table 3.3.

Notations of Formulae for Family Unit Kinship Composition Patterns

Formula (Symbol)	Ego with or without reference notation(s)		Genealogical Stem	Core Constituents			Nuclear Subunits		
(1)	(2)		(3)	(4)			(5)		
0.0 (K)	(E		) (F.../M.../B/S/Z.../D...)				(H,	W)	(K)
0.1 (N₀)	(EuF/M, Eme,	Efe	) (	) (			) (H, W, Z,	D	)
0.2 (N₁)	(EuF/M, Eme,	Efe	) (	) (			) (H, W, Zu, Du)		
1.3 (P₃)	(Eu, Emeᵏ, E'uM, EmeᵃWF/WB,	EfeᵏF/B EfeᵃH	(F.../B/Z...))	(M,	S,	D)	(H, W, Zu, Du)		
1.2 (P₂)	(Eu, Emeᵏ, E'uM, —,	EfeᵏF/B EfeᵃH	(F.../B/Z...))	(M,	S,	D)	(W, Zu, Du)		
1.1 (P₁)	(Eu, Emeᵏ, —, EmeᵃWF/WB,	EfeᵏF/B EfeᵃH	(F.../B/Z...))	(M,	S,	D)	(H, W		)
1.0 (P₀)	(Eu, Emeᵏ, —, —,	— EfeᵃH	(F.../B/Z...))	(M,	Su,	Du)	(W		)
4.0 (A)	(EuF, Emeᵏ, —, —,	— EfeᵃH	(M.../S̲/D...))	(	B̄e, Z̄e)		(W, Zu, Du)		
3.1 (T₁)	(EuF, EmeᵏM, E'u, —,	Efeᵏ EfeᵃH	(M.../S/D...))	(	B,	Z)	(W, Zu, Du)		
3.0 (T₀)	(—, EmeᵏM, E'u, —,	Efeᵏ —	(M.../S/D...))	(	B,	Z)	(		)
3.2 (T₂)	(—, EmeᵏM, E'u, EmeᵃW,	Efeᵏ —	(M.../S/D...))	(	B,	Z)	(H		)
2.0 (M₀)	(—, —, E'u, EmeᵃW,	Efeᵏ —	(M.../S/D...))	(F,	Bu,	Zu)	(H		)
2.1 (M₁)	(—, EmeᵏM, E'u, EmeᵃW,	Efeᵏ EfeᵃH	(M.../S/D...))	(F,	B,	Z)	(H, W,		)
2.2 (M₂)	(EuF, EmeᵏM, E'u, EmeᵃW,	Efeᵏ EfeᵃH	(M.../S/D...))	(F,	B,	Z)	(H, W, Zu, Du)		

We notice the following essential characteristics of the kinship patterns from Table 3.3:

1. The *Ego reference points,* parentheses (column 2), vary in number and specification in a cyclic manner.

2. The *stem of genealogical extensions* of the patterns in the male or the female line, as shown in parentheses (column 3), varies in a systematic manner, with a specific phase noted for the avunculocal (*A*) pattern.

3. The *core kinship constituents*—located at different points of generational and collateral extension for the various patterns, as given in parentheses (column 4)—vary in a cyclical and systematic manner, with the distinctive phases noted for the *A* pattern.

4. The formation of *nuclear sub units* specific to the respective patterns, as given in parentheses (column 5), finally substantiates that the kinship patterns form a pattern among themselves.

Thus we see that by adopting the population approach one may precisely and unequivocally classify family units according to their kinship composition in the light of our prior and subsequent knowledge about the phenomena. We also see with this approach that the course of classification will always be comprehensive with respect to the known and the knowable variations. However, the formulae of the kinship patterns may suggest that the procedure of classification would be complicated and therefore beyond the reach of individual researchers; but that assumption would not be correct. All that is required during the field investigation is an extension of Schedule 3.1 as indicated by columns 4 and 5 of that schedule. In whichever manner the family units are identified and whoever among the family members is selected as the Ego of the unit, column 1 of Block 1 in Schedule 3.2 will be filled in with reference to the information in columns 2–5 of Schedule 3.1. Next, the Ego will be qualified in column 2 of that block as male or female, as unmarried or ever-married, and as kin or as affinal member of the family. Afterwards, the remaining rows under that column will be filled in with reference to the Master Chart which has been prepared by considering the 13 kinship patterns and is given in Appendix 3B.

Although Schedule 3.2 has been prepared with reference to the 13 kinship patterns we have discussed, more patterns may be specified and the Master Chart may be correspondingly expanded, for example to account for the variations noted by Murdock with reference to the avunculocal pattern (Murdock 1949: 35). Thus the point to note is that on the basis of the null position given by the formula 0.0, the scope of detectable patterns of intra-family relations remains theoretically infinite and, therefore, the scope of classification remains infinite but enumerable and flexible but comprehensive. The Master Chart in Appendix 3B shows that, based on the respective formulae and the genealogical relations given in Appendix 3A, it can precisely and comprehensively enumerate all possible kinship notation series with reference to any consistent pattern of intra-family relations. Hence, Block 1 of Schedule 3.2 may specify alternative or additional kinship patterns for the members of a family unit, while the task of filling in Block 2 of that schedule would follow routinely. This we may explicate by using that block for the 13 kinship patterns we have presented.

We notice, first, that while the 13 patterns could combine in 8,191 ($2^{13}-1$) ways according to the notation series of the family members of the person selected as the Ego of the unit, only 38 combinations occur in the Master Chart for the extended family structures (i.e., excluding the two nuclear patterns, N_0 and N_1). Secondly, while various patterns within each of sets N, P, T, and M occur in combinations, they represent certain invariant relations among themselves and are therefore reduced to a single pattern symbol in each set when only one of these notations occurs in a unit. Thus:

1. Within the N set, "N_0" occurring alone denotes the N_0 pattern; and "N_0" occurring with "N_1" denotes the N_1 pattern.

Schedule 3.2: Blocks 1 and 2: Tabulation 1.

Block 1

According to unit characteristics of family, write kinship notation for each family member from Schedule 3.1 col. (2), using appropriate symbols F, M, Bu, Be, Su, Se, Zu, Ze, Du, De, H, W.

Circle the appropriate symbol for Ego on Line (1), col. (2).

For each notation series in col. (1) see Master Chart (Appendix 3B) and circle all appropriate symbols of kinship patterns in col. (2). (Circle X for series not included in Master Chart.)

(1)	(2)

	Eu	$E'u$	$E''u$	Eme^k	Eme^a	Efe^k	Efe^a
1. Ego = reference point							
2.	N_0 N_1 P_3 P_2 P_1 P_0 A T_1 T_0 T_2 M_0 M_1 M_2 X
3.	N_0 N_1 P_3 P_2 P_1 P_0 A T_1 T_0 T_2 M_0 M_1 M_2 X
4.	N_0 N_1 P_3 P_2 P_1 P_0 A T_1 T_0 T_2 M_0 M_1 M_2 X
5.	N_0 N_1 P_3 P_2 P_1 P_0 A T_1 T_0 T_2 M_0 M_1 M_2 X
6.	N_0 N_1 P_3 P_2 P_1 P_0 A T_1 T_0 T_2 M_0 M_1 M_2 X
7.	N_0 N_1 P_3 P_2 P_1 P_0 A T_1 T_0 T_2 M_0 M_1 M_2 X

No. of symbols circled in each column:

S = Total number of notations in col. (1), excluding Ego =

Block 2

   S = 0: Circle 0 = Nonfamilial unit.   S 〉 0: Circle 1 = Family unit
Circle the family's kinship pattern as N_0 when $S = N_0 \rangle N_1$.   Circle N_1 when $S = N_0 = N_1$.
Otherwise circle (below) the single or the combined set of kinship pattern(s) according to whether S equals the single or a combined set:

P_0	P_1	P_2	A	T_1	M_0
P_0M_1	P_1M_1	$P_2T_0M_0$	$A T_0M_1$	T_1M_1	M_1
	P_1M_2	$P_2T_0M_1$	$A T_1M_1$	T_1M_2	M_2
$P_0T_0M_1$			$A T_1M_2$		
$P_0T_1M_1$	$P_1T_0M_0$	$P_2T_1M_1$			
$P_0T_1M_2$	$P_1T_0M_1$	$P_2T_1M_2$		U = unspecified
$P_0T_2M_1$	$P_1T_1M_1$			(S does not equal
$P_0A T_0M_1$	$P_1T_1M_2$	T_0	T_2	to any one of
$P_0A T_1M_1$	$P_1T_2M_0$	P_3	T_0M_0	T_2M_0	these patterns)
$P_0A T_1M_2$	$P_1T_2M_1$	$P_3T_2M_0$	T_0M_1	T_2M_1	

2. Within the P set, "P_0," invariably occurring with "P_1," "P_2," and "P_3," denotes the P_0 pattern; "P_1," invariably occurring with "P_2" and "P_3" or with "P_3" alone (with P_0 = 0 in both cases) denotes the P_1 pattern; "P_2" occurring only with "P_3" (i.e., $P_0 = P_1 = 0$) denotes the P_2 pattern; and "P_3" occurring alone denotes the P_3 pattern.

3. Within the T set, "T_0" invariably occurring with "T_1" and "T_2" denotes the T_0 pattern; and "T_1" and "T_2" occurring alone denote their respective patterns.

4. Within the M set, "M_0" invariably occurring with "M_1" and "M_2," denotes the M_0 pattern; "M_1" occurring with "M_2" (i.e., with $M_0 = 0$) denotes the M_1 pattern; and "M_2" by itself of course denotes the M_2 pattern.

The 38 possible combinations of these kinship patterns shown in column 1 of Table 3.4 are therefore simplified and reduced to 37 combinations of only 1 to 4 patterns in column 2 of that table. Now, at the extreme, only one of these 37 combinations can occur in a family when the unit is composed of 2 persons, the Ego and another. Such a situation can also occur with more than 2 persons in a family, while a family may comprise several combinations of the kinship patterns registered in Block 1 of Schedule 3.2. In the latter case, one or some of these patterns would be common to all family members and thus denote the "family pattern." Otherwise the family would not represent any one of the 13 patterns under consideration; this is a possibility denoted in Block 2 of that schedule by the symbol U.

Block 2 of Schedule 3.2 therefore allows all possibilities, including the possibility of only one of the patterns A, T_0, T_1, T_2, and M_0 occurring, although they are not shown in Table 3.4 to occur exclusively. The block is so designed that, first, it registers whether the family represents a nuclear kinship pattern or not. If a unit represents N_1 and/or N_0 as the common pattern for all its members, it represents one of the two nuclear patterns irrespective of any common occurrence of the patterns of lineal and affinal relations. Hence, if a family failed to demonstrate a nuclear pattern, it would represent one of the remaining 13 patterns (singly or in combination) or it would not consistently represent any one of the patterns and would therefore be categorized as U (i.e., it would represent a pattern not yet known but knowable). The scope of classification would thus be precise and comprehensive and at the same time amenable to incorporating further knowledge about kinship patterns in family units.

It can be seen, however, from Schedule 3.2 that a set of family units may register not just one pattern but a combination of patterns. For a given place-time-people situation (i.e., in a particular society at a given point or period of time), the combinations may be interpreted against a common pattern or a few frequently occurring patterns. For example, while the P_0 pattern can occur in combination with A, T_0, T_1, T_2, M_1, and M_2, for societies on the plains of North India, the A and T sets of patterns may be regarded as totally irrelevant and the M set of patterns as only marginally relevant. At the same time, the P_1, P_2, and P_3 patterns may deserve particular attention in these societies, irrespective of possible combinations of these patterns with the variants of T and M sets. On the other hand, the A pattern in combination with the P, T, and M sets of patterns may be of specific relevance for appraising the dynamics of family organization in some African societies, as will be the case for the T set in combination with the M and P sets in South India, or the M set in combination with the P set in the northeastern hill areas of India.

The validity of such selections will be tested from empirical investigations and, in that context, the course of classification based on Schedule 3.2 will be

Table 3.4.
Derivation of Extended Family Kinship Patterns

All Combinations of Kinship Patterns											Derived Patterns			
(1)											(2)			
P_3	P_2	P_1	P_0	A	T_1	T_0	T_2	•	M_1	M_2	P_0	A	T_0	M_1
P_3	P_2	P_1	P_0	A	T_1	•	•	•	M_1	M_2	P_0	A	T_1	M_1
P_3	P_2	P_1	P_0	A	T_1	•	•	•	•	M_2	P_0	A	T_1	M_2
P_3	P_2	P_1	P_0	•	T_1	T_0	T_2	•	M_1	M_2	P_0	•	T_0	M_1
P_3	P_2	P_1	P_0	•	T_1	•	•	•	M_1	M_2	P_0	•	T_1	M_1
P_3	P_2	P_1	P_0	•	T_1	•	•	•	•	M_2	P_0	•	T_1	M_2
P_3	P_2	P_1	P_0	•	•	•	T_2	•	M_1	M_2	P_0	•	T_2	M_1
P_3	P_2	P_1	P_0	•	•	•	•	•	M_1	M_2	P_0	•	•	M_1
P_3	P_2	P_1	P_0	•	•	•	•	•	•	•	P_0	•	•	•
P_3	P_2	P_1	•	•	T_1	T_0	T_2	M_0	M_1	M_2	P_1	•	T_0	M_0
P_3	P_2	P_1	•	•	T_1	T_0	T_2	•	M_1	M_2	P_1	•	T_0	M_1
P_3	P_2	P_1	•	•	T_1	•	•	•	M_1	M_2	P_1	•	T_1	M_1
P_3	P_2	P_1	•	•	T_1	•	•	•	•	M_2	P_1	•	T_1	M_2
P_3	P_2	P_1	•	•	•	•	T_2	M_0	M_1	M_2	P_1	•	T_2	M_0
P_3	•	P_1	•	•	•	•	T_2	M_0	M_1	M_2	P_1	•	T_2	M_0
P_3	•	P_1	•	•	•	•	T_2	•	M_1	M_2	P_1	•	T_2	M_1
P_3	•	P_1	•	•	•	•	•	•	M_1	M_2	P_1	•	•	M_1
P_3	•	P_1	•	•	•	•	•	•	•	M_2	P_1	•	•	M_2
P_3	P_2	P_1	•	•	•	•	•	•	•	•	P_1	•	•	•
P_3	•	P_1	•	•	•	•	•	•	•	•	P_1	•	•	•
P_3	P_2	•	•	•	T_1	T_0	T_2	M_0	M_1	M_2	P_2	•	T_0	M_0
P_3	P_2	•	•	•	T_1	T_0	T_2	•	M_1	M_2	P_2	•	T_0	M_1
P_3	P_2	•	•	•	T_1	•	•	•	M_1	M_2	P_2	•	T_1	M_1
P_3	P_2	•	•	•	T_1	•	•	•	•	M_2	P_2	•	T_1	M_2
P_3	P_2	•	•	•	•	•	•	•	•	•	P_2	•	•	•
P_3	•	•	•	•	•	•	T_2	M_0	M_1	M_2	P_3	•	T_2	M_0
P_3	•	•	•	•	•	•	•	•	•	•	P_3	•	•	•
				A	T_1	T_0	T_2	•	M_1	M_2		A	T_0	M_1
				A	T_1	•	•	•	M_1	M_2		A	T_1	M_1
				A	T_1	•	•	•	•	M_2		A	T_1	M_2
					T_1	T_0	T_2	M_0	M_1	M_2			T_0	M_0
					T_1	T_0	T_2	•	M_1	M_2			T_0	M_1
					T_1	•	•	•	M_1	M_2			T_1	M_1
					T_1	•	•	•	•	M_2			T_1	M_2
							T_2	M_0	M_1	M_2			T_2	M_0
							T_2	•	M_1	M_2			T_2	M_1
									M_1	M_2				M_1
										M_2				M_2

unrestrictedly amenable to the consolidation of our prior and subsequent knowledge on the known and knowable variations. Indeed, the classificatory procedure is seen to enter directly into the sphere of knowable variations. The appraisal of all possible family formations in specific societies will therefore be efficient and, at the same time, the data base for cross-cultural and longitudinal studies on the family will be comprehensive and remain free from ambiguity by recording all possible combinations of kinship patterns for each unit in all societies.

This is beyond the scope of any typological classification. Moreover, these possibilities of various pattern formations of intra-family relations, which can be unfolded only by adopting the population approach, lead us to another sphere of classification which is relevant and necessary for studying the dynamics of family organization.

3 PATTERN FORMATION

The possibility of detecting different patterns of intra-family relations in one and the same family unit suggests that there are processual changes in family patterns. This is evident from the interrelations among the 13 kinship patterns in Figure 3.1, particularly the sets they form around the symbols P, M, and T. Another aspect of developing classification from the known to the knowable characteristics of family organization would, therefore, be in the formation of family pattern as distinct from the patterns formed.

The process of pattern formation obviously involves both a *basic* pattern and the *directions* of change from the base. Our attention, accordingly, should be directed toward *deviations* from a pattern with a high probability of occurrence. For example, the T_0 kinship pattern is considered to represent the norm of family organization of the Chetlat Islanders in the Arabian Sea, but the data supplied by Roy Burman (1967: 80-82) indicate that out of 56 family units forming coresident and commensal kin groups, 28 (50%) represent the T_0 pattern; 21 (38%) the T_2 pattern, which leans toward M_0; 6 (10%) the N_1 pattern; and 1 (2%) the T_1 pattern, which tends toward P_0. Clearly, from the historically known structural base of T_0, pattern formations develop in three directions represented by T_2, N_1 and T_1, particularly T_2. This is contrary to the common belief in the universality of family nuclearization and change from all forms of matrilineage to patrilineage. However, if we seek the reasons for different directions in family organization changes among the Chetlat Islanders, we should first consolidate our knowledge about the relative importance of the directions recorded and, therefore, categorize the T_2, N_1, and T_1 family units in terms of the *nature* and the *extent* of deviations they register from the T_0 pattern.

A similar course of classification would be relevant even where the dominant pattern is nuclear. For example, Parsons and Bales (1956: 10) may be justified in considering the "American family in the total society" to be represented by nuclear coresident and commensal kin groups, but it can be calculated from US Bureau of the Census figures that in 1953 as many as 14% of all family households in the United States displayed non-nuclear structures (Glick 1957: 2). A typologist may ignore the variations inherent to these "deviant" families, but it would be useful to ascertain such knowable characteristics as: *(a)* the *nature* of deviation registered on the husband's or the wife's side, or both; and *(b)* the *extent* of deviation spreading within or beyond the parental nuclear unit of the husband, wife, or both. The typological approach to classification cannot systematically elicit such familial properties, while the population approach must not stop at merely categorizing the established kinship patterns. The knowable but not classified properties cannot be covered by the spontaneous explanations, although the explanations may be generally valid.

Thus, there is evidence to suggest that the process of change from T_0 to T_2 on Chetlat Island is governed by changes in the economic organization of society, but the economic forces may also cause change from T_0 to T_1 or N_1. Therefore, any clarification of how and why certain social forces are operating more forcibly than others would be appropriate if the *relative* incidence of different pattern formations provides the background for it. Moreover, mere "cultural definitions of the genealogical relationships" (Nagata 1972: 437) would not be adequate to unfold social reality in this context.

For example, there are the concepts of the wife-centered family in the United States, an emerging "matrifocial" family on Chetland Island and in Puerto Rico, and so on (e.g., Kunstadter 1963; Roy Burman 1967: 82-84; Safa 1965). These concepts may, to an extent, provide us with a static description but do not lead us very far in appreciating the dynamics of family organization. Moreover, such an attempt to dovetail an assumed "cultural" aspect into a structural analysis may end in inept discussion, as for example, with reference to the functional disparity between the household and the family on Chetlat Island (Roy Burman 1967: 110-111). Instead, the answers to the "why" and "what will be" questions on family organization would be more systematic, unequivocal, and comprehensive if we proceeded beyond the noticeable kinship patterns (which would retain their intrinsic merit for classification) and categorize the process of pattern formation with reference to the nature and extent of deviation from the materially and/or ideologically determined normative pattern.

This course of categorization, which is possible only by adopting the population approach, may be essential in macrosituations. While various kinship patterns may be discerned in research dealing with extensive, large-scale data, an appreciable number of family units may be found to register no consistent pattern of intra-family relations. Moreover, many such families may not demonstrate any consistent pattern. They may register casual fluctuations in the course of change from the dominant pattern or in maintaining the status quo. In either case, the nature and extent of deviations from the dominant pattern will substantiate the emergence of new patterns or the continuation of the "normative" pattern under the given circumstances.

For example, in a random sample of 1,497 extended families (forming co-resident and commensal kin groups) in West Bengal in 1960–61, 440 (or 29%) were not found to conform to the patrilineal-patrivirolocal pattern that the remaining 71% of the sample did (R. Mukherjee 1977a: 29, 51). Some but not all of these 440 family units could be classified as variations of the P_0 structure: 27% of them were of the P_1 structure, 29% were of P_2, and a negligible number P_3, while the remaining 44% did not register any consistent pattern (ibid.: 54). The typologists may ignore these variations from P_0 and thus jeopardize the comparability of data for determining cross-cultural and longitudinal variations. However, the population approach also would be incomplete if we stop "dividing and collecting" the kinship characteristics of the family units at this point. Instead, we should explore the processual variations in these structures, irrespective of the fact that the *kulin* (P_2 pattern) is obsolete in West Bengal society and Murdock's matripatrilocal type (P_1) was never socially prescribed there. Different social needs may lead to identical pattern formations or casual fluctuations around a base pattern, and an appraisal of these needs can follow from a classification of these variations.

The possibility of formation of an *extended family complex* (i.e., a family which does not register a consistent pattern formation) is accommodated in Block 2 of Schedule 3.2 by the symbol *U*. In case that symbol is circled, the value of *S* in Block 1 nearest to that of any known pattern would appear to provide the cue to search for new pattern(s); but that will not be operationally efficient and conceptually useful.

As noted, so long as a family unit consistently represents one or more kinship patterns of the extended variety, its members will be unequivocally qualified as ever-married kin or affines in the family or as the unmarried offspring of the male kinsman and a female affine (u), a male affine and a female kin (u'), or of male and female affines (u''). For example, if in a unit consisting of a man (1), his wife (2), his unmarried son (3), and his father's widowed brother (4) — (1) is denoted as me^k, then (2) will automatically be fe^a, (3) will be *mu*, and (4) will be me^k. Alternatively, the qualification of (1) as me^a would automatically qualify (2) as fe^k, (3) as mu', and (4) as me^a, to denote a consistent pattern of kinship relations in that unit. But if (1) is me^a and (2) is fe^a, the family unit must include some other person as its kin member and that person cannot be a blood relative of any one of the four family members we have listed because all of them would have an affinal status in the unit.

We have seen that the qualification of family members as kin or affines is unnecessary only with the nuclear pattern. But the family unit comprising the first four persons enumerated above does not represent that pattern and, therefore, with reference to the nuclear pattern the unit represents two variations: (1) if any one of the first three are selected as the Ego of the unit, it will form a N_1 complex because of the presence of the father's widowed brother; and (2) if this last person is selected as the Ego, it will form a nonfamilial ($=nfu$) complex because the other three family members do not belong to his nuclear structure.

Thus it is that a unit fails to register a consistent pattern of kinship relations and turns itself into a family complex, raising an issue about categorization that cannot be resolved by ignoring the kinship or affinal status of the family members. On the contrary, that qualification of the family members allows us to take into consideration any extended kinship pattern in order to categorize variations in those family units which do not register any consistent pattern of intra-family relations. Each and every such family unit, therefore, would implicitly include at least one kin member.

Let us suppose that the person we search for as the kin member of the family unit, of which the first and second persons listed above are me^a and fe^a, respectively, is the man's wife's sister's husband (6). This person would be sequentially enumerated as the sixth member of the family, the fifth being the man's wife's ever-married sister (5). In that case, depending on whether the persons numbered (1), (2), and (6) are qualified as kin or affines in the family, the other family members will be duly qualified as affines or kin by their relationships with these three. In the three possible cases the family unit will assume three different configurations shown in Table 3.5.

Hence, if a family unit is labelled U in Block 2 of Schedule 3.2, either its categorization will end at that stage as a kindred or else a particular member of the unit will have to be stipulated as its Ego in order to detect any process of pattern formation in the unit with respect to that person located in the *base,* i.e., the trunk of the family tree under analysis. Clearly, the Ego will be characterized either as a kin member or an affine of the family unit because any one

Table 3.5.
Configurations of Alternate Kin/Affine Relationships of Members of a Sample Family Unit.

Serial Number of Unit Members (See text)	Stipulated kinmember of family unit for each configuration is italicized.					
	Configuration 1		Configuration 2		Configuration 3	
	Core	Deviants	Core	Deviants	Core	Deviants
(1)	(2)	(3)	(4)	(5)	(6)	(7)
1	me^k		me^a			me^a
2	fe^a		fe^k			fe^a
3	mu		mu'			mu''
4	me^k			me^a		me^a
5		fe^a	fe^k		fe^a	
6		me^a	me^a		me^k	
Family Category Formed:	Patrilineal-patrivirilocal extended family complex (P$_o$ complex)		Matrilineal-matriutrolocal extended family complex (M$_o$ complex)		Nuclear family complex (N$_1$ complex)	

See text for explanation of serial numbers and symbols of family members.

of its members may be stipulated as Ego in order to maintain complete flexibility in the course of categorization.

The stipulation of a particular person as the Ego of a family unit implies that he or she may not register any one of the known kinship patterns with other family members. As we find from field research (R. Mukherjee 1977a), this possibility is not restricted to the case cited above. In all such cases, therefore, the unit will be categorized as a nonfamilial ($= nfu$) complex. Otherwise the base (the trunk of the family tree) will be characterized as P_0, M_0, N_1, etc., with reference to some members of the unit (as illustrated), and so the unit will be categorized as a complex of the kinship pattern represented by the base. It follows that the remaining family members will be conceived as *adherents* of the unit. They would form branches, subbranches, etc., off the trunk of the family tree. Their characteristics registering deviations from the base pattern will either reveal the direction(s) and the extent of changes taking place toward new pattern formations or merely denote casual fluctuations around the base pattern.

The operational aspect of categorizing a set of family complexes can thus be made efficient by stipulating one particular person in each of these units as its ego. Obviously, the selection of the Ego will be based on conceptual grounds, important as the means for bringing all the family units (whether forming a complex family or not) under this stipulated family member. For example, the Ego may be that person around whom all other family members congregate to form the respective units. He or she may be the principal or the only provider for the unit, its centralized authority, the symbol of "the effective minimal lineage," and so on.

Corresponding to the stipulation of an Ego for each one of the family complexes, its base pattern also may be stipulated. Operationally this may be efficient because the subjective judgment of a researcher may be involved in deciding how large the largest of the frequencies of the known kinship patterns must be (as found from Schedule 3.2) in order to select it as the base pattern on purely empirical grounds. Moreover, on conceptual grounds, too, the stipulation of a base pattern would be useful.

As we have pointed out with reference to the *taravad* organization among the Chetlat Islanders, the nuclear organization among the North Americans, and the patrilineal-patrivirilocal organization in India generally, it would be useful to analyze the dynamics of the family when the stipulated pattern is historically know to form the desired or probabilistically normative family organization in a society. Hence, that particular family organization may be stipulated for all the family units brought under analysis, whether or not they form family complexes with reference to the design of Schedule 3.2, in order that the course of classification regarding pattern formation (and *not* regarding the pattern(s) formed) can be standardized and made uniform. Obviously, in this context, Schedule 3.2 will be revised and the Master Chart in Appendix 3B will be simplified with reference only to that pattern of intra-family relations which is stipulated.

However, even though a particular pattern of lineal and/or affinal relations is stipulated, some family units may consistently represent the N_1 pattern. As noted, the N_0 pattern may be logically consistent with a lineal pattern only (e.g., with reference to the T_0 pattern), but that would be a rare possibility. On the other hand, with reference to all the 13 patterns we have discussed, N_1 may form component(s) of a family unit. Hence, while examining pattern formation with reference to a base pattern stipulated for the family units, we must keep room for three possibilities with respect to each unit; namely, it may form (1) a family complex of the stipulated pattern of lineal and affinal relations, (2) a N_1 complex, or (3) a nonfamilial complex. The design of Block 1 of

Schedule 3.3: Block 1: Tabulation 2. (with examples)

Write the symbol for stipulated Ego as *Eu*, *Eu'*, *Eu"*, *Eme^k*, *Eme^a*, *Efe^k*, or *Efe^a*	Write the notation series of each of Ego's family members, noting his/her marital status and the sequential order of notations in each series	Consult Master Chart for each notation series and circle N_1 and/or s for the deduced or stipulated pattern, X for residual category	Give the series coded X in col. (3) new serial numbers and put the previous ones in parentheses	Family complex category: *nfu* when $N_1 = s = O$, N_1 when $O \langle N_1 \rangle s$, s when $O \langle s \rangle N_1$
(1)	(2)	(3)	(4)	(5)

		Base Pattern N_1		
Eu	1 F	N_1 s X		N_1
	2 M	N_1 s X		
	3 FS1De1	N_1 s X	1(3) FS1De1	
	4 Be1	N_1 s X	2(4) Be1	
	5 Se1	N_1 s X	3(5) Se1	
	6 MB1Ze1	N_1 s X	4(6) MB1Ze1	
Count the numbers of N_1, s, and X:		2 2 4		

		Base Pattern P_0		
Efe^a	1 H	N_1 s X		$s = P_0$
	2 Ze1	N_1 s X		
	3 Z1W	N_1 s X		
	4 HFB1De1	N_1 s X	1(4) HFB1De1	
	5 HFB1De2 D1H	N_1 s X	2(5) HFB1D2D1H	
	6 Se1	N_1 s X	3(6) Se1	
Count the numbers of N_1, s, and X:		1 3 3		

Schedule 3.3 will show that these possibilities can be easily accommodated in the course of analyzing family units.

Schedule 3.3: Block 1.—continued
Base Pattern M_0

Eme[a]	1 W	N_1	s	X		$s = M_0$
	2 De1	N_1	s	X		
	3 De1H1	N_1	s	X		
	4 WMS1Ze1	N_1	s	X	1(4) WMS1Ze1	
	5 WMS1Ze2Z1W	N_1	s	X	2(5) WMS1Ze2Z1W	
	6 Be1	N_1	s	X	3(6) Be1	

Count the numbers of N_1, s, and X:		1	3	3

Base Pattern T_0

Eu'	1 M	N_1	s	X		$s - T_0$
	2 Be1	N_1	s	X		
	3 Se2	N_1	s	X		
	4 MS1Z1De1	N_1	s	X	1(4) MS1Z1De1	
	5 MB1WS1D2Z1	N_1	s	X	2(5) MB1WS1D2Z1	
	6 S1D1Z1D1HF	N_1	s	X	3(6) S1D1Z1D1HF	

Count the number of N_1, s, and X:		1	3	3

Base Pattern A

Eme[k]	1 W	N_1	s	X		$s = A$
	2 MBe1	N_1	s	X		
	3 M	N_1	s	X	1(3) M	
	4 S1D1H	N_1	s	X	2(4) S1D1H	
	5 S1Zu1	N_1	s	X	3(5) S1Zu1	
	6 S2Z1Ze1	N_1	s	X	4(6) S2Z1Ze1	
	7 D1De1	N_1	s	X	5(7) D1De1	
	8 D1Ze1	N_1	s	X	6(8) D1Ze1	
	9 MBu1	N_1	s	X	7(9) MBu1	
	10 Bu1	N_1	s	X	8(10) Bu1	
	11 B1Z1W	N_1	s	X	9(11) B1Z1W	
	12 B1Z2WF	N_1	s	X	10(12) B1Z2WF	
	13 B2D1H	N_1	s	X	11(13) B2D1H	
	14 B2De2	N_1	s	X	12(14) B2De2	
	15 WMBe1	N_1	s	X	13(15) WMBe1	
	16 Z1WSu1	N_1	s	X	14(16) Z1WSu1	

Count the numbers of N_1, s, and X:		0	2	14

Note: The symbol *s* refers to the stipulated base pattern, to be recorded along with N_1 whether stipulated or not. The symbol X refers to any pattern not covered in Master Chart, the symbol *nfu,* for "non-familial unit."

Now, the trunks of the family complexes being identified with respect to the stipulated ego, the *nature and extent of deviation* registered by the adherents (i.e., the adhering branches of the family tree) can be specified with reference to the empirically or conceptually determined basic kinship pattern. For illustrative purposes we may examine these characteristics of deviation with reference to five major kinship patterns given by the symbols N_1, P_0, M_0, T_0, and A. Other patterns also could be considered, but we notice that the nature of deviation from P_0 leads to a certain extent to P_1, P_2, and P_3, but not entirely; and so it is from M_0 to M_1 and M_2, or from T_0 to T_1 and T_2. The nature of deviations from any one particular kinship pattern would thus denote the usefulness of this categorization, bearing in mind the immense possibilities for forming patterns in the given universe of variation.

From the nuclear pattern the deviations can occur only with reference to the husband or the wife forming the nucleus of the unit. From the P_0, M_0, and T_0 patterns, the nature of deviations can be of various kinds. The deviant kinship constituents may be affiliated with the lineal strain of the pattern, even though this is not prescribed for it. These *lineal deviants* would be: (1) for P_0, any ever-married sister or daughter (and/or her progeny) of the male members of the family; (2) for M_0, any ever-married brother or son (and/or his progeny) of the female members of the family; and (3) for T_0, any progeny of the male members of the family. Similarly, with respect to the avunculocal *A* pattern, they would be *(a)* any female related as (or traced through) the mother or sister of the ever-married male members of the family, *(b)* the unmarried sons of these female relatives, *(c)* the ever-married children of the male members already listed, and *(d)* the progeny of these children.

The deviant kinship constituents may also be affiliated with the affinal relations prescribed for the base pattern or, if the pattern does not include any affinal relation, the type of affinal relation that follows from the prescribed lineal relations. With respect to the five patterns under examination, these *affinal deviants* can be ascertained as follows: (1) any kin or affines of the ever-married female members of the family (excluding their progeny), for P_0 and *A;* (2) any kin or affines of the ever-married male members of the family (excluding their progeny), for M_0; and (3) any consort and his or her kin or affines (excluding the progeny of the consorts) of the prescribed members of the family, for T_0.

Furthermore, such kinship constituents may be found in a family complex, forming affinal relations with its basic substructure only through such persons who themselves have deviated from the lineal kinship composition of the unit. These *lineally linked affinal* deviants are, in the first instance, the consorts of the lineal deviants and, in the second, the kin and affines of these consorts (exluding their own progeny). With respect to the P_0 complex, these deviants are related to any male member located in the trunk of the family tree, such as SH, DHB, and FBDHF. With respect to other kinds of family complexes, the lineally linked affinal deviants will be enumerated in Table 3.6.

With respect to some base patterns, the nature of deviation may be further distinguished. For example, the kinship constituents registering affinal deviation from P_1, P_2, and P_3 patterns may be categorized "agnatic-affinal" or "uterine-affinal," depending on whether they are related to the constituents of the basic substructure through the husbands of the ever-married female kin or through the ever-married female affines, respectively. Similar categorizies of the affinal deviants can be made for the M_1 and M_2 or T_1 and T_2 patterns with reference to the ever-married male kin and affines. The lineal kin deviants from the A pattern can be categorized as (1) "ancestral," if they refer to (or are traced through) the mothers and sisters of the ever-married males of the basic structure, or (2) "filial," if they refer to the ever-married children (or the progeny of these children) of these male members. Corresponding to these lineal kin deviants, the lineally linked affinal deviants from the A pattern could also be "ancestral" or "filial."

Thus, with reference to any base pattern, there would be various ways of specifying the nature of deviant relationships which a family complex may incorporate severally or in combination. We should formulate these strains of deviation precisely in order to indicate how the possibility of *(a)* new pattern formations can be detected, *(b)* the lingering influence of any previous pattern can be ascertained, and *(c)* how the range of casual fluctuations around a central tendency can be specified.

We shall demonstrate the utility of this course of categorization in the next chapter. For the moment we may show that the deviant kinship constituents can be detected from the extensions of the formulae given in Table 3.3. We shall therefore illustrate this procedure with respect to the N_1, P_0, M_0, T_0 and A patterns by extending the formulae 0.2, 1.0, 2.0, 3.0, and 4.0 of that table in Table 3.6. The extended formulae are so constructed for each kinship pattern that (1) the first set of brackets in column 4 denotes the trunk of the family tree, (2) the second set the lineal *or* the affinal deviants as appropriate to a formula, and (3) the third set the lineally linked affinal deviants. Each one of the sets of brackets is divided, where necessary, into parenthetical components in order to register the sequential extensions of the trunk and the adhering branches of the family tree. Moreover, so as to specify the direction of deviant relations, some notations in these formulae are overlined to indicate that one of them must occur in the composition of the kinship notation series. For the formulae 4.0.12 and 4.0.2, S and Ze are underlined because Ze cannot occur without S preceding it.

Just as the Master Chart in Appendix 3B is prepared on the basis of the formulae given in Table 3.3 for the 13 kinship patterns, so with reference to the formulae given in Table 3.6 (and those which can be devised in the same manner) master charts can be prepared to denote the nature of deviation from any kinship pattern. A schedule can therefore be constructed to register whether a family unit in a set conforms to a consistent pattern of intra-family relations or deviates from the base pattern, and what strain(s) of deviant relations it incorporates. Such a schedule may not require the preparation of additional master charts, while it may denote the extent of deviation represented by the relevant kinship constituents in each family unit. The procedure is shown in the design of Schedule 3.3, Blocks 2 and 3.

The extent of deviation can be examined with reference to the foliation of the adherent branches of a family tree; for example, (1) how many branches have been formed on the trunk of the family tree by the deviant kinship constituents?, (2) have the branches forked out from the same or different points of contact with the trunk?, (3) to what extent have the deviant kinship constituents extended the family tree into branches, subbranches, sub-subbranches?, and so on. These characteristics will allow recording of distinctions among the

Table 3.6.
Deviations from kinship patterns

Kinship Pattern	Nature of Deviation	Formula	Constituents
(1)	(2)	(3)	(4)
N_l	Husband's side	0.2.1	[(EuF, Eme, EfeH)] [(F, M, B, S)] [(K)]
	Wife's side	0.2.2	[(EuM, EmeW, Efe)] [(F, M, B, S)] [(K)]
P_0	Lineal & Lineally linked affinal	1.0.1	[(Eu, Eme^k, Efe^{a}H) (F.../B/Z...)] [($\overline{\text{Se}}$, $\overline{\text{De}}$) (Z.../D...)] [($\overline{\text{H}}$,$\overline{\text{W}}$) (K)]
	Affinal	1.0.2	[(Eu, Eme^k, Efe^{a}H) (F.../B/Z...) ($\overline{\text{M}}$, $\overline{\text{W}}$)] [(K)]
M_0	Lineal & Lineally linked affinal	2.0.1	[(E'u, Eme^{a}W, Efe^k) (M.../S/D...)] [($\overline{\text{Be}}$, $\overline{\text{Ze}}$) (Z.../D...)] [($\overline{\text{H}}$, $\overline{\text{W}}$) (K)]
	Affinal	2.0.2.	[(E'u, Eme^{a}W, Efe^k) (M.../S/D...) ($\overline{\text{F}}$, $\overline{\text{H}}$)] [(K)]
T_0	Lineal & Lineally linked affinal	3.0.1.	[(E'u, Eme^{k}M, Efe$\underline{^k}$) (M.../S/D...) ($\overline{\text{B}}$, $\overline{\text{Z}}$)] [(Z.../D...)] [($\overline{\text{H}}$, $\overline{\text{W}}$) (K)]
	Affinal	3.0.2	[(E'u, Eme^{k}M, Efe^k) (M.../S/D...) (B, Z)] [($\overline{\text{F}}$, $\overline{\text{H}}$, $\overline{\text{W}}$) (K)]
A	Lineal & Lineally linked affinal: Ancestral	4.0.11	[(Euf, Eme^k, Efe^{a}H)] [($\overline{\text{M}}$.../$\overline{\text{S}}$/D...) (Bu, Zu)] [($\overline{\text{F}}$, $\overline{\text{H}}$) (K)]
	Filial	4.0.12	[(EuF, Eme^k, Efe^{a}H) (M.../$\underline{\text{S}}$/D...) (Be, $\underline{\text{Z}}$e)] [($\overline{\text{Ze}}$.../$\overline{\text{De}}$...)] [($\overline{\text{H}}$, $\overline{\text{W}}$) (K)]
	Affinal	4.0.2	[(EuF, Eme^k, Efe^{a}H) (M.../$\underline{\text{S}}$/D...) (Be, $\underline{\text{Z}}$e) (W)] [(K)]

Schedule 3.3: Block 2: Computation 1. (for base pattern N_1, with an illustration)

Write the symbol for Ego from Schedule 3.3, Block 1, col. (1).	Write all notation series in Block 1, col. (4).	Write the first notation and number of each series in col. (2).	Count all F/M/B/S/Z/D from col. (2) but *exclude* Zu/Du if *last* for all series, *and* F/M if *first* in the series, when Eu is Ego.	Circle appropriate code according to Ego's symbol in col. (1), when the first notation in col. (3) is			
				F for Eu, H for Efe, *or* F/M/ B/S for Eme as Ego.	M for Eu, W for Eme, *or* F/M/ B/S for Efe as Ego.	B for Eu *and* Z for Eme or Efe as Ego.	S for Eu *and* D for Eme or Efe as Ego.
(1)	(2)	(3)	(4)	(5)	(6)	(7)	(8)
Eu	1. FS1De1	F	2	1	2	3	4
	2. Be1	Be1	1	1	2	3	4
	3. Se1	Se1	1	1	2	3	4
	4. MB1Ze1	M	2	1	2	3	4

Count the number of different notations in col. (3):* $\beta = 4$ ($\propto$ is always 1)   Max. value $= \delta = 2$ Display circled numbers sequentially for nature of deviation: 1—2—3—4

Code: Adherents from: 1 = husband-father's side   2 = wife-mother's side
                                   3 = brother-son's side   4 = sister-daughter's side
Note: / = and/or.
*See page 151 for explanation of notation.

deviant kinship constituents in terms of their forming mutually exclusive clusters of that pattern of intra-family relations that is regarded as the base pattern. Thus by denoting the linkage of these clusters among themselves as well as with the basic structure of the respective family units, these characteristics of deviation will suggest incipient patterns, casual fluctuations around the basic kinship pattern, or anomalous situations.

It will be seen from Table 3.6 that the point(s) of contact of the adherents to the trunk of the family tree are given by the first set of brackets in each formula. Since the trunk of the family tree for the nuclear pattern N_1 consists of only one person (viz. Ego as the husband, the wife, or any one of their unmarried children), there is only one point of contact for the adherents, given by the single set of parentheses within the first set of brackets in the formulae 0.2.1 and 0.2.2. Similarly, the "ancestral" strain of deviations for the avunculocal A pattern emerges directly with reference to the Ego denoted as Eme[k]. For all other formulae in the table the possible elaborations of the respective family trees and, consequently, of various points of contact for the adherents are shown by the subsequent sets of parentheses within the first set of brackets.

Schedule 3.3: Block 2.—*continued*—(for base pattern P_0, with an example)

Write Ego's symbol from Block 1, col. (1): Efe[a] For each series in Block 1, col. (4), put its notations and numbers sequentially under appropriate columns; but for Efe as Ego, all notation series beginning with F/M/B/S put under col. (7), with W in col. (6).							Write that part of the series which falls under Cols. (1)-(6)-(4),	Cols. (1)-(6)	Count the number of M/W/S/D in cols. (5)-(7), but *not* M/W/ Su/Du if *last* notation	Circle appropriate code if notation occurs *in col. (5)* in with *no* H/W H/W (6)/ in in (7) col. col. (7) (7)		
H	F-s*	B	Z-s*	S/D	M/W	Other						

(1)	(2)	(3)	(4)	(5)	(6)	(7)	(8)	(9)	(10)	(11)	(12)	(13)
1. H	F	B1		De1			HFB1	HFB1De1	1	1	2	3
2. H	F	B1		De2		D1H	HFB1	HFB1De2	2	1	2	3
3.			W	Se1		W	W	W	2	1	2	3

Count the notation series in cols. (8) and (9), respectively, with different notations/numbers:			$\alpha = 2$	$\beta = 3$	Max. value $\delta = 2$	Nature of deviation: 1—2—3

Code: 1 = lineal adherent, 2 = lineally linked affinal, 3 = affinal adherent
Note: / = and/or.
*F-s = FF...; Z-s = ZZ....
**See p. 151 for explanation of notation.

Schedule 3.3: Block 2.—*continued*—(for base pattern M_0, with an example)

Write Ego's symbol from Block 1, col. (1): Eme[a] For each series in Block 1, col. (4), put its notations and numbers sequentially under appropriate columns; but for Eme as Ego, all notation series beginning with F/M/B/S put under col. (7), with H in col. (6).							Write that part of the series which falls under Cols. (1)-(4), (6)	Cols. (1)-(6)	Count the number of F/H/B/Z in cols. (5)-(7), but *not* F/H/Bu/ Zu if *last* notation	Circle appropriate code if notation occurs *in col. (5)* in cols. with *no* H/W H/W (6)/ in in (7) col. col. (7) (7)		
W	M-s*	S	D-s*	B/Z	F/H	Other						

(1)	(2)	(3)	(4)	(5)	(6)	(7)	(8)	(9)	(10)	(11)	(12)	(13)
1. W	M	S1		Ze1			WMS1	WMS1Ze1	1	1	2	3
2. W	M	S1		Ze2		Z1W	WMS1	WMS1Ze2	2	1	2	3
3.			H	Be1		H	H	H	2	1	2	3

Count the notation series in cols. (8) and (9), respectively, with different notations/numbers:‡		$\alpha = 2$	$\beta = 3$	Max. value $\delta = 2$	Nature of deviation: 1—2—3

Code: 1, 2, and 3 are same as for base pattern P_0.
Note: / = and/or.
* M-s = MM...; D-s = DD....
‡See p. 151 for explanation of notation.

Schedule 3.3: Block 2.—*continued*—(for base pattern T_0, with an example)

Write Ego's symbol from Block 1, col. (1): Eu'							Write that part of the series which falls under Cols. (1)–(4).	Count the number of F/H/W/Z/D occurs in cols. (5)–(7), but *not* Z/D if it follows S/D in these columns.	Circle appropriate code if notation occurs		
For each series in Block 1, col. (4), put its notations and numbers sequentially under appropriate columns.									in col. (5) but *not* in col. (6)	in col. (5) *and* in col. (6)	in col. (6). but *not* in col. (5).
M-s*	S	D-s*	Z-s B/Z D-s* after cols. (1–4)	F H W	Other						
(1)	(2)	(3)	(4)	(5)	(6)	(7)	(8)	(9)	(10)	(11)	(12)
1. M	S1		Z1	De1			MS1Z1	1	1	2	3
2. M			B1		W	S1D2Z1	MB1	1	1	2	3
3.	S1	D1	Z1	De1	H	F	S1	3	1	2	3
Count the notation series in col. (8) with different notation and numbers:**						$\alpha = \beta = 3$		Max. value $\delta = 3$	Nature of deviation: 1—2—3		

Code: 1, 2, and 3 are same as for base pattern P_0 and M_0.
Note: / = and/or.
* M-s = MM...; D-s = DD...; Z-s/D-s = any combination of Z and/or D = ZZ....
** See p. 151 for explanation of notation.

As noted, the lineal strain of adherents may fork into more than one branch from the same point of contact with the trunk of the family tree. This we notice from the overlined notations within the second set of brackets for the formulae 1.0.1, 2.0.1, and 4.0.12 in Table 3.6. Overlined notations of this kind are irrelevant for the second set of brackets in formula 3.0.1 because all sons and daughters of the overlined notations B and Z—belonging to the trunk of the T_0 complex—should belong to the respective *taravads* of each B's and Z's wife. For the other kinds of family complexes, the lineal branches from the same point of contact with the trunk of the family tree include (1) FSe_1, FSe_2, $FBDe_1$, $FBDe_2$, etc., for the P_0 complex; (2) MBe_1, MBe_2, $MSZe_1$, $MSZe_2$, etc., for the M_0 complex; (3) Ze_1, Ze_2, $MBDe_1$, $MBDe_2$, etc., to depict the filial strain of lineal deviations from the A complex.

Table 3.6 shows further that a lineally linked affinal adherent would follow that branch of the family tree denoted by the lineal deviants to which it is linked, whereas a directly linked affinal adherent would follow that branch denoted by its point of contact with the trunk of the family tree. However, with all the varieties of adherents, the possibility of foliation of the family tree is virtually infinite because it refers to the whole network of the kinship system. The adherents, therefore, may also be characterized according to where they attach—singly, in clusters, or en block—to the trunk(s) of the family tree(s),

Schedule 3.3: Block 2.—*continued*—(for base pattern A, with an example)

Write Ego's symbol from Block 1, col. (1):	Eme^k	For
For each series in Block 1, col. (4), put its notations and numbers sequentially under appropriate columns, but do not place *Ze* in col. (8) and *De* in col. (6) unless *Se* occurs in col. (4). For *Efe* as Ego, all notation series beginning with F/M/B/S put under col. (11), with *W* in col. (9).	For series with notation in col. (8), write that part under	series without notation in col. (8), write its first notation and number.

											For series with notation in col. (8), write that part under		
		Bu,		Zu,		Zu, Be,	H,	Ze,			cols. (1)–(9)	cols. (1)–(10)	
F/H*	M-s**	Su	Se	Du	De-s**Du	Ze	W	De	Other				
(1)	(2)	(3)	(4)	(5)	(6)	(7)	(8)	(9)	(10)	(11)	(12)	(13)	(14)
1.	M												M
2.		S1		D1			H						S1
3.		S1	Zu1										S1
4.		S2				Z1		Ze1			S2Z1	S2Z1Z1	
5.								De1	De1				D1
6.								De1	Ze1				D1
7.	M	Bu1											M
8.		Bu1											Bu1
9.						B1		Ze1	W	B1	B1Z1		
10.						B1		Ze2	WF	B1	B1Z2		
11.						B2		De1	H	B2	B2D1		
12.						B2		De2		B2	B2D2		
13.							W		MBe1				W
14.								Ze1	WSu1				Z1

Count the parts of series in cols. (12), (13), and (14), respectively, which are different in notation and/or number; but count all Bu/Su in col. (14) as 1:***	$\alpha_1 = 3$ $\beta_1 = 5$ $\beta_2 = 6$ **** $\alpha_2 = 1$ ***** $\alpha = 4$ $\beta = \beta_1 + \beta_2 = 11$

Note: / = and/or.
* For Eu/Efe as Ego.
** M-s = MM...; De-s = DeDe....
*** See p. 151 for explanation of notation.
**** $\alpha_2 = 0$ or 1 if β_2 is 0 or greater.
***** $\alpha = \alpha_1 + \alpha_2$.

for which the basic structure of kinship relations has been empirically determined from Schedule 3.2 or conceptually stipulated. Accordingly, we may enumerate the number of trunks of family trees which an adherent has bypassed in order to belong to the family complex which is being categorized. The procedure is illustrated here with the patrilineal-patrivirilocal pattern, i.e., the P_0 complex, as it is the most commonly encountered pattern of extended families in world society.

Let there be three persons who are related to any point of contact on the trunk of the P_0 family complex, labelled X, as: (1) DZe, (2) DDH, and (3) WBWSDe. DZe will denote the *first* branch from the trunk of X because this lineal adherent to the family complex belongs to that P_0 structure of which his

Schedule 3.3: Block 3: Computation 2 (for base pattern A, with an example)

For each notation series in Block 2, cols. (1)–(11) write its parts in the appropriate columns below.	For series *without* notation in col. (2), count *the number of*	For series *with* nota-tion in col. (2), count the number of F/M/	Circle appropriate code for the series with notation in		
			col. (1) but *not* in (2)	col. (2) but *not* in (3) *or* only in col. (4)	cols. (2)–(4) *or* cols. (1)–(4) *or* cols. (3)–(4) only
Cols. Col. Col. Cols. (2)–(7) (8) (9) (10)–(11)	M/S/ F/M/ Add Bu/ B/S/ col. De Ze/ (5) in De and col. in col. (1) col. (6) (4)	B/S/Ze/De in col. (4).	with *no* H/W in cols. (3)–(4).	with H/W in col. (3) or (4)	
			col. (4)	with *no* H/W in col. (4)	with H/W in col. (4)

(1)	(2)	(3)	(4)	(5)	(6)	(7)	(8)	(9)	(10)	(11)	(12)	(13)
1. M				1	–	1	–	11	12	21	22	30
2. S1D1		H		2	–	2	–	11	12	21	22	30
3. S1Zu1				1	–	1	–	11	12	21	22	30
4. S2	Z1	Ze1		–	–	–	1	11	12	21	22	30
5.		D1De1		–	2	2	–	11	12	21	22	30
6.		D1Ze1		–	2	2	–	11	12	21	22	30
7. MBu1				2	–	2	–	11	12	21	22	30
8. Bu1				1	–	1	–	11	12	21	22	30
9.	B1	Z1W		–	–	–	1	11	12	21	22	30
10.	B1	Z2WF		–	–	–	2	11	12	21	22	30
11.	B2	D1H		–	–	–	1	11	12	21	22	30
12.	B2	De2		–	–	–	1	11	12	21	22	30
13.		W	MBe1	–	2	2	–	11	12	21	22	30
14.			Z1WSu1	–	2	2	–	11	12	21	22	30

Write the maximum value in col. (7) and col. (8), respectively:*

$$\alpha_1 = 2 \quad \alpha_2 = 2$$
$$\alpha = \max.\alpha_1, \alpha_2 = 2$$

Nature of deviation: 11–12–21–22–30

Code: 11 = lineal adherent (ancestral) 12 = lineally linked adherent (ancestral)
      21 = lineal adherent (filial)   22 = lineally linked adherent (filial)
      30 = affinal adherent
Note: / = and/or.
*See page 151 for explanation of notation.

mother De is a member after her marriage with DH. DDH would be attached to the first branch of the P_0 structure of DH and the *second* branch of family X because DH would have been a lineally linked affinal adherent to this unit. WBWSDe would be attached to the first branch of the P_0 structure of WBWSe since the former was married; sequentially, WBWSDe would refer to the second branch of the P_0 structure of WBe because WBWSe forms its first af-final branch; and, following the sequence, WBWSDe would refer to the *third* branch of X because WBe was an affinal adherent to this unit.

Figure 3.2.
Trunk and Foliation of a Patrilineal-patrivirilocal (P_0) Complex Family Tree

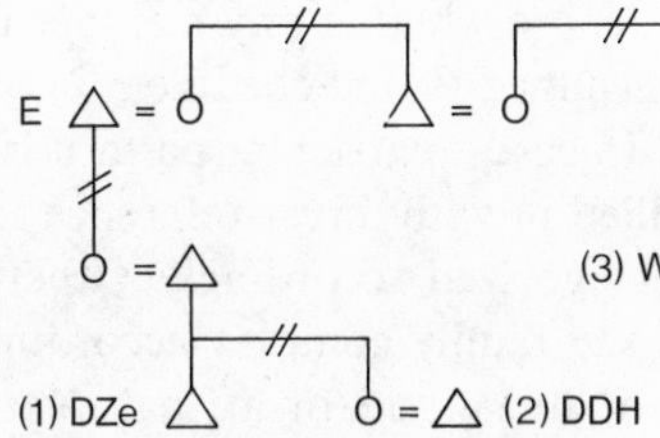

Note: // denotes branch, subbranch, sub-subbranch from the P_0 trunk of Ego (E) and corresponding P_0 branch, subbranch)

Thus, by following the population approach, the nature and extent of deviation can be categorized in various ways for those families that do not totally conform to any one (including the stipulated) pattern of kinship relations. We have illustrated some forms of categorization in this context; others can be designed to advance the course of family structure classification. We may note, however, that with the categorization of family complexes according to the extent of deviation registered by their constituent adherents, we enter into the sphere of quantification of the attributes of classification.

A variate $\propto$ can be constructed to denote the number of points of contact of the adherents to the trunk of the family tree. The value of $\propto$ will be zero for a family unit which consistently registers the empirically found or the conceptually stipulated kinship pattern. Otherwise the variate may attain any value from 1 upwards for the family complexes, and the units may be classified according to these values.

The total number of branches emerging from the family tree, with reference to the points of contact of the adherents to the trunk of the family tree, can be given by another variate, say, β. The value of this variate also will be zero when $\propto$ equals zero; otherwise its value will be equal to or greater than that of $\propto$, and, on that basis, the family complexes may be further classified.

As illustrated by the formation of the first branch, the second branch (= subbranch), the third branch (= sub-subbranch), and so on, the foliation of a family tree will be given by the distance (d) of each adherent from the trunk with respect to the pattern of intra-family relations empirically ascertained or stipulated for the units under analysis. Hence, the maximum of these d distances can be denoted by a variate, say, δ, which would be zero when $\propto = \beta = 0$. Otherwise, irrespective of the nature of deviation registered by the respective adhesions (as it is in the case of $\propto$ and β values), and also irrespective of the values of $\propto$ and β, the value of δ can be from 1 upwards. The family complexes may, therefore, be classified according to the value of this variate in order to denote the maximum spread of the respective family trees.

We may, thus, obtain a more and more precise and comprehensive picture of the family structures under analysis, by proceeding in their classification from a qualitative to a quantitative appraisal of their attributes of *being* and *becoming.* The computational procedure for this course of classification would be a routine task, as seen from Schedule 3.3, Blocks 2 and 3.

Block 1 of Schedule 3.3 can denote whether any member in a family unit deviates from the empirically determined (vide Schedule 3.2) or the stipulated base pattern of kinship relations. In case a particular pattern is not stipulated, Schedule 3.3, column 3 will be filled in with direct reference to Schedule 3.2, and the family complex will be categorized accordingly. Otherwise, column 5 will denote the categorization of the family complex according to whether it represents the stipulated pattern of lineal and/or affinal relations, or the N_l pattern, or none (= non-familial complex). However, whether or not the base pattern is stipulated, column 4 of the block will arrange the deviant kinship constituents for categorizing the family complexes according to the nature and the extent of deviation registered by their respective sets of adherents.

Block 2 of Schedule 3.3 would vary according to the particular kinship pattern empirically determined or stipulated for categorizing the nature and extent of deviation registered by the adherents in a family complex. This block, therefore, has been designed separately for the N_1, P_0, M_0, T_0, and A patterns. For the avunculocal A pattern, another block (Schedule 3.3., Block 3) has been designed to facilitate the computation of the complicated nature and extent of deviation of kinship constituents from this peculiar pattern of intra-family relations. Thus, by comprising two or more blocks, Schedule 3.3 can be designed for any and all kinds of pattern formation in order to systematically categorize the family units by following the population approach.

4   KINSHIP DISTANCE

The inductive process of classification can be pursued further to categorize all family units in terms of the kinship distance registered by their respective members, whether or not they belong to the core of the units or are deviants, and whichever kinship patterns these units depict or deviate from. This course of categorization would involve "genealogical relations" which, as Radcliffe-Brown pointed out, is an important but virgin field in family studies; we have explained why it has remained a virtually untouched area for family structure classification.

The deductive process of classification and the typological approach generally would block our entry into this area of classification, because it has to begin with the measurement of all possible kinship distances among the members in each family unit, and thus proceeds from the bottom, as it were, from these indivisible attributes of classification. To illustrate, the patrilineal pattern sorts out the relationship between a "nephew" or a "niece" and his/her "uncle" by utilizing only the variants *FB, FFBZ, FFFBZZ,* and so on, from the total field comprising the other variants: *MB, MMBZ,* . . . ; *FSH, FFSDH, FFSZ,* . . . ; *MSH, MMSDH, MMSZ,* . . . ; and so on. However, no extant or immanent kinship pattern distinguishes the family units in accordance with the knowable variations in the degree of collaterality of such relationships (e.g., that between a nephew/niece and his/her uncle); yet these variations are relevant to appraising the dynamics of the family system, as we have discussed.

Now, once the concept of kinship distance has been introduced, the manner in which the distance is measured and the scale evolved for this purpose may be made more and more precise and efficient. For the moment, we shall discuss only the broad outlines of classification of family structures on the dimension of kinship distance.

We should, first, conceive of a family matrix (R. Mukherjee 1959: 133-140). Let any one of the n number of individuals in a family be considered as its Ego (E), and let him or her be placed at the focal point 00 of a matrix which, with respect to E, gives the "ancestral," "own" (= zero), and "descendant" generation levels on its y-y' axis and the collateral extension of each generation level on its x axis. Accordingly, if the Ego's ancestral generation levels (i) be given by values varying from 0 to 3, the descendant generation levels (i') by values from 0 to 3, and the collateral extension (j) in each of the generation levels by values from 0 to 3, then the matrix will take the shape shown in Table 3.7, in which (1) the i' values are given in negative numerals in order to distinguish them from the corresponding i values, and (2) in each number the left-hand figure indicates the generation level and the right hand one the degree of collateral extension on that level.

In such a matrix formation, the position of the Ego's consort(s) will be at the point 00, since there cannot be any generational or collateral distance among them. The location of the remaining family members at particular points of the matrix will be given by the number of times the notations (F or M, B or S, and Z or D) occur in their respective kinship notation series with respect to the Ego; i.e., by say, p for the number of occurrences of the notation F or M; r for B or S; and q for Z or D. The number of times the notations H or W occur in these series will be of no concern to us in the present context, since these notations will not increase the intra-matrix distance between Ego and the relative in question. On the other hand, the figure p-q as a positive quantity will denote the i value, but as a negative quantity the i' value; and the j value

Table 3.7.

**Generational-Collateral
Distance Matrix**

		Collateral			
		30	31	32	33
	Ancestral	20	21	22	23
		10	11	12	13
Generational		*00*	01	02	03
		-10	-11	-12	-13
	Descendant	-20	-21	-22	-23
		-30	-31	-32	-33

will be given by $q + r$ when p-q is positive, by $p + r$ when p-q is negative, and by $q + r$ or $p + r$ when p equals q.

Thus, with reference to one of the family members selected as the Ego for the unit, all other family members will occupy definite places in the matrix. If Ego is selected on the basis of a specific familial role (as illustrated earlier), then it may be desirable to categorize the family unit of n members in terms of the n-1 kinship distances formed around the stipulated Ego. If, on the other hand, the particular role of Ego in the family is of no relevance, the scheme of categorization may refer to *all* the kinship distances $[n(n-1)/2]$ in these units and not just to those which one family member has with the other members. In that case, n-1 matrices will have to be drawn successively for a family. Like the matrix of Table 3.7, drawn with respect to a stipulated Ego, the first matrix will comprise n-1 kinship distances; the second, however, will comprise n-2 kinship distances, because the distance between its Ego and the Ego of the first matrix has already been accounted for; the third matrix will correspondingly comprise n-3 kinship distances; the n-1 matrix will record only 1 kinship distance, and the nth matrix none at all.

However, the enumeration of n-1 family matrices encounters an operational problem. The inter-generational distance between two family members will be denoted differently according to which of the two serves as the point of reference (the Ego) for recording the kinship notation series. For example, between a "father" and a "son," the inter-generational distance with the former as the point of reference will be denoted by $i = 0$, $i' = 1$, and with the latter as the point of reference, by $i = 1$, $i' = 0$. This distinction in the corresponding values of i and i' is useful to record for the n-1 kinship distances drawn with reference to the stipulated Ego for a family, viz. to ascertain whether the parental-filial relationship refers to his/her "father" or "son." But when all kinship distances in a family are taken into account, the dyadic relationships are represented complementarily; for example, the parental-filial relationship will refer to the "father" of a person, who will be referred to by his "father" as "son." The different ways of representing inter-generational distance by the corresponding values of i and i' will, therefore, be irrelevant and will only complicate the enumeration of all kinship distances in a family.

The problem can be solved by arranging serially all the family members in such a manner that their numbering proceeds from the lowest generation level represented in the family to the highest. According to this arrangement, the kinship distances will be measured, first, from the person at the top of the list to the remaining ones; second, from the person next on the list to the remaining ones; and so on, ending with the distance from the person next to last to the last one on the list. The dyadic relationships in the family will thus be arranged in one direction only, with the value of i' remaining consistently zero. In this way, the operational difficulty will be removed without causing any loss of information.

Thus, by taking either the three variates i, i', and j into account (where the Ego's role in the families is of some relevance) or only the variates i and j, a set of families may be categorized in terms of their constituent kinship distances. The scope of categorization, however, remains wide, to the point of being unwieldy. The maximum of inter-generational distances among the members in a set of families (G_m) may be 4; the maximum of collateral distances (Y_m) may be 3. Within this overall coverage, the inter-generational distances registered by the respective subsets of family units will be ($G =$) 1, 2, 3, up to a maximum of 4, and the collateral distances ($Y =$) 0, 1, 2, and 3.

While the values of G will be given by the maximum i values ($= x + 1$), if all the kinship distances in the respective family units are taken into account in the manner described earlier, G will be given by the maximum values of i and i' ($= x + x' + 1$), if only those kinship distances are taken into account which refer to the location of family members around the stipulated Ego for the respective units. In the latter instance, further variations are possible within a given value of G. For example, when $G = 4$, the values of X and X' may be 3 and 0, 2 and 1, 1 and 2, or 0 and 3. Finally, although the values of X, X', and Y may be distinctly specified, variations will occur depending on whether the points of kinship distance fall within the specified area of the matrix or not. For example, even for a simple situation as given by $G = 1$, $X = X' = 0$, and $Y = 2$, the matrix may assume either of the two configurations: (00 01 02) or (00   02).

These possibilities will increase at a very rapid rate with the rise in the value of the variates X, X', Y, G, G_m, and Y_m. This may be ascertained from the following three formulae which give the possible number of different configurations *(C)* of the matrix under two situations: $G = (X + X' + 1)$, and $G = (X + 1)$ with X' consistently zero. The value of C can be calculated also for combinations of these variates other than those given by the three formulae (R. Mukherjee 1959: 133-140); however, for the present, we need not be concerned with them. Needless to say, where $G_m = G = 1$ and $X = X' = Y = Y_m = 0$, C will always by 1.

$$C_{(G_m, Y_m)} = (2^{G_m(Y_m + 1) - 1}) + (G_m - 1)(2^{(Y_m + 1)} - 1)(2^{(G_m - 1)(Y_m + 1) - 1}) \tag{5.0}$$

where the second term will cease to exist when X' is consistently zero for the enumeraiton of G values.

$$C_{(G, Y)} = (2^{G-1})(2^{GY-1}) - (2^{(G-1)} - 1)(2^{(G-1)Y-1}) \tag{6.0}$$
$$+ (G-1)[(2^G - 1)(2^{GY-1}) - (2^{(G-1)} - 1)(2^{(G-1)Y-1})]$$
$$+ (G-2)[2^Y - 1)(2^{(G-2)Y-1}) - (2^{(Y+1)} - 1)(2^{(G-2)(Y+1)-1})]$$

where: (1) the terms beginning with G-1 and G-2 will cease to exist when X' is consistently zero for the enumeration of G values; and

(2) the term beginning with (G-2) will cease to exist when $G = 1$.

$$(7.0)$$

$$C_{(X, X',Y)} = (2^{G(Y+1)-2}) + (2^{(G-1)}-1)(2^Y-1)(2^{(G-1)Y-1})$$
$$-\gamma[(2^{(G-1)}-1)(2^{(G-1)Y-1}) - (2^{(G-2)}-1)(2^{(G-2)Y-1})]$$

where $\gamma = 0$ for $XX' = 0$, and $\gamma = 1$ for $XX' \rangle 0$.

The problem of too many different possibilities of categorization can be circumvented by undertaking the task in two stages. In the first stage we may categorize the families according to the *peripheral* characteristics of their respective sets of kinship distance. In the second stage we may examine the varying configurations delimited by these peripheral characteristics. Besides simplifying the operation, this procedure has the further advantage that on many occasions adequate results will be obtained at the first stage, making it unnecessary to proceed with the second.

In this context, however, the construction of $n-1$ matrices for a family unit, in the manner suggested above, will confuse the issue. When the kinship distances recorded in these matrices are pooled together, there will be no ambiguity in denoting the maximum inter-generational distance in the unit, for the focal point 00 of the successive matrices will be shifted from the person(s) at the lowest generation level to the next higher, and so on, and, thus, the descendant generation levels will not be taken into account. On the other hand, along with the shifting of the focal point, what would be recorded as the maximum collateral spread in an ancestral generation level with respect to any person located in the lowest generation level of the family may be denoted as the maximum collateral spread at the 0 generation level with respect to a person of a higher generation located at the focal point of a successively drawn matrix. For example, in a family unit comprising a man, his brother, and his son, the collateral spread of 1 degree will be recorded at the first ancestral generation level when the son is at the focal point of the first matrix; but with the man at the focal point of the second matrix, the collateral spread will be at the 0 generation level. The delineation of the peripheral characteristics of all kinship distances in a family may thus become ambiguous.

This possibility will be clearly seen from Block 5 of the specimen Schedule 3.4 below, while Block 6 of that schedule shows that the $n-1$ distances with respect to any person at the lowest generation level of a family unit will provide us with the maximum possible generational and collateral spread of the unit in terms of the kinship distances it contains. The peripheral characteristics of the kinship distances in a family unit should therefore be recorded with respect to a stipulated Ego and/or with respect to any one family member belonging to its lowest generation level. The two alternatives are demostrated in Sub blocks 4.1 and 4.2, respectively, of Schedule 3.4, in the light of identifying in Block 2 the respective sets of points from which to draw the kinship distances; while Sub block 4.3 records the third alternative of considering all the kinship distances $[(n(n-1)/2]$ in the light of the data from successively drawn $n-1$ matrices as depicted in Block 3 of that schedule.

Now, the peripheral characteristics of kinship distances in a family unit may be denoted by the following variates:

Let x_e represent the maximum inter-generational distance along the direct ancestral line of any family member from Ego. This variate will register the maximum extension in a family of that line of relationships which proceeds from a person to his or her parents, grandparents, great-grandparents, and so on. We may construct an expression for this,

$$_g(x_e-2)_{gp},$$

where the first g stands for the word "great," the second g for "grand," and p for "parent."

Thus, when $x_e = 4$, that unit registers the presence of a great-great-grandparental (g^2gp) relationship at the maximum; when $x_e = 3$, a great grandparental (g^1gp) relationship at the maximum; when $x_e = 2$, a grandparental $(g^0gp = gp)$ relationship at the maximum; when $x_e = 1$, parental $(g^{-1}gp = gp/g = p)$ relationship at the maximum; and with $x_e = 0$, no relationships at all $(g^{-2}gp = gp/gg = 0)$ in the given line.

Let y_e represent the maximum collateral distance in the direct ancestral line of any family member from Ego, in order to specify that point of kinship distance on the x and y coordinates of the matrix in which the variate x_e occurs. Obviously, y_e will always be zero, since it refers to the direct ancestral line of the respective family members.

Let x_h represent the maximum inter-generational distance along the collateral ancestral line of any family member from Ego. This variate will delimit the maximum extension of that line of relationships in the unit which proceeds from a person to his or her uncle/aunt, granduncle/aunt, great-granduncle/aunt, and so on. We may construct an expression, $_g(x_h-2)_{gu}$, where u stands for "uncle/aunt."

Then $x_h = 4$ will denote the presence of a great-great-granduncle/aunt relationship in the unit at the maximum; and proceeding in the same manner as described for x_e, with $x_h = 1$ the unit will register, at the maximum, the uncle/aunt relationship, and with $x_h = 0$, no relationship at all in the given line.

Let y_h represent the degree of maximum collateral spread for x_h, thus specifying the point of kinship distance for locating x_h, just as y_e does for x_e. The variate y_h, however, can assume any value from 0 upward and thus indicate the maximum degree of collateral distance of the avuncular relationship denoted by x_h. We may, accordingly, reconstruct the previously derived expression as

$$_g(x_h-2)_{gu_{y_h}},$$

so that, with $x_h = 2$ and $y_h = 1$, the unit will register the presence of a granduncle/aunt reltionship of the first order only, at the maximum, while x_h

$= 2$ and $y_h = 2$ will register at the maximum the avuncular relationship of the second order.

Let y_s represent the maximum collateral distance in the ancestral line of any family member from Ego and let x_s denote the maximum inter-generational distance at which y_s is located. We may, then, construct an expression,

$$g^{(x_s-2)} gu_{y_s},$$

to denote how far removed any avuncular relationship exists in the family.

For example, the values of $x_h = 3$, $y_h = 1$, $x_s = 1$ and $y_s = 2$ for a family unit will register the presence in the unit of avuncular relationships that at their maximum inter-generational distance represent the great-granduncle/aunt relationship of the first order while including also the second order avuncular relationship of the uncle/aunt variety only.

Let y_o represent the maximum collateral distance from Ego of any family member in Ego's generation level, so that the variate x_o, which with y_o, specifies the point of kinship distance, remains consistently zero. The variate y_o will register the maximum extension of the sibling-cousin line of relationships in the family. If we construct an expression for this, $s_{y_o}-1$, the value of $y_o = 4$ will register the presence in the unit of an inter-cousin relationship of the third degree (s_3) at the maximum. Correspondingly, $y_o = 3$ will register the presence of an inter-cousin relationship of the second degree (s_2) at the maximum, $y_o = 2$ the presence of an inter-cousin relationship of the first degree only, $y_o = 1$ the presence of an inter-sibling relationship only and no inter-cousin relationship, and $y_o = 0$ the absence of any inter-sibling or inter-cousin relationship.

Thus the variates x_e, x_h, x_s, y_h, y_s, and y_o (with x_o and y_e remaining consistently zero) will denote the peripheral characteristics of all kinship distances in each family, and these characteristics will register the varying structural integration of the respective units in terms of the maximum generational and collateral extensions of their intra-family relations. If, however, only those kinship distances are considered for each unit which its $n-1$ family members have with the remaining member stipulated as its Ego, then five more variates will have to be taken into account to denote the peripheral characteristics of the $n-1$ kinship distances of the respective units, because the kinship distances will now represent the direct and collateral lines of relationships with reference to both the ancestral and descendant generations of the stipulated Ego. Thus the relationships denoted by the expressions

$$g^{(x_e-2)} gp, \qquad g^{(x_h-2)} gu_{y_h}, \qquad \text{and} \qquad g^{(x_s-2)} gu_{y_s}$$

may have their complements in the descendant generation of the Ego, as given by the expressions

$$g^{(x'_e-2)} gc, \qquad g^{(x'_h-2)} gn_{y'_h} \qquad \text{and} \qquad g^{(x'_s-2)} gn_{y'_s}$$

respectively, where c stands for the word "child" and n for "nephew/niece."

Also, since the stipulated Ego is likely to have a distinctive role in the family organization (as mentioned before), it may be desirable to register his or her specific position in the given lines of relationships through these expressions. Accordingly, the variate x'_e will denote the presence in the unit of the Ego's child(ren), grandchild(ren), great-grandchild(ren), and so on, at the maximum, just as the presence of the Ego's parent(s), grandparent(s), and so on at the maximum will be given by x_e. Similarly, the set of variates x'_h, y'_h, x'_s, and y'_s will denote the presence in the unit of the Ego's nephew/niece, grandnephew/niece, and the other more distant such relatives at the maximum generational and collateral expansion, just as the set of variates, x_h, y_h, x_s, and y_s, will denote the corresponding presence of the Ego's uncle/aunt, granduncle/aunt, and the other more removed such relatives.

Obviously, the variate y'_e, specifying the point of kinship distance for the variate x'_e will remain consistently zero, like y_e. Also the inter-sibling and inter-cousin relationships will be denoted in either situation by the variate y_0 only. Therefore, depending on whether all the kinship distances or only a particular set of $n-1$ kinship distances are taken into account for each family unit, the six variates (x_e, x_h, x_s, y_h, y_s, and y_0) or the eleven variates (the preceding six plus x'_e, x'_h, x'_s, y'_h, and y'_s) will usefully denote the peripheral characteristics of the given set of kinship distances. These variates can be derived from a simple computation of the i, i', and j values of the kinship distances for each family unit in order to obtain their maximum values.

Thus,

$$x_e = [\, i - (i \times j)\,] \text{ max.}$$
$$x_h = [\, (i \times j)/j\,] \text{ max.}$$
$$x_s = (w - y_s^2)$$

where

$$w = \left[\frac{(i + j^2)\,(i \times j)}{(i \times j)}\right] \text{max.}$$

and

$$y_s = [\,(i \times j)/i\,] \text{ max.}$$
$$y_h = (v - x_h^2)$$

where

$$v = \left[\frac{(i^2 + j)\,(i \times j)}{(i \times j)}\right] \text{max.}$$

and

$$y_0 = [\, j - (i \times j)\,] \text{ max.}$$

$$x'_e = [\, i' = (i' \times j)\,] \text{ max.}$$
$$x'_h = [\, (i' \times j)/j\,] \text{ max.}$$
$$x'_s = (w' - y'^2_s)$$

where

$$w' = \left[\frac{(i' + j^2)\,(i' \times j)}{(i' \times j)}\right] \text{max.}$$

and

$$y'_s = [\,(i' \times j)/i'\,] \text{ max.}$$
$$y'_h = (v' - x'^2_h)$$

where

$$v' = \left[\frac{(i'^2 + j)\,(i' \times j)}{(i' \times j)}\right] \text{max.}$$

Thus, depending upon the mode of analysis, the set of 6 or 11 variates may be calculated and employed for the categorization of family units in terms of the kinship distances they contain. The possibilities of categorization may still appear to be large, viz. one set of categories for each variate. The variates X or X', however, will rarely assume a value greater than 3: Y will rarely be greater than 2. Within these limits, the variates x_h, x_s, y_h, y_s and x'_h, x'_s, y'_h, y'_s can be considered in clusters, since their individual values are interdependent.

Where the set of 6 variates is to be used, two orders of classification will have to be formulated: one for the variates x_e and y_0 separately, and the other for x_h, x_s, y_h, and y_s taken together. Where the set of 11 variates is to be used, three or four classificatory orders will be required. The categories of the four orders of classification are detailed in Table 3.8. It will be seen that Orders 1 and 2 may be combined to produce 30 categories (10 x 3 of Orders 1 and 2). Alternatively, where $x'_e = 0$ consistently, a classificatory order of 12 categories may be made of the values of x_e and y_0, because Order 1 will be represented by only four categories, listed in Table 3.8 as 1, 5, 8, and 10.

The computation of these variates from the field data is simple, as will be seen from Schedule 3.4, the structure of which has already been explained. The point to note is that a course of categorization by these variates may effectively register the structural integration of respective family units in terms of the successively more remote and diverse orders of intra-family relations they contain. For example, while dealing with a sample of 3,731 randomly selected family units (coresident and commensal kingroups) in West Bengal in 1960–61, 85 different configurations were detected in the family matrices drawn with reference to a stipulated Ego (the "head" of each unit). Of these, 53 (or 62%

Table 3.8

Classification of Kinship Distance Variates

Category for each order of classification	Order 1		Order 2	Order or Order 3		4	
	values of x_e x'_e		value of y_0	x_h or x'_h	y_h or y'_h	x_s or x'_s	y_s or y'_s
(1)	(2)	(3)	(4)	(5)	(6)	(7)	(8)
1	0	0	0	0	0	0	0
2	0	1	1	1	1	1	1
3	0	2	2	1	2	1	2
4	0	3	——	2	1	1	2
5	1	0		2	1	2	1
6	1	1		2	2	2	2
7	1	2		3	1	1	2
8	2	0		3	1	2	2
9	2	1		3	1	3	1
10	3	0		3	2	3	2

of the total) were reproduced exactly by the values of the 11 peripheral variates, and these configurations accounted for 3,662 (or 98% of the total) family
units. Further categorization of these units in terms of the *internal* characteristics of kinship distances was, therefore, of little importance.

Schedule 3.4: Block 1: Field Data
(Illustrated with a hypothetical case)

Block 1 Write the kinship relations of family members with respect to any one of them selected *or* stipulated as the Ego.	Circle appropriate symbol for the family member
	Unmarried male = mu Unmarried female = fu Ever-married male = me Ever-married female = fe
(1)	(2)
1. Ego	mu / fu / me / fe
2. Wife	mu / fu / me / fe
3. Daughter's husband	mu / fu / me / fe
4. Daughter's son	mu / fu / me / fe
5. Mother	mu / fu / me / fe
6. Mother's sister	mu / fu / me / fe
7. Father's brother's daughter	mu / fu / me / fe
8. Father's mother	mu / fu / me / fe

Schedule 3.4: Block 2.
Transfer of Reference Point to *Any* Family Member in the Lowest Generation Level of a Family Unit

Block 2

Turn each relation in Block 1, col. (1), into a notation series by writing a notation for each kinship term, where

father = F, mother = M,
brother = B, sister = S,
son = Z, daughter = D,
husband = H, wife = W.

Add *u* to the notation if the person concerned is unmarried in col. (2) of Block 1. Add *e* if ever married.

Count the number of times F and/or M occur in each notation in col. (1), and write the figure in col. (2). Count the number of times Z and/or D occur in each series in col. (1), and write the figure in col. (3). Subtract the figure in col. (3) from that in col. (2), and write the remainder (g) in col. (4).

Place that notation series from col. (1) first which has the lowest *g* value (= the maximum minus or, if all other *g* values are positive, 0). Place, next, that series which has the next lowest *g* value, and thereafter all series in col. (1) in order of their *g* values (from maximum minus to 0, and then to maximum plus).

If two or more series have the same *g* value, place them one after another, in any order.

Write in parentheses after each series its serial number in col. (1).

Write against each series in col. (5) the symbol circled in Block 1, col. (2) for the person to whom the series refers.

(1)	F/M (2)	Z/D (3)	g (4)	(5)	(6)
1. Ego = Ee	0	0	0	1. DZu	(4)	mu
2. We	0	0	0	2. DHe	(3)	me
3. DHe	0	1	-1	3. Ee	(1)	me
4. DZu	0	2	-2	4. We	(2)	fe
5. Me	1	0	1	5. FBDu	(7)	fu
6. MSe	1	0	1	6. Me	(5)	fe
7. FBDu	1	1	0	7. MSe	(6)	fe
8. FMe	2	0	2	8. FMe	(8)	fe

Note: / = and/or.

Schedule 3.4: Block 3.
All Kinship Relations in a Family Unit with Respect to Any Family Member as the Point of Reference

Block 3
Write in col. (1) the notation series from Block 2, col. (5). Put, in brackets, under each series its symbol from Block 2, col. (6).

For each notation series in col. (1), write in col. (2) all the series in col. (1) that have serial numbers higher than the series in question.

Each row of cols. (1) and (2) will then have a pair of notation series: 1. and 2,..., 1. and 3,..., 2. and 3,..., etc.

Compare and record the parts of the two notation series in each row of cols. (1) and (2) that are:

	different in	
the same.	col. (1) than col. (2).	col. (2) than col. (1).

Write the notations only, from *right to left,* of each series in col. (4). Add the last notation in the series in same row in col. (3). If col. (3) is blank, add Ego's symbol in Block 1, col. (2).

Refer to Block 3, Chart 1 and write the reciprocal of each pair in col. (6). Add notations only (from left to right) of the series in same row in col. (5). See Block 3, Chart 2 and bracket compound notations.

Refer to Block 3, Chart 2 and write the single notation for each compound notation, and repeat all notation series from col. (7) after simplification. Add symbol *u* or *e,* as given in the same row in col. (5).

(1)	(2)	(3)	(4)	(5)	(6)	(7)	(8)
1. DZu	2. DHe	D	Zu	He	ZD	(MH)	1. Fe
(mu)	3. Ee	–	DZu	Ee	ZDme	M(FE)	2. MFe
	4. We	–	DZu	We	ZDme	M(FW)	3. MMe
	5. FBDu	–	DZu	FBDu	ZDme	MFFBD	4. MFFBDu
	6. Me	–	DZu	Me	ZDme	MFM	5. MFMe
	7. MSe	–	DZu	MSe	ZDme	MFMS	6. MFMSe
	8. FMe	–	DZu	FMe	ZDme	MFFM	7. MFFMe

(1)	(2)	(3)	(4)	(5)	(6)	(7)	(8)
2. DHe	3. Ee	–	DHe	Ee	HDme	W(FE)	8. WFe
(me)	4. We	–	DHe	We	HDme	W(FW)	9. WMe
	5. FBDu	–	DHe	FBDu	HDme	WFFBD	10. WFFBDu
	6. Me	–	DHe	Me	HDme	WFM	11. WFMe
	7. MSe	–	DHe	MSe	HDme	WFMS	12. WFMSe
	8. FMe	–	DHe	FMe	HDme	WFFM	13. WFFMe
3. Ee	4. We	–	Ee	We	Eme	W	14. We
(me)	5. FBDu	–	Ee	FBDu	Eme	FBD	15. FBDu
	6 Me	–	Ee	Me	Eme	M	16 Me
	7 MSe	–	Ee	MSe	Eme	MS	17 MSe
	8 FMe	–	Ee	FMe	Eme	FM	18 FMe
4. We	5. FBDu	–	We	FBDu	Wme	HFBD	19 HFBDu
(fe)	6. Me	–	We	Me	Wme	HM	20 HMe
	7 MSe	–	We	MSe	Wme	HMS	21 HMSe
	8 FMe	–	We	FMe	Wme	HFM	22 HFMe
5. FBDu	6. Me	–	FBDu	Me	DBFme	FB(ZM)	23 FBWe
(fu)	7. MSe	–	FBDu	MSe	DBFme	FB(ZM)S	24 FBWSe
	8 FMe	F	BDu	Me	DBF	F(BM)	25 FMe
6. Me	7. MSe	M	e	Se	M	S	26 Se
(fe)	8 FMe	–	Me	FMe	Mme	(ZF)M	27 HMe
7. MSe	8. FMe	–	MSe	FMe	SMme	S(ZF)M	28 SHMe
(fe)							

Schedule 3.4: Block 3: Chart 1 (with reference to col. 7)

Chart 1   Read each series in Block 3, col. (6), from left to right, taking two consecutive nottions at a time until all the notations have been taken into account. For example, read the series HDZB first as H on the left and D on the right, next as D on the left and Z on the right, and last as Z on the left and B on the right. For HDZ(me), the third stage will be Z on the left and (me) on the right.

The reciprocal notation for each pair is obtained from the relevant cell of the chart. For example, in both cases above, the first reciprocal notation is W, the second F, and the third F.

Left-Hand Notation	Right-Hand Notation										
	None	mu/me	fu/fe	F	M	B	S	Z	D	H	W
(1)	(2)	(3)	(4)	(5)	(6)	(7)	(8)	(9)	(10)	(11)	(12)
E	–	–	–	–	–	–	–	–	–	–	–
F	–	Z	D	Z	D	Z	D	Z	D	Z	D
M	–	Z	D	Z	D	Z	D	Z	D	Z	D
B	–	B	S	B	S	B	S	B	S	B	S
S	–	B	S	B	S	B	S	B	S	B	S
Z	–	F	M	F	M	F	M	F	M	F	M
D	–	F	M	F	M	F	M	F	M	F	M
H	–	H	W	H	W	H	W	H	W	H	W
W	–	H	W	H	W	H	W	H	W	H	W

Note: / = and/or

Schedule 3.4: Block 3: Chart 2 (with reference to cols. 7 and 8)

Chart 2   Compound notations are listed on the left side of each column; on the right side of each column are the single notations for the compound ones. For example, FZ = B, ME = M. Longer compound notations are reduced, pair by pair, into shorter ones, e.g., FWHZ = MHZ = FZ = B.

Compound Notations and Their Equivalent Single Notations							
(1)	(2)	(3)	(4)	(5)	(6)	(7)	(8)
FE = F	ME = M	HE = H	WE = W	BE = B	SE = S	ZE = Z	DE = D
FZ = B	MZ = B	HZ = Z	WZ = Z	BF = F	SF = F	ZF = H	DF = H
FD = S	MD = S	HD = D	WD = D	BM = M	SM = M	ZM = W	DM = W
FH = F	MH = F	HH = H	WH = H	BB = B	SB = B	ZB = Z	DB = Z
FW = M	MW = M	HW = W	WW = W	BS = S	SS = S	ZS = D	DS = D
				BH = B	SW = S	ZH = Z	DW = D

Schedule 3.4: Subblock 4.1.
Kinship Distances of Family Members with Reference to the Stipulated Ego for the Family Unit

Notation of each Series in Block 2, col. (1).	Number of			p-q		$q+r$, if $i \geq 0$; $p+r$, if $i'>0$ $=j$	Value of j when		
	F/M = p	Z/D = q	B/S = r	plus = i	minus = i'		$i=0$	$i>0$	$i'>0$
(1)	(2)	(3)	(4)	(5)	(6)	(7)	(8)	(9)	(10)
1. E	0	0	0	0	–	0	0	–	–
2. W	0	0	0	0	–	0	0	–	–
3. DH	0	1	0	–	1	0	–	–	0
4. DZ	0	2	0	–	2	0	–	–	0
5. M	1	0	0	1	–	0	–	0	–
6. MS	1	0	1	1	–	1	–	1	–
7. FBD	1	1	1	0	–	2	2	–	–
8. FM	2	0	0	2	–	0	–	0	–
Maximum value in the column				2	2	2	2	1	0
symbol				X	X'	Y	y_o	y_s	y'_s

Series as above	When j=0,		When j>0,			when $i>0$, and $j>0$		When $i'>0$ and $j>0$	
	i	i'	i	i'	j	i^2+j	$i+j^2$	i'^2+j	$i'+j^2$
	(11)	(12)	(13)	(14)	(15)	(16)	(17)	(18)	(19)
1. E	0	–	–	–	–	–	–	–	–
2. W	0	–	–	–	–	–	–	–	–
3. DH	–	1	–	–	–	–	–	–	–
4. DZ	–	2	–	–	–	–	–	–	–
5. M	1	–	–	–	–	–	–	–	–
6. MS	–	–	1	–	1	2	2	–	–
7. FBD	–	–	0	–	2	–	–	–	–
8. FM	2	–	–	–	–	–	–	–	–

	(11)	(12)	(13)	(14)	(15)	(16)	(17)	(18)	(19)
Maxi- mum Value	2	2	1	0	2	2	2	0	0
Symbol	x_e	x'_e	x_h	x'_h		v	w	v'	w'

Note: / = and/or

Schedule 3.4: Subblock 4.2.
Kinship Distances of Family Members with Reference to One of Them Belonging to the Latest Generation of the Family Unit

Notation of Each series in Block 3, col. (8), referring to **first** series in col. (1)	Number of			p-q		$q+r$, if $i \geqslant 0;/$ $p+r$, if $i' \rangle 0$	Value of j when		
	F/M	Z/D	B/S	plus	minus				
	=	=	=	=	=	=	$i=0$	$i \rangle 0$	$i' \rangle 0$
	p	q	r	i	i'	j			
(1)	(2)	(3)	(4)	(5)	(6)	(7)	(8)	(9)	(10)
1. Ego	0	0	0	0	-	0	0	-	-
2. F	1	0	0	1	-	0	-	0	-
3. MF	2	0	0	2	-	0	-	0	-
4. MM	2	0	0	2	-	0	-	0	-
5. MFFBD	3	1	1	2	-	2	-	2	-
6. MFM	3	0	0	3	-	0	-	0	-
7. MFMS	3	0	1	3	-	1	-	1	-
8. MFFM	4	0	0	4	-	0	-	0	-
Maximum value in the column				4	-	2	0	2	-
Symbol				X		Y	y_o	y_s	-

Series as above	When j = 0		When j>0,			When i>0, and j>0		When i'>0 and j>0	
	i	i'	i	i'	j	i^2+j	$i+j^2$	i'^2+j	$i'+j^2$
	(11)	(12)	(13)	(14)	(15)	(16)	(17)	(18)	(19)
1. Ego	0	-	-	-	-	-	-	-	-
2. F	1	-	-	-	-	-	-	-	-
3. MF	2	-	-	-	-	-	-	-	-
4. MM	2	-	-	-	-	-	-	-	-
5. MFFBD	-	-	2	-	2	6	6	-	-
6. MFM	3	-	-	-	-	-	-	-	-
7. MFMS	-	-	3	-	1	10	4	-	-
8. MFFM	4	-	-	-	-	-	-	-	-
Maximum Value	4	-	3	-	2	10	6	-	-
Symbol	x_e		x_h			v	w		

Schedule 3.4: Subblock 4.3.
Kinship Distances among All Members in a Family Unit

Notation of Each Series in Block 3, col. (8).	Numbers			p–q		q + r, if i>0, p + r, if i'>0 = j	Value of j			When j = 0	
								when			
	F/M = p	Z/D = q	B/S = r	plus = i	minus = i'		i=0	i>0	i'>0	i	i'
(1)	(2)	(3)	(4)	(5)	(6)	(7)	(8)	(9)	(10)	(11)	(12)
1. F	1	0	0	1	-	0	-	0	-	1	-
2. MF	2	0	0	2	-	0	-	0	-	2	-
3. MM	2	0	0	2	-	0	-	0	-	2	-

(1)	(2)	(3)	(4)	(5)	(6)	(7)	(8)	(9)	(10)	(11)	(12)
4. MFFBD	3	1	1	2	–	2	–	2	–	–	–
5. MFM	3	0	0	3	–	0	–	0	–	3	–
6. MFMS	3	0	1	3	–	1	–	1	–	–	–
7. MFFM	4	0	0	4	–	0	–	0	–	4	–
8. WF	1	0	0	1	–	0	–	0	–	1	–
9. WM	1	0	0	1	–	0	–	0	–	1	–
10. WFFBD	2	1	1	1	–	2	–	2	–	–	–
11. WFM	2	0	0	2	–	0	–	0	–	2	–
12. WFMS	2	0	1	2	–	1	–	1	–	–	–
13. WFFM	3	0	0	3	–	0	–	0	–	3	–
14. W	0	0	0	0	–	0	0	–	–	0	–
15. FBD	1	1	1	0	–	2	2	–	–	–	–
16. M	1	0	0	1	–	0	–	0	–	1	–
17. MS	1	0	1	1	–	1	–	1	–	–	–
18. FM	2	0	0	2	–	0	–	0	–	2	–
19. HFBD	1	1	1	0	–	2	2	–	–	–	–
20. HM	1	0	0	1	–	0	–	0	–	1	–
21. HMS	1	0	1	1	–	1	–	1	–	–	–
22. HFM	2	0	0	2	–	0	–	0	–	2	–
23. FBW	1	0	1	1	–	1	–	1	–	–	–
24. FBWS	1	0	2	1	–	2	–	2	–	–	–
25. FM	2	0	0	2	–	0	–	0	–	2	–
26. S	0	0	1	0	–	1	1	–	–	–	–
27. HM	1	0	0	1	–	0	–	0	–	1	–
28. SHM	1	0	1	1	–	1	–	1	–	–	–
Maximum value in column				4		2	2	2		4	
Symbol				X		Y	y_o	y_s		x_e	

Schedule 3.4: Subblock 4.3.—*continued*
Kinship Distances among All Members in a Family Unit

Notation	i	i′	j	i	i′	j	i² + j	i + j²	i′² + j	i′ + j²
				When j>0, value of			When i≥0, and j>0		When i′>0 and j>0	
(1)	(5)	(6)	(7)	(13)	(14)	(15)	(16)	(17)	(18)	(19)
1. F	1	–	0	–	–	–	–	–	–	–
2. MF	2	–	0	–	–	–	–	–	–	–
3. MM	2	–	0	–	–	–	–	–	–	–
4. MFFBD	2	–	2	2	–	2	6	6	–	–
5. MFM	3	–	0	–	–	–	–	–	–	–
6. MFMS	3	–	1	3	–	1	10	4	–	–
7. MFFM	4	–	0	–	–	–	–	–	–	–
8. WF	1	–	0	–	–	–	–	–	–	–
9. WM	1	–	0	–	–	–	–	–	–	–
10. WFFBD	1	–	2	1	–	2	3	5	–	–
11. WFM	2	–	0	–	–	–	–	–	–	–
12. WFMS	2	–	1	2	–	1	5	3	–	–
13. WFFM	3	–	0	–	–	–	–	–	–	–
14. W	0	–	0	–	–	–	–	–	–	–
15. FBD	0	–	2	0	–	2	2	4	–	–
16. M	1	–	0	–	–	–	–	–	–	–
17. MS	1	–	1	1	–	1	2	2	–	–
18. FM	2	–	0	–	–	–	–	–	–	–
19. HFBD	0	–	2	0	–	2	2	4	–	–
20. HM	1	–	0	–	–	–	–	–	–	–
21. HMS	1	–	1	1	–	1	2	2	–	–
22. HFM	2	–	0	–	–	–	–	–	–	–
23. FBW	1	–	1	1	–	1	2	2	–	–
24. FBWS	1	–	2	1	–	2	3	5	–	–

Notation	i	i'	j	i	i'	j	i²+j	i+j²	i'²+j	i'+j²
(1)	(5)	(6)	(7)	(13)	(14)	(15)	(16)	(17)	(18)	(19)
25. FM	2	–	0	–	–	–	–	–	–	–
26. S	0	–	1	0	–	1	1	1	–	–
27. HM	1	–	0	–	–	–	–	–	–	–
28. SHM	1	–	1	1	–	1	2	2	–	–
Maximum value				3		2	10	6		
Symbol				x_h			v	w		

Schedule 3.4: Block 5.
Peripheral Characteristics of Kinship Distances

Block 5. From the maximum values obtained in block 4, determine peripheral characteristics of kinship distances when: *a)* the Ego is stipulated for the family (Subblock 4.1); *b)* Ego = any person in the latest (lowest) generation-level, so as to measure the maximum collateral spread of all kinship distances among family members. (Subblock 4.2); *c)* Ego = each family member from the lowest generation-level to the highest in the family, except the last person thus arranged, and excluding successively those already analyzed as an Ego (Subblock 4.3).	Subblock		
	4.1	4.2	4.3
	(a)	(b)	(c)

(1)	(2)	(3)	(4)
1. Maximum extension of ancestral generations of Ego $= X$	2	4	4
2. Maximum extension of descendant generations of Ego $= X'$	2	–	–
3. Total generations in the family $= (X+X'+1)$	5	5	5
4. Maximum degree of collateral spread in the family $= Y$	2	2	2
5. Maximum extension of ancestral generations in direct line of Ego (with collateral spread $y_e = 0$) $= x_e$	2	4	4
6. Maximum extension of ancestral generations in collateral lines of Ego $= x_h$	1	3	3
7. Maximum collateral spread in x_h generation level $= y_h = (v - x^2_h)$	1	1	1
8. Topmost ancestral generation level recording maximum collateral spread from Ego $= x_s = (w - y^2_s)$	1	2	2
9. Maximum collateral spread in x_s generation level $= y_s$	1	2	2
10. Maximum collateral spread in the generation level of Ego (with generational extension $x_o = 0$) $= y_o$	2	0	2
11. Lowest descendant generation level recording maximum collateral spread from Ego $= x'_s = (w' - y'^2_s)$	0	–	–
12. Maximum collateral spread in x'_s generation level $= y'_s$	0	–	–
13. Maximum extension of descendant generations in collateral lines of Ego $= x'_h$	0	–	–
14. Maximum collateral spread in x'_h generation level $= y'_h = (v' - x'^2_h)$	0	–	–
15. Maximum extension of descendant generations in direct line of Ego (with collateral spread $y'_e = 0$) $= x'_e$	2	–	–

Schedule 3.4: Block 6.
Generational and Collateral Configurations of Family Matrix

Under Separate Conditions 1, 2, and 3, place from Subblocks 4.1, 4.2, and 4.3, respectively, the corresponding values of i (or i' in negative numerals) and j: the left-hand figure in each number will denote the i (ancestral), or O (Ego's) or i' (descendant) generation, and the right-hand figure will denote the collateral spread by j.

The conditions are as follows:

Condition 1. Ego is stipulated as a specific person in the family unit

(Subblock 4.1);

Condition 2. Ego belongs to the lowest generation of the family unit

(Subblock 4.2);

Condition 3. Ego is shifted from one family member to another from the lowest to successively higher generation levels

(Subblock 4.3).

Condition 1 (a)			*Condition 2* (b)		*Condition 3* (c)		
			40		40		
			30	31	30	31	
20			20	22	20	21	22
10	11		10		10	11	12
Ego: *00*		02	Ego: *00*		Ego: *00*	01	02
− 10							
− 20							

If, however, we wish to proceed further, we may now ascertain, in the light of the sample of family units available for analysis, whether it will be feasible and useful to categorize them with reference to all the kinship distances incorporated in each family. In reference to the values of the peripheral variates, the possible number of different configurations of the matrices (C, as previously denoted) will be reduced drastically from those obtained by formulae 5.0–7.0. This will be seen from the following formula:

(8.0)

$$C = (2^{(x_e + x_h y_h + x_s(y_s - y_h)) \;+\; y_o + x'_e + x'_h y'_h + x'_s(y'_s - y'_h) - \phi}),$$

where ϕ stands for the total number of terms out of the seven presented as additive powers of 2—viz. x_e, $x_h y_h$, $x_s (y_s - y_h)$, y_o, x'_e, $x'_h y'_h$, $x'_s (y'_s - y'_h)$—which have values greater than zero.

Whether or not a course of categorization takes into account the internal characteristics of kinship distances in the family units, it will be useful to develop some secondary variates to further measure the integration of the family structures. For example, we may derive a variate $\lambda = (Z - X)$, where $Z = (i + j)$ max., in order to denote the missing number of parental generations at the top of which all the existing collateral relatives have common ancestors or a group of common ancestors.

To illustrate, let there be 3 family units comprising: (1) a man (Ego) and his brother's son (BZ); (2) a man (Ego) and his father's brother's son (FBZ); and (3) a man (Ego) and his brother's son's wife (BZW). The values of λ as 1, 2, and 1 for the respective family units show that the common ancestor of the two members of the first family is located in the first parental generation of F and M of Ego; of the second family, in the second parental generation of FF and FM of Ego; and, in the case of the third family, a group of common ancestors is located in the first parental generation of F, M, BWF, and BWM of Ego.

The usefulness of this variate is manifest for a society in which a consistent pattern formation of intra-family relations is an invariant or prevailing phenomenon. In that case, the value of λ will indicate whether the source of the family tree is present in the current family organization (with $\lambda = 0$), and if not what is the *measure of tenacity* of the collateral relatives in forming one family organization even though their common source is an extint generation level, as given by any value of λ from 1 upwards. This variate, therefore, will yield valuable information on its own merits as well as in reference to the vital institutions, customs, and codes affecting the life of the people in the economic, social, and ideological spheres. For example, the lawgivers may suggest particular configurations of the family matrix in relation to, say, the devolution of ancestral property; it may be of interest to examine the extent to which the 'ideal' family structure is preserved (see Buehler 1886: 366–367; Shamasastry 1951: 181–182 in reference to Hindu society in India). The usefulness of this variate can be noted in connection with *(a)* the rules of exogamy in Hindu marriage and the organization of kingroups, *(b)* the changes in the joint family structure in India, and *(c)* the formulation of the previously mentioned concepts of 'vertically extended' and 'laterally joint' families (see Kapadia 1947: 273ff; Nimkoff 1959: 32–38; R. Mukherjee 1977a). Parallel uses for many other societies can be cited.

Moreover, while dealing with the units categorized as the family complex, it will be useful to compare the values of the peripheral and the secondary variates for the basic substructure and the deviant relations considered en bloc. The comparison will show whether the structural ramification of the deviant kinship constituents exceeds that of the basic kinship constituents and, if not, to what extent the former remain submerged within the generational and collateral coverage of the latter; for example, the latter ones may register avuncular relationship of the second degree but the deviant relations only the first degree of inter-cousin relationship or merely the sibling or sibling-in-law relationship. The kinship distances of the deviant relations from the Ego of the family complex will also help in detecting any new pattern formation of the intra-family relations or the lingering influence of any previously operating pattern in the society, as mentioned earlier.

Thus, by following the inductive process of categorization and the population approach, we may pursue the classification of family structures in a hitherto unexplored field of variation. The method and the scale of measurement of the kinship distances can be systematically improved along with our ever-accumulating knowledge on the subject. And the formation of peripheral characteristics of the kinship distances in each family, and all other characteristics concerned with this field of variation, can be made more and more precise and effective. The scope of classification will remain infinite in concept yet enumerable in practice; and, at any stage in the development of our knowledge about the subject, the course of categorization will be objectively valid and not constrained in any manner whatsoever.

Appendix 3A.

Genealogical Charts for 13 Kinship Patterns

Figure 0.1.

N_0 = Nuclear (absolute) pattern in which parents and children (married or not), but not children's spouses, live together.

Formula: (EuF/M, Eme, Efe) (H, W, Zu, Ze, Du, De)

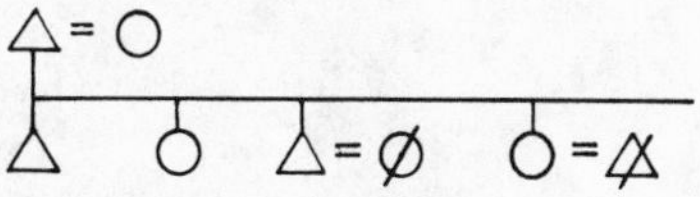

Figure 0.2.

N_1 = Nuclear (specific) pattern in which only parents and unmarried children live in the household.

Formula: (EuF/M, Eme, Efe) (H, W, Zu, Du)

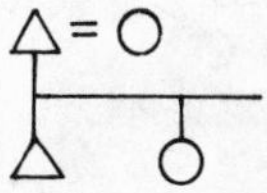

Figure 1.0.

P_0 = Patrilineal-patrivirilocal pattern in which ever-married female affines live with children in husbands' family of orientation.

Formula: (Eu, Eme^k, Efe^{a}H) (F.../B/Z...) (M, Su, Du) (W)

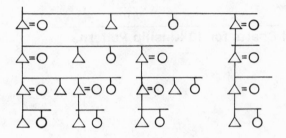

Figure 1.1.

P_1 = Matripatrilocal (transitory) pattern in which ever-married female kin, their husbands, but not their children, stay in patrilineal-patrivirilocal family.

Formula: (Eu, Eme^k, Eme^{a}WF/WB, Efe^{k}F/B, Efe^{a}H)
(F.../B/Z...) (M, S, D) (H, W)

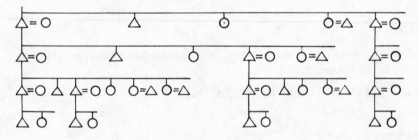

Figure 1.2.

P_2 = Matripatrilocal (truncated) pattern in which ever-married female kin and their unmarried children, but not their husbands, stay in patrilineal-patrivirilocal family.

Formula: (Eu, E'uM, Eme^k, Efe^kF/B, Efe^aH)
(F.../B/Z...) (M, S, D) (W, Zu, Du)

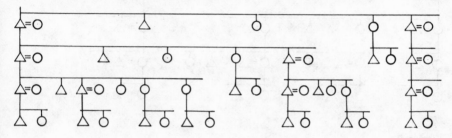

Figure 1.3.

P_3 = Matripatrilocal (durable) pattern in which ever-married female kin, their husbands and unmarried children stay in patrilineal-patrivirilocal family.

Formula: (Eu, E'uM, Eme^k, Eme^aWF/WB, Efe^kF/B, Efe^aH)
(F.../B/Z...) (M, S, D) (H, W, Zu, Du)

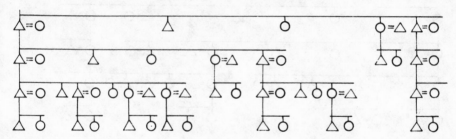

Figure 2.0.

M_0 = Matrilineal-matriutrolocal pattern in which ever-married male affines live with wives and children in wives' family of orientation.

Formula: (E′u, Eme^{a}W, Efe^k) (M.../S/D...) (F, Bu, Zu) (H)

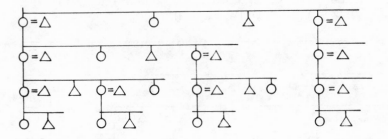

Figure 2.1.

M_1 = Patrimatrilocal (transitory) pattern in which ever-married male kin and their wives, but not their children, stay in matrilineal-matriutrolocal family.

Formula: (E′u, Eme^{k}M, Eme^{a}W, Efe^k, Efe^{a}H) (M.../S/D...) (F, B, Z) (H, W)

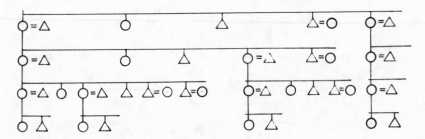

Figure 2.2.

M_2 = Patrimatrilocal (durable) pattern in which ever-married male kin, their wives and unmarried children stay in matrilineal-matriutrolocal family.

Formula: (EuF, E'u, Eme^{k}M, Eme^{a}W, Efe^k, Efe^{a}H)
(M.../S/D...) (F, B, Z) (H, W, Zu, Du)

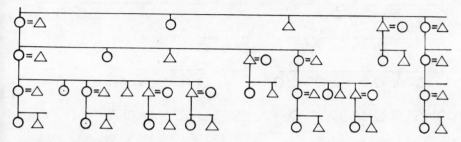

Figure 3.0.

T_0 = Natolocal (*taravad*) pattern in which siblings live jointly through generations and without spouses but with the female siblings' progeny.

Formula: (E'u, Eme^{k}M, Efe^k) (M.../S/D...) (B, Z)

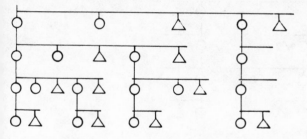

Figure 3.1.

T_1 = Natolocal (variant 1 towards P_0) pattern in which the male siblings, their wives and their unmarried children live in *taravad*.

Formula: (EuF, E'u, Eme^{k}M, Efe^k, Efe^{a}H) (M.../S/D...) (B, Z) (W, Zu, Du)

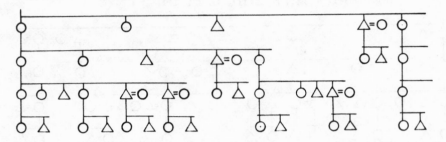

Figure 3.2.

T_2 = Natolocal (variant 2 towards M_0) pattern in which the female siblings live with their children and husbands in *taravad*.

Formula: (E'u, Eme^{k}M, Eme^{a}W, Efe^k) (M.../S/D...) (B, Z) (H)

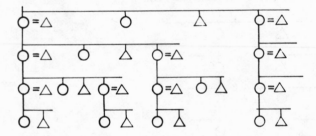

Figure 4.0.

A = Avunculocal pattern in which ever-married males with wives and unmarried children live with their mothers' ever-married brothers, their wives and unmarried children.

Formula: (EuF, Eme^k, Efe^{a}H) (M.../$\underline{S}$/D...) ($\overline{B}$e, $\overline{Z}$e) (W, Zu, Du)

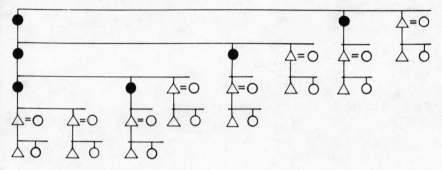

● do not belong to the family unit.

Master Chart for 13 Kinship Patterns

Table 1.1.
Ego = Unmarried child of me^k & fe^a = *Eu*

Relation	Kinship Pattern								
	N_0	N_1	P_3	P_2	P_1	P_0	A	T_1	M_2
F	N_0	N_1	P_3	P_2	P_1	P_0	A	T_1	M_2
F...F			P_3	P_2	P_1	P_0			
F...FM			P_3	P_2	P_1	P_0			
FM...M								T_1	M_2
FM...MF									M_2
FM...MBu								T_1	M_2
FM...MBe							A	T_1	M_2
FM...MBW							A	T_1	M_2
FM...MBZu							A	T_1	M_2
FM...MBDu							A	T_1	M_2
FM...MSu								T_1	M_2
FM...MSe								T_1	M_2
FM...MSH									M_2
FM...MSZu								T_1	M_2
FM...MSZe							A	T_1	M_2
FM...MSZW							A	T_1	M_2
FM...MSZZu							A	T_1	M_2
FM...MSZDu							A	T_1	M_2
FM...MSD...Du								T_1	M_2
FM...MSD...De								T_1	M_2
FM...MSD...DH									M_2
FM...MSD...DZu								T_1	M_2
FM...MSD...DZe							A	T_1	M_2
FM...MSD...DZW							A	T_1	M_2
FM...MSD...DZZu							A	T_1	M_2
FM...MSD...DZDu							A	T_1	M_2
FBu			P_3	P_2	P_1	P_0		T_1	M_2
F...FBu			P_3	P_2	P_1	P_0			
FBe			P_3	P_2	P_1	P_0	A	T_1	M_2
F...FBe			P_3	P_2	P_1	P_0			
FBW			P_3	P_2	P_1	P_0	A	T_1	M_2
F...FBW			P_3	P_2	P_1	P_0			

Table 1.1 — *continued*

	N_0	N_1	P_3	P_2	P_1	P_0	A	T_1	M_2
FBZu			P_3	P_2	P_1	P_0	A	T_1	M_2
F...FBZ...Zu			P_3	P_2	P_1	P_0			
F...FBZ...Ze			P_3	P_2	P_1	P_0			
F...FBZ...ZW			P_3	P_2	P_1	P_0			
F...FBZ...ZDu			P_3	P_2	P_1	P_0			
F...FBZ...ZDe			P_3	P_2	P_1				
F...FBZ...ZDH			P_3		P_1				
F...FBZ...ZDZu			P_3	P_2					
F...FBZ...ZDDu			P_3	P_2					
FBDu			P_3	P_2	P_1	P_0	A	T_1	M_2
F...FBDu			P_3	P_2	P_1	P_0			
F...FBDe			P_3	P_2	P_1				
F...FBDH			P_3		P_1				
F...FBDZu			P_3	P_2					
F...FBDDu			P_3	P_2					
FSu			P_3	P_2	P_1	P_0		T_1	M_2
F...FSu			P_3	P_2	P_1	P_0			
FSe			P_3	P_2	P_1			T_1	M_2
F...FSe			P_3	P_2	P_1				
FSH			P_3		P_1				M_2
F...FSH			P_3		P_1				
FSZu			P_3	P_2				T_1	M_2
F...FSZu			P_3	P_2					
FSZe							A	T_1	M_2
FSZW							A	T_1	M_2
FSZZu							A	T_1	M_2
FSZDu							A	T_1	M_2
FSDu			P_3	P_2				T_1	M_2
F...FSDu			P_3	P_2					
FSD...Du								T_1	M_2
FSD...De								T_1	M_2
FSD...DH									M_2
FSD...DZu								T_1	M_2
FSD...DZe							A	T_1	M_2
FSD...DZW							A	T_1	M_2
FSD...DZZu							A	T_1	M_2
FSD...DZDu							A	T_1	M_2
M	N_0	N_1	P_3	P_2	P_1	P_0	A	T_1	M_2
Bu	N_0	N_1	P_3	P_2	P_1	P_0	A	T_1	M_2
Be	N_0		P_3	P_2	P_1	P_0			
BW			P_3	P_2	P_1	P_0			
BZu			P_3	P_2	P_1	P_0			
BZ...Zu			P_3	P_2	P_1	P_0			
BZ...Ze			P_3	P_2	P_1	P_0			
BZ...ZW			P_3	P_2	P_1	P_0			
BZ...ZDu			P_3	P_2	P_1	P_0			
BZ...ZDe			P_3	P_2	P_1				
BZ...ZDH			P_3		P_1				
BZ...ZDZu			P_3	P_2					
BZ...ZDDu			P_3	P_2					

Table 1.1 — *continued*

BDu	P_3	P_2	P_1	P_0
BDe	P_3	P_2	P_1	
BDH	P_3		P_1	
BDZu	P_3	P_2		
BDDu	P_3	P_2		

Su	N_0	N_1	P_3	P_2	P_1	P_0	A	T_1	M_2
Se	N_0		P_3	P_2	P_1				
SH			P_3		P_1				
SZu			P_3	P_2					
SDu			P_3	P_2					
Any other series of kinship notations	X								

Table 1.2.
Ego = Unmarried child of me^a & fe^k = *Eu'*

Relation	Kinship Pattern								
F	N_0	N_1	P_3			T_2	M_0	M_1	M_2
M	N_0	N_1	P_3	P_2	T_1T_0	T_2	M_0	M_1	M_2
MM			P_3	P_2	T_1T_0	T_2	M_0	M_1	M_2
M...M					T_1T_0	T_2	M_0	M_1	M_2
M...MF						T_2	M_0	M_1	M_2
MF...F			P_3	P_2					
MF...FM			P_3	P_2					
MF...FBu			P_3	P_2					
MF...FBe			P_3	P_2					
MF...FBW			P_3	P_2					
MF...FBZ...Zu			P_3	P_2					
MF...FBZ...Ze			P_3	P_2					
MF...FBZ...ZW			P_3	P_2					
MF...FBZ...ZDu			P_3	P_2					
MF...FBZ...ZDe			P_3	P_2					
MF...FBZ...ZDH			P_3						
MF...FBZ...ZDZu			P_3	P_2					
MF...FBZ...ZDDu			P_3	P_2					
MF...FBDu			P_3	P_2					
MF...FBDe			P_3	P_2					
MF...FBDH			P_3						
MF...FBDZu			P_3	P_2					
MF...FBDDu			P_3	P_2					
MF...FSu			P_3	P_2					
MF...FSe			P_3	P_2					
MF...FSH			P_3						
MF...FSZu			P_3	P_2					
MF...FSDu			P_3	P_2					

Table 1.2—*continued*

	N₀	N₁	P₃	P₂	T₁T₀	T₂	M₀	M₁	M₂
MBu			P_3	P_2	T_1T_0	T_2	M_0	M_1	M_2
M...MBu					T_1T_0	T_2	M_0	M_1	M_2
MBe			P_3	P_2	T_1T_0	T_2		M_1	M_2
M...MBe					T_1T_0	T_2		M_1	M_2
MBW			P_3	P_2	T_1			M_1	M_2
M...MBW					T_1			M_1	M_2
MBZu			P_3	P_2	T_1				M_2
M...MBZu					T_1				M_2
MBDu			P_3	P_2	T_1				M_2
M...MBDu					T_1				M_2
MBDe			P_3	P_2					
MBDH			P_3						
MBDZu			P_3	P_2					
MBDDu			P_3	P_2					
MBZ...Zu			P_3	P_2					
MBZ...Ze			P_3	P_2					
MBZ...ZW			P_3	P_2					
MBZ...ZDu			P_3	P_2					
MBZ...ZDe			P_3	P_2					
MBZ...ZDH			P_3						
MBZ...ZZu			P_3	P_2					
MBZ...ZDu			P_3	P_2					
MSu			P_3	P_2	T_1T_0	T_2	M_0	M_1	M_2
M...MSu					T_1T_0	T_2	M_0	M_1	M_2
MSe			P_3	P_2	T_1T_0	T_2	M_0	M_1	M_2
M...MSe					T_1T_0	T_2	M_0	M_1	M_2
MSH			P_3	P_1		T_2	M_0	M_1	M_2
M...MSH						T_2	T_0	M_1	M_2
MSZu			P_3	P_2	T_1T_0	T_2	M_0	M_1	M_2
M...MSZu					T_1T_0	T_2	M_0	M_1	M_2
M...MSZe					T_1T_0	T_2		M_1	M_2
M...MSZW					T_1			M_1	M_2
M...MSZZu					T_1				M_2
M...MSZDu					T_1				M_2
MSDu			P_3	P_2	T_1T_0	T_2	M_0	M_1	M_2
M...MSD...Du					T_1T_0	T_2	M_0	M_1	M_2
M...MSD...De					T_1T_0	T_2	M_0	M_1	M_2
M...MSD...DH						T_2	M_0	M_1	M_2
M...MSD...DZu					T_1T_0	T_2	M_0	M_1	M_2
M...MSD...DZe					T_1T_0	T_2		M_1	M_2
M...MSD...DZW					T_1			M_1	M_2
M...MSD...DZZu					T_1				M_2
M...MSD...DZDu					T_1				M_2
Bu	N_0	N_1	P_3	P_2	T_1T_0	T_2	M_0	M_1	M_2
Be					T_1T_0	T_2		M_1	M_2
BW					T_1			M_1	M_2
BZu					T_1				M_2
BDu					T_1				M_2
Su	N_0	N_1	P_3	P_2	T_1T_0	T_2	M_0	M_1	M_2
Se	N_0				T_1T_0	T_2	M_0	M_1	M_2
SH						T_2	M_0	M_1	M_2

Table 1.2—*continued*

SZu	T_1T_0	T_2	M_0	M_1	M_2
SZe	T_1T_0	T_2		M_1	M_2
SZW	T_1			M_1	M_2
SZZu	T_1				M_2
SZDu	T_1				M_2
SD...Du	T_1T_0	T_2	M_0	M_1	M_2
SD...De	T_1T_0	T_2	M_0	M_1	M_2
SD...DH		T_2	M_0	M_1	M_2
SD...DZu	T_1T_0	T_2	M_0	M_1	M_2
SD...DZe	T_1T_0	T_2		M_1	M_2
SD...DZW	T_1			M_1	M_2
SD...DZZu	T_1				M_2
SD...DZDu	T_1				M_2
Any other series of kinship notations	X				

Table 1.3.
Ego = Unmarried child of me[a] & fe[a] = *Eu″*

Relation	Kinship Pattern
F	N_0N_1
M	N_0N_1
Bu	N_0N_1
Su	N_0N_1
Be	N_0
Se	N_0
Any other series of kinship notations	X

Table 2.1.
Ego = Ever-married male kin = *Eme[k]*

Relation								
			Kinship Pattern					
F	N_0	P_3	P_2	P_1	P_0	T_2	M_1	M_2
F...F		P_3	P_2	P_1	P_0			
F...FM		P_3	P_2	P_1	P_0			
F...FBu		P_3	P_2	P_1	P_0			
F...FBe		P_3	P_2	P_1	P_0			
F...FBW		P_3	P_2	P_1	P_0			

Table 2.1—*continued*

	N	P₃	P₂	P₁	P₀	A	T₁	T₀	T₂	M₁	M₂
F...FBZ...Zu		P_3	P_2	P_1	P_0						
F...FBZ...Ze		P_3	P_2	P_1	P_0						
F...FBZ...ZW		P_3	P_2	P_1	P_0						
F...FBZ...ZDu		P_3	P_2	P_1	P_0						
F...FBZ...ZDe		P_3	P_2	P_1							
F...FBZ...ZDH		P_3		P_1							
F...FBZ...ZDZu		P_3	P_2								
F...FBZ...ZDDu		P_3	P_2								
F...FBDu		P_3	P_2	P_1	P_0						
F...FBDe		P_3	P_2	P_1							
F...FBDH		P_3		P_1							
F...FBDZu		P_3	P_2								
F...FBDDu		P_3	P_2								
F...FSu		P_3	P_2	P_1	P_0						
F...FSe		P_3	P_2	P_1							
F...FSH		P_3		P_1							
F...FSZu		P_3	P_2								
F...FSDu		P_3	P_2								
M	N_0	P_3	P_2	P_1	P_0		T_1	T_0	T_2	M_1	M_2
M...M							T_1	T_0	T_2	M_1	M_2
M...MF									T_2	M_1	M_2
M...MBu							T_1	T_0	T_2	M_1	M_2
M...MBe						A	T_1	T_0	T_2	M_1	M_2
M...MBW						A	T_1			M_1	M_2
M...MBZu						A	T_1				M_2
M...MBDu						A	T_1				M_2
M...MSu							T_1	T_0	T_2	M_1	M_2
M...MSe							T_1	T_0	T_2	M_1	M_2
M...MSH									T_2	M_1	M_2
M...MSZu							T_1	T_0	T_2	M_1	M_2
M...MSZe						A	T_1	T_0	T_2	M_1	M_2
M...MSZW						A	T_1			M_1	M_2
M...MSZZu						A	T_1				M_2
M...MSZDu						A	T_1				M_2
M...MSD...Du							T_1	T_0	T_2	M_1	M_2
M...MSD...De							T_1	T_0	T_2	M_1	M_2
M...MSD...DH									T_2	M_1	M_2
M...MSD...DZu							T_1	T_0	T_2	M_1	M_2
M...MSD...DZe						A	T_1	T_0	T_2	M_1	M_2
M...MSD...DZW						A	T_1			M_1	M_2
M...MSD...DZZu						A	T_1				M_2
M...MSD...DZDu						A	T_1				M_2
Bu	N_0	P_3	P_2	P_1	P_0		T_1	T_0	T_2	M_1	M_2
Be	N_0	P_3	P_2	P_1	P_0	A	T_1	T_0	T_2	M_1	M_2
BW		P_3	P_2	P_1	P_0	A	T_1			M_1	M_2
BZu		P_3	P_2	P_1	P_0	A	T_1				M_2
BZ...Zu		P_3	P_2	P_1	P_0						
BZ...Ze		P_3	P_2	P_1	P_0						
BZ...ZW		P_3	P_2	P_1	P_0						

Table 2.1. — *continued*

Relation	N_0	N_1	P_3	P_2	P_1	P_0	A	T_1	T_0	T_2	M_1	M_2
BZ...ZDu			P_3	P_2	P_1	P_0						
BZ...ZDe			P_3	P_2	P_1							
BZ...ZDH			P_3		P_1							
BZ...ZDZu			P_3	P_2								
BZ...ZDDu			P_3	P_2								
BDu			P_3	P_2	P_1	P_0	A	T_1				M_2
BDe			P_3	P_2	P_1							
BDH			P_3		P_1							
BDZu			P_3	P_2								
BDDu			P_3	P_2								
Su	N_0		P_3	P_2	P_1	P_0		T_1	T_0	T_2	M_1	M_2
Se	N_0		P_3	P_2	P_1			T_1	T_0	T_2	M_1	M_2
SH			P_3		P_1					T_2	M_1	M_2
SZu			P_3	P_2				T_1	T_0	T_2	M_1	M_2
SZe							A	T_1	T_0	T_2	M_1	M_2
SZW							A	T_1			M_1	M_2
SZZu							A	T_1				M_2
SZDu							A	T_1				M_2
SDu			P_3	P_2				T_1	T_0	T_2	M_1	M_2
SD...Du								T_1	T_0	T_2	M_1	M_2
SD...De								T_1	T_0	T_2	M_1	M_2
SD...DH										T_2	M_1	M_2
SD...DZu								T_1	T_0	T_2	M_1	M_2
SD...DZe							A	T_1	T_0	T_2	M_1	M_2
SD...DZW							A	T_1			M_1	M_2
SD...DZZu							A	T_1				M_2
SD...DZDu							A	T_1				M_2
Zu	N_0	N_1	P_3	P_2	P_1	P_0	A	T_1				M_2
Ze	N_0		P_3	P_2	P_1	P_0						
ZW			P_3	P_2	P_1	P_0						
Z...Zu			P_3	P_2	P_1	P_0						
Z...Ze			P_3	P_2	P_1	P_0						
Z...ZW			P_3	P_2	P_1	P_0						
Z...ZDu			P_3	P_2	P_1	P_0						
Z...ZDe			P_3	P_2	P_1							
Z...ZDH			P_3		P_1							
Z...ZDZu			P_3	P_2								
Z...ZDDu			P_3	P_2								
Du	N_0	N_1	P_3	P_2	P_1	P_0	A	T_1				M_2
De	N_0		P_3	P_2	P_1							
DH			P_3		P_1							
DDu			P_3	P_2								
DZu			P_3	P_2								

Table 2.1.—*continued*

Relation	Kinship Pattern									
W	N_0	N_1	P_3	P_2	P_1	P_0	A	T_1	M_1	M_2
Any other series of kinship notations X										

Table 2.2. Ego = Ever-married male affine = *Eme*[a]

Relation	Kinship Pattern							
	N_0	N_1	P_3	P_1	T_2	M_0	M_1	M_2
Zu	N_0	N_1	P_3		T_2	M_0	M_1	M_2
ZZu								M_2
ZDu								M_2
Ze	N_0				T_2		M_1	M_2
ZW							M_1	M_2
Du	N_0	N_1	P_3		T_2	M_0	M_1	M_2
D...Du					T_2	M_0	M_1	M_2
De	N_0				T_2	M_0	M_1	M_2
D...De					T_2	M_0	M_1	M_2
D...DH					T_2	M_0	M_1	M_2
D...DZu					T_2	M_0	M_1	M_2
D...DZe					T_2		M_1	M_2
D...DZW							M_1	M_2
D...DZZu								M_2
D...DZDu								M_2
W	N_0	N_1	P_3	P_1	T_2	M_0	M_1	M_2
WF			P_3	P_1	T_2	M_0	M_1	M_2
WF...F			P_3	P_1				
WF...FM			P_3					
WF...FBu			P_3	P_1				
WF...FBe			P_3	P_1				
WF...FBW			P_3	P_1				
WF...FBZ...Zu			P_3	P_1				
WF...FBZ...Ze			P_3	P_1				
WF...FBZ...ZW			P_3	P_1				
WF...FBZ...ZZu			P_3	P_1				
WF...FBZ...ZDu			P_3	P_1				
WF...FBZ...ZDe			P_3	P_1				
WF...FBZ...ZDH			P_3	P_1				
WF...FBZ...ZDZu			P_3					
WF...FBZ...ZDDu			P_3					
WF...FBDu			P_3	P_1				
WF...FBDe			P_3	P_1				
WF...FBDH			P_3	P_1				
WF...FBDZu			P_3					
WF...FBDDu			P_3					

Table 2.2.—*continued*

Relation	Kinship Pattern					
WF...FSu	P_3	P_1				
WF...FSe	P_3	P_1				
WF...FSH	P_3	P_1				
WF...FSZu	P_3					
WF...FSDu	P_3					
WM	P_3	P_1	T_2	M_0	M_1	M_2
WM...M			T_2	M_0	M_1	M_2
WH...MF			T_2	M_0	M_1	M_2
WM...MBu			T_2	M_0	M_1	M_2
WM...MBe			T_2		M_1	M_2
WM...MBW					M_1	M_2
WM...MBZu						M_2
WM...MBDu						M_2
WM...MSu			T_2	M_0	M_1	M_2
WM...MSe			T_2	M_0	M_1	M_2
WM...MSH			T_2	M_0	M_1	M_2
WM...MSZu			T_2	M_0	M_1	M_2
WM...MSZe			T_2		M_1	M_2
WM...MSZW					M_1	M_2
WM...MSZZu						M_2
WM...MSZDu						M_2
WM...MSD...Du			T_2	M_0	M_1	M_2
WM...MSD...De			T_2	M_0	M_1	M_2
WM...MSD...DH			T_2	M_0	M_1	M_2
WM...MSD...DZu			T_2	M_0	M_1	M_2
WM...MSD...DZe			T_2		M_1	M_2
WM...MSD...DZW					M_1	M_2
WM...MSD...DZZu						M_2
WM...MSD...DZDu						M_2
WBu	P_3	P_1	T_2	M_0	M_1	M_2
WBe	P_3	P_1	T_2		M_1	M_2
WBW	P_3	P_1			M_1	M_2
WBZu	P_3	P_1				M_2
WBZ...Zu	P_3	P_1				
WBZ...Ze	P_3	P_1				
WBZ...ZW	P_3	P_1				
WBZ...ZDu	P_3	P_1				
WBZ...ZDe	P_3	P_1				
WBZ...ZDH	P_3	P_1				
WBZ...ZDZu	P_3					
WBZ...ZDDu	P_3					

Table 2.2.—*continued*

Relation	Kinship Pattern						
WBDu	P_3	P_1					M_2
WBDe	P_3	P_1					
WBDH	P_3	P_1					
WBDZu	P_3						
WBDDu	P_3						
WSu	P_3	P_1	T_2	M_0	M_1	M_2	
WSe	P_3	P_1	T_2	M_0	M_1	M_2	
WSH	P_3	P_1	T_2	M_0	M_1	M_2	
WSZu	P_3		T_2	M_0	M_1	M_2	
WSZe			T_2		M_1	M_2	
WSZW					M_1	M_2	
WSZZu						M_2	
WSZDu						M_2	
WSDu	P_3		T_2	M_0	M_1	M_2	
WSD...Du			T_2	M_0	M_1	M_2	
WSD...De			T_2	M_0	M_1	M_2	
WSD...DH			T_2	M_0	M_1	M_2	
WSD...DZu			T_2	M_0	M_1	M_2	
WSD...DZe			T_2		M_1	M_2	
WSD...DZW					M_1	M_2	
WSD...DZZu						M_2	
WSD...DZDu						M_2	
Any other series of kinship notations X							

Table 3.1. Ego = Ever-married female kin = *Efe*[k]

Relation	Kinship Pattern							
F	N_0	P_3	P_2	P_1	T_2	M_0	M_1	M_2
F...F		P_3	P_2	P_1				
F...FM		P_3	P_2	P_1				
F...FBu		P_3	P_2	P_1				
F...FBe		P_3	P_2	P_1				
F...FBW		P_3	P_2	P_1				
F...FBZ...Zu		P_3	P_2	P_1				
F...FBZ...Ze		P_3	P_2	P_1				
F...FBZ...ZW		P_3	P_2	P_1				
F...FBZ...ZDu		P_3	P_2	P_1				
F...FBZ...ZDe		P_3	P_2	P_1				
F...FBZ...ZDH		P_3		P_1				
F...FBZ...ZDZu		P_3	P_2					
F...FBZ...ZDDu		P_3	P_2					

Table 3.1.—*continued*

Relation		N_0	P_3	P_2	P_1	T_1	T_0	T_2	M_0	M_1	M_2
F...FBDu			P_3	P_2	P_1						
F...FBDe			P_3	P_2	P_1						
F...FBDH			P_3		P_1						
F...FBZDu			P_3	P_2							
F...FBDDu			P_3	P_2							
F...FSu			P_3	P_2	P_1						
F...FSe			P_3	P_2	P_1						
F...FSH			P_3		P_1						
F...FSZu			P_3	P_2							
F...FSDu			P_3	P_2							
M		N_0	P_3	P_2	P_1	T_1	T_0	T_2	M_0	M_1	M_2
M...M						T_1	T_0	T_2	M_0	M_1	M_2
M...MF								T_2	M_0	M_1	M_2
M...MBu						T_1	T_0	T_2	M_0	M_1	M_2
M...MBe						T_1	T_0	T_2		M_1	M_2
M...MBW						T_1				M_1	M_2
M...MBZu						T_1					M_2
M...MBDu						T_1					M_2
M...MSu						T_1	T_0	T_2	M_0	M_1	M_2
M...MSe						T_1	T_0	T_2	M_0	M_1	M_2
M...MSH								T_2	M_0	M_1	M_2
M...MSZu						T_1	T_0	T_2	M_0	M_1	M_2
M...MSZe						T_1	T_0	T_2		M_1	M_2
M...MSZW						T_1				M_1	M_2
M...MSZZu						T_1					M_2
M...MSZDu						T_1					M_2
M...MSD...Du						T_1	T_0	T_2	M_0	M_1	M_2
M...MSD...De						T_1	T_0	T_2	M_0	M_1	M_2
M...MSD...DH								T_2	M_0	M_1	M_2
M...MSD...DZu						T_1	T_0	T_2	M_0	M_1	M_2
M...MSD...DZe						T_1	T_0	T_2		M_1	M_2
M...MSD...DZW						T_1				M_1	M_2
M...MSD...DZZu						T_1					M_2
M...MSD...DZDu						T_1					M_2
Bu		N_0	P_3	P_2	P_1	T_1	T_0	T_2	M_0	M_1	M_2
Be		N_0	P_3	P_2	P_1	T_1	T_0	T_2		M_1	M_2
BW			P_3	P_2	P_1	T_1				M_1	M_2
BZu			P_3	P_2	P_1	T_1					M_2
BZ...Zu			P_3	P_2	P_1						
BZ...Ze			P_3	P_2	P_1						
BZ...ZW			P_3	P_2	P_1						
BZ...ZDu			P_3	P_2	P_1						
BZ...ZDe			P_3	P_2	P_1						
BZ...ZDH			P_3		P_1						
BZ...ZDZu			P_3	P_2							
BZ...ZDDu			P_3	P_2							

Table 3.1.—*continued*

Relation	N_0	N_1	P_3	P_2	P_1	T_1	T_0	T_2	M_0	M_1	M_2
BDu			P_3	P_2	P_1	T_1					M_2
BDe			P_3	P_2	P_1						
BDH			P_3		P_1						
BDZu			P_3	P_2							
BDDu			P_3	P_2							
Su	N_0		P_3	P_2	P_1	T_1	T_0	T_2	M_0	M_1	M_2
Se	N_0		P_3	P_2	P_1	T_1	T_0	T_2	M_0	M_1	M_2
SH			P_3		P_1			T_2	M_0	M_1	M_2
SZu			P_3	P_2		T_1	T_0	T_2	M_0	M_1	M_2
SZe						T_1	T_0	T_2		M_1	M_2
SZW						T_1				M_1	M_2
SZZu						T_1					M_2
SZDu						T_1					M_2
SDu			P_3	P_2		T_1	T_0	T_2	M_0	M_1	M_2
SD...Du						T_1	T_0	T_2	M_0	M_1	M_2
SD...De						T_1	T_0	T_2	M_0	M_1	M_2
SD...DH								T_2	M_0	M_1	M_2
SD...DZu						T_1	T_0	T_2	M_0	M_1	M_2
SD...DZe						T_1	T_0	T_2		M_1	M_2
SD...DZW						T_1				M_1	M_2
SD...DZZu						T_1					M_2
SD...DZDu						T_1					M_2
Zu	N_0	N_1	P_3	P_2		T_1	T_0	T_2	M_0	M_1	M_2
ZZu						T_1					M_2
ZDu						T_1					M_2
Ze	N_0					T_1	T_0	T_2		M_1	M_2
ZW						T_1				M_1	M_2
Du	N_0	N_1	P_3	P_2		T_1	T_0	T_2	M_0	M_1	M_2
D...Du						T_1	T_0	T_2	M_0	M_1	M_2
De	N_0					T_1	T_0	T_2	M_0	M_1	M_2
D...De						T_1	T_0	T_2	M_0	M_1	M_2
D...DH								T_2	M_0	M_1	M_2
D...DZu						T_1	T_0	T_2	M_0	M_1	M_2
D...DZe						T_1	T_0	T_2		M_1	M_2
D...DZW						T_1				M_1	M_2
D...DZZu						T_1					M_2
D...DZDu						T_1					M_2
H	N_0	N_1	P_3		P_1			T_2	M_0	M_1	M_2
Any other series of kinship notations X											

Table 3.2. Ego = Ever-married female affine = *Efe*[a]

Relation	Kinship Pattern									
	N_0	N_1	P_3	P_2	P_1	P_0	A	T_1	M_1	M_2
Zu	N_0	N_1	P_3	P_2	P_1	P_0	A	T_1		M_2
Z...Zu			P_3	P_2	P_1	P_0				
Z...Ze			P_3	P_2	P_1	P_0				
Z...ZW			P_3	P_2	P_1	P_0				
Z...ZDu			P_3	P_2	P_1	P_0				
Z...ZDe			P_3	P_2	P_1					
Z...ZDH			P_3		P_1					
Z...ZDZu			P_3	P_2						
Z...ZDDu			P_3	P_2						
Du	N_0	N_1	P_3	P_2	P_1	P_0	A	T_1		M_2
De	N_0		P_3	P_2	P_1					
DH			P_3		P_1					
DZu			P_3	P_2						
DDu			P_3	P_2						
H	N_0	N_1	P_3	P_2	P_1	P_0	A	T_1	M_1	M_2
HF			P_3	P_2	P_1	P_0			M_1	M_2
HF...F			P_3	P_2	P_1	P_0				
HF...FM			P_3	P_2	P_1	P_0				
HF...FBu			P_3	P_2	P_1	P_0				
HF...FBe			P_3	P_2	P_1	P_0				
HF...FBW			P_3	P_2	P_1	P_0				
HF...FBZ...Zu			P_3	P_2	P_1	P_0				
HF...FBZ...Ze			P_3	P_2	P_1	P_0				
HF...FBZ...ZW			P_3	P_2	P_1	P_0				
HF...FBZ...ZZu			P_3	P_2	P_1	P_0				
HF...FBZ...ZDu			P_3	P_2	P_1	P_0				
HF...FBZ...ZDe			P_3	P_2	P_1					
HF...FBZ...ZDH			P_3		P_1					
HF...FBZ...ZDZu			P_3	P_2						
HF...FBZ...ZDDu			P_3	P_2						
HF...FBDu			P_3	P_2	P_1	P_0				
HF...FBDe			P_3	P_2	P_1					
HF...FBDH			P_3		P_1					
HF...FBDZu			P_3	P_2						
HF...FBDDu			P_3	P_2						
HF...FSu			P_3	P_2	P_1	P_0				
HF...FSe			P_3	P_2	P_1					
HF...FSH			P_3		P_1					
HF...FSZu			P_3	P_2						
HF...FSDu			P_3	P_2						
HM			P_3	P_2	P_1	P_0		T_1	M_1	M_2
HM...M								T_1	M_1	M_2
HM...MF									M_1	M_2

Table 3.2.— *continued*

Relation	Kinship Pattern							
HM...MBu						T_1	M_1	M_2
HM...MBe					A	T_1	M_1	M_2
HM...MBW					A	T_1	M_1	M_2
HM...MBZu					A	T_1	M_1	M_2
HM...MBDu					A	T_1	M_1	M_2
HM...MSu						T_1	M_1	M_2
HM...MSe						T_1	M_1	M_2
HM...MSH							M_1	M_2
HM...MSZu						T_1	M_1	M_2
HM...MSZe					A	T_1	M_1	M_2
HM...MSZW					A	T_1	M_1	M_2
HM...MSZZu					A	T_1		M_2
HM...MSZDu					A	T_1		M_2
HM...MSD...Du						T_1	M_1	M_2
HM...MSD...De						T_1	M_1	M_2
HM...MSD...DH							M_1	M_2
HM...MSD...DZu						T_1	M_1	M_2
HM...MSD...DZe					A	T_1	M_1	M_2
HM...MSD...DZW					A	T_1	M_1	M_2
HM...MSD...DZZu					A	T_1		M_2
HM...MSD...DZDu					A	T_1		M_2
HBu	P_3	P_2	P_1	P_0		T_1	M_1	M_2
HBe	P_3	P_2	P_1	P_0	A	T_1	M_1	M_2
HBW	P_3	P_2	P_1	P_0	A	T_1	M_1	M_2
HBZu	P_3	P_2	P_1	P_0	A	T_1		M_2
HBZ...Zu	P_3	P_2	P_1	P_0				
HBZ...Ze	P_3	P_2	P_1	P_0				
HBZ...ZW	P_3	P_2	P_1	P_0				
HBZ...ZDu	P_3	P_2	P_1	P_0				
HBZ...ZDe	P_3	P_2	P_1					
HBZ...ZDH	P_3		P_1					
HBZ...ZDZu	P_3	P_2						
HBZ...ZDDu	P_3	P_2						
HBDu	P_3	P_2	P_1	P_0	A	T_1		M_2
HBDe	P_3	P_2	P_1					
HBDH	P_3		P_1					
HBDZu	P_3	P_2						
HBDDu	P_3	P_2						
HSu	P_3	P_2	P_1	P_0		T_1	M_1	M_2
HSe	P_3	P_2	P_1			T_1	M_1	M_2
HSH	P_3		P_1				M_1	M_2

Table 3.2.—*continued*

Relation	Kinship Pattern					
HSZu	P_3	P_2		T_1	M_1	M_2
HSZe			A	T_1	M_1	M_2
HSZW			A	T_1	M_1	M_2
HSZZu			A	T_1		M_2
HSZDu			A	T_1		M_2
HSDu	P_3	P_2		T_1	M_1	M_2
HSD...Du				T_1	M_1	M_2
HSD...De				T_1	M_1	M_2
HSD...DH					M_1	M_2
HSD...DZu				T_1	M_1	M_2
HSD...DZe			A	T_1	M_1	M_2
HSD...DZW			A	T_1	M_1	M_2
HSD...DZZu			A	T_1		M_2
HSD...DZDu			A	T_1		M_2
Any other series of kinship notations	X					

Chapter 4
Utility

1 FAMILY IN INDIA: AN EXAMPLE

In the last chapter we have illustrated how by adopting the population approach a measure variable can be treated in a flexible and comprehensive manner to meet the objectives of classification. We have shown how the nominal distinctions drawn with respect to a measure variable, and the typology of ordinal series, evolving from the accumulation of knowledge about the phenomenon to which the variable refers, can be systematized from a theoretically infinite but enumerable field of variation in the relevant properties. And we have shown that, conceived in this manner, the population approach can be used to enter into hitherto unclassified regions of knowable variations that are qualitative to begin with but can be increasingly quantified so that the categorization of the measure variable can be ever more precise, unequivocal, and comprehensive. The synchronization of various objectives of classification with the numerous ways of categorizing the measure variable will not, therefore, suffer from any constraint.

This facility, as we have indicated in Chapter 2, is not an inherent feature of the typological approach to classification. We have pointed out, however, that so long as research on a phenomenon is geared merely to the *search* for information or data with reference to one particular context or a simple cross-classification of several contexts, the typological approach may adequately serve for classification. But, restricted in this manner, the scope of such research is now inadequate to appraise social reality. As we have discussed in

Chapter 1, social research must now be geared to *research* into a data space which will not refer to just one or another contextual explanation, or some form of cross-classification of a few such explanations. The data space must now be explored with reference to a systematized *series* of available and enumerable explanations for the phenomenon examined. This lies beyond the search for information or data with respect to one contextual explanation or even a cross-classification of several such contexts.

In this perspective, the content aspect of classification no longer draws our exclusive attention. The consideration of the measure variable, therefore, becomes only one part of an efficient procedure of classification. The other part deals with the categorization of relevant context variables, which must be systemized and integrated with the corresponding measure variables from the grass-roots level on up. The item, unit, and object aspects of classification thus come under a simultaneous examination that is of importance equal to that of the content aspect. The first three aspects, as pointed out in Chapter 2, refer to the context variable. Thus, an efficient procedure of classification must not only treat the measure variables in a flexible and comprehensive manner but also accomodate and integrate all possible variations in the relevant context variables, the respective properties of which need to refer to the alternative explanations of the phenomenon examined.

This requirement, as we have pointed out in Chapter 2, cannot be met unambiguously by the typological approach to classification. We have briefly pointed out in Chapter 3 how the population approach can better attend to it. In this chapter we shall illustrate the utility of the population approach with reference to available and enumerable series of context variables.

For this purpose we propose to deal with the family as an example, because in the last chapter we used the measure variable of kinship characteristics of family units as an illustration. The other reason for this selection is that sharply different explanations are given with respect to the structure, function, and process of this primordial social institution in virtually all configurations of world society. We have mentioned this in the last three chapters while discussing the central point that the objective of classification is to organize the available knowledge in such a manner that research can venture into hitherto unexplored regions of knowledge. For that purpose, the analysis of data must refer to an ever more efficient link between the prior and the subsequent knowledge of the known and the knowable variations inherent in and associated with a phenomenon.

We shall, however, confine ourselves to a place–time–people set of variation in order that we may clearly but concisely demonstrate the utility of the population approach for dealing with the context variables. We choose, therefore, contemporary Indian society and show in this chapter how the ultimate objective of classification can be met by the population approach. For this purpose, we shall examine the variations in family structures illustrated in Chapter 3 with respect to the alternate explanations posited to reveal the dynamics of family organization in contemporary India. We shall show how these explanations can be systemized into a numerable series of context variables in order that we may categorize the properties of the measure variables in a manner such that one can unequivocally deduce the key features of contemporary family organization and, furthermore, draw efficient inferences on what will be the family in India in the near future.

2 ALTERNATIVE EXPLANATIONS

Views and counterviews are held on the fact and the process of nuclearization of the patrilineal-patrivirilocal joint family system in India. The fact of nuclearization is assumed, primarily, from the relative incidence of the joint and nuclear family types at a point in time or over a series of time points. The context is the unit characterization of families as forming coresident and commensal kin groups.

On that basis, and under the unanimous assumption that the coresident and commensal joint family structures represented the traditional and the probabilistic norm for the Indian society, some scholars like Nimkoff and K.M. Kapadia stated in the 1950s that nuclearization is not taking place (Kapadia 1956; Nimkoff 1959). Their antagonists maintained that microstudies such as that of Kapadia did not represent the overall Indian scene, and Nimkoff's remarks were not backed by empirical data.

The prevailing viewpoint, therefore, is that Indian joint family structures are nuclearized over time. The process, accepted in the light of the rising incidence of nuclear families in the society, is explained with particular reference to the economic and psychological changes in the society which are often posited under the tradition–modernity schema. In using the typological approach to categorize the empirical data in these contexts of unit and object characteristics of classification, we may consider only the joint–nuclear dichotomy or evolve another type of "quasi-joint" family in the same manner as noted in Chapter 3 with regard to Chattopadhyay's "intermediate family" which may be "vertically extended" or "laterally joint".

One of the best known applications of this approach is found in W.A. Morrison's article on Maharashtrian families. He concluded (1959: 67):

Types of familism in Badlapur are quite clearly related to various well defined cultural types. The data presented lead to the conclusion that the Joint and Quasi-Joint Family patterns are "traditional middle class" village phenomena, patterns of living which are closely associated with certain multi-caste groups, certain traditional occupations, and certain educational levels. In addition, the Nuclear Family is very closely associated with both the upper and lower socio-economic and cultural groupings of the village. The Nuclear Family appears both among the better educated, more non-traditional, middle and upper status caste groupings, as well as among the lower socio-economic levels of poorer villagers. The former group reflects in its familism the influence of "urban-industrial" non-traditional values and attitudes of modern life, whereas the latter group reflects a poverty-stricken way of life which in most cases does not permit larger family groups than the nuclear.

It will be noticed that this analysis of family types in Badlapur does not represent a systematic division and collection of the measure variable of kinship characteristics of the family units. It will also be noticed that the explanatory contexts of economic and cultural variables are not systematically arranged with respect to their relevant properties. Lastly, the economic and cultural variables are not integrated with the measure variable: these are merely cross-classified in the manner we have pointed out in Chapters 1 and 2. As a result, the categorization of the measure variable in the context of the kinship patterns formed and in formation is incomplete; the categorization of the economic and cultural characteristics of the context variables is superficial.

Clearly, what is required is a systematic and integrated examination of the indivisible properties of the three interacting measure variables of kinship, economic, and cultural characteristics from the last stage of their division through their successive consolidation with reference to the contexts of forming (a.) coresident and commensal kin groups, and (b.) a systematic series of social class categories of economic and cultural valuation. Failing to apply the population approach to classification, the deduced correlations among the family and social class typologies remain imprecise, while the references to "traditional middle class" and "urban-industrial" non-traditional values takes the study into the realm of conjecture.

Contrary pictures are presented by other sets of data, such as those of Kapadia for Gujarat (a neighboring state of Maharashtra). Kapadia's study is not usually accepted as representing all of Indian society; but that comment would be equally applicable to Morrison's study, and both are based on typologies. All-India studies in these contexts—based on the typological or the population approach to classification—are not available. For the state of West Bengal, however, large-scale sample survey data on 26,735 family units and nonfamilial units, forming coresident and commensal kin groups over the 20 years of 1946–66, have been dealt with utilizing the population approach to classification. While not claiming to represent Indian society as a whole, this macrostudy can provide a minimax situation vis-a-vis Morrison's Maharashtra and Kapadia's Gujarat. This is so because (a.) up to the 1950s, at any rate, the urban and industrial development of West Bengal was rapid, as was claimed for Kapadia's region in Gujarat; (b.) the "traditional middle class," found in Morrison's Maharashtrian village and no less available in Kapadia's Gujarat region, is well entrenched in rural and urban West Bengal; and (c.) the "heterodox" Bengalis, somewhat like the Maharashtrians, although perhaps less like the Gujaratis, have always been regarded as less imbued with the "traditional" Indian cultural values in any of its forms.

The 1960–61 survey of West Bengal showed that the percentage incidence of the joint plus quasijoint extended family, along with the incidence of the nuclear family and the nonfamilial unit, was the same for the urban and rural areas (34.98 ± 4.98 and 32.08 ± 2.09, respectively). But the relative incidence of the extended family is larger for the urban than the rural area (46.12 ± 4.07 and 35.33 ± 3.87, respectively) if the nonfamilial units (which are overwhelmingly found in the urban areas) are excluded (R. Mukherjee 1977a: 60). The urban-industrial areas—including the metropolis of Calcutta, which came under the influence of the West from the beginning of British rule in India and which harbor the bulk of the nonfamilial units—are thus seen to be no less influenced by the "traditional" joint family system.

By systematically sorting the family units with references to their economic, demographic, caste-religious, and educational-cultural characteristics, social categories could be formed from the bottom of the social space, that is, by gathering these characteristics, starting from their primary categorization through successively more inclusive categories (R. Mukherjee, 1977a: 59-90). In association with their family organization, therefore, social groups could be discerned in West Bengal society as more or less associated with the incidence of the extended family structure. These groups, however, cannot be clearly distinguished as representing either the "traditional middle class" village phenomena or the urban-industrial nontraditional values and attitudes of modern life (R. Mukherjee, 1977a: 89-91). We notice, moreover, that in both rural and urban areas, the nonagricultural illiterate gentry and literate commoners register a high incidence of the extended family when only the nuclear and the extended family types are taken into account, but a very low incidence if the typology also includes the nonfamilial units (R. Mukherjee, 1977a: 91). This indicates that many in these social strata also subscribe to the joint family organization and, at the same time, are largely responsible for the generation of single-member ($=$ nonfamilial) units in the context of unit characterization of the family as forming coresident and commensal kin groups.

The nonfamilial units are predominantly males who, as the survey data tell us, live alone either because they have been socially atomized or in order to earn money for their "families" located elsewhere (R. Mukherjee, 1977a: 29-31). Now, in order to test the validity of either hypothesis, we are required to conceive the formation of family units in another context, namely, whom the heads of households (including the single-member households) consider to belong to his/her family. The kinship characteristics of these units in the perspective of the specified individuals may denote an extended or a nuclear family; alternatively, these units also may be nonfamilial in the cases where the specified individuals refuse to consider any kin or affines to be their "family members."

The two contexts for unit characterization must, however, by synchronized and integrated with the measure variable in order that the consolidation of knowledge by means of this course of classification not be imprecise or equivocal. We must bear in mind that a specified individual may live in a nuclear family (a coresident and commensal kin group) but the mental image of his/her family may be a "joint" one, or vice versa. Also, whether or not physically living in a family unit, he/she may be living alone in the psychological dimension. And, while living as a nonfamilial unit, he/she may have the mental image of living in a nuclear or extended family—for the maintenance of which he/she lives alone elsewhere. There may be other reasons for living apart from one's family, but these were found in the West Bengal study to be of virtually no relevance to the people concerned.

We find from a course of analysis that employs this procedure of classification of the data, as outlined in Table 2.2, that, with minor variations the following holds true: (1) In both urban and rural areas, those who form an extended family consider it also as their family organization. (2) Predominantly, those who live by forming a nuclear family consider it also as their family organization, except an appreciable proportion in the urban (and not the rural) areas whose mental affiliation is with their extended family of the patrilineal-patrivirilocal variety. (3) In both urban and rural areas, the female nonfamilial units (whose representation in the society is small) are nonfamilial both physically and psychologically. But (4), while in the rural areas the relatively small number of male nonfamilial units are physically and psychologically nonfamilial, those in the urban areas have mostly their far-away patrilineal-patrivirilocal joint family in their minds, and next most likely their absent nuclear family; only a quarter of them form truly nonfamilial units, both physically and psychologically (R. Mukherjee 1977a: 163). Clearly, the dominant role of the joint family system is thus further substantiated by considering these two contexts of the unit characterization of the family in a systemic framework of classification.

As has been discussed, the typological approach to classification would fail to consolidate our knowledge in this manner. It can be seen, therefore, that the typologists who would refute the thesis of nuclearization of the joint family system nevertheless must agree, first, that the joint family system is not tenable at the present time for forming coresident and commensal kin groups; and, then, they use the outlook of the individuals or else what they conceive to be "familial integration" as the context of family unit formation. They thus employ the latter contexts in isolation and not in a systemic relation to the context already discussed, nor to any other. The result is a distorted or equivocal appraisal of the contextual reality.

G.C. Hallen and G.A. Theodorson (1961/65) investigated how "modern" college students are in India and the United States by conducting opinion studies on the basis of identical questionnaire schedules. The preferred family organization of the students was elicited from a set of questions in the schedule; it was found that, as in most other aspects of their personal and social organization, the Indian students are far more "modern" than the U.S. students, such as in choosing their consorts, practicing the custom of the honeymoon, living separately from their parents after marriage, and so on.

I.P. Desai (1964) was more cautious in employing the context of familial integration in his study of a town in Gujarat. He identified the family units as

coresident and commensal kin groups, typed them as nuclear or different varieties of extended families, and traced over time the extent to which the extended families of their ancestors have separated. He then employed some
shared attributes of privilege and obligation (e.g., mutual assistance from the
segments of family with ancestral links on special occasions like the marriage
of girls) to denote the incidence of familial integration. He deduced, on that
basis, that the joint family system is holding its ground in Indian society.
Prima facie, then, Desai's context of familial integration becomes a matter of
interpretation: where does kinship integration end and familial integration begin?

We have in this case two interacting fields of variation in kinship and family. The two fields refer to both the measure variables (i.e., the contents of kinship and family relations, respectively, although the two systems are not
disparate) and the context variables (i.e., the kinship units and family units, respectively, whether or not some of the latter are traced from ancestral families). Since Desai's typology fails to systematize these two fields of variation,
his assertion of the persistence of the joint family system is equivocal.

Desai, however, has raised a moot point on the "jointness" of family
units. It has, therefore, been taken up by family researchers who, significantly,
indicate beforehand that they believe that as far as coresident and commensal
kin groups the joint families may have been nuclearized. Their system of classification, thus, tends to convey a decisive change in the unit characterization
of the family, beginning with the cross-classification of two contexts. We may
recall that the typologists cannot but shift from one context to another, or
merely cross-classify a number of contexts, instead of systematizing a series of
contexts and integrating them with the measure variables, as pointed out earlier.

Any study of the "jointness" of family units will, on the other hand, be
imprecise and equivocal unless the researcher (a.) attends to these interacting
variations in kinship and family with reference to the item, unit, and content
aspects of classification, and (b.) systematize, furthermore, the context variables referring to the object aspect of classification. In the latter respect, we
should consider the following logical sequence:

1. The minimal criterion by which to ascertain a lack of jointness in families is set in terms of their forming coresident and commensal kin groups of the
joint *or* the nuclear type, *but* at the *critical limit of replacement* of the joint
families by the nuclear families (or nonfamilial units) *without feedback*. We
shall explain and demonstrate this critical limit of replacement without feedback in the following pages.

2. The subsequent criterion of *functional* jointness is set in regard to the
familial (and not kinship) privileges and obligations. These may be shared less
and less, over time, by those coresident and commensal nuclear families (and

nonfamilial units) which have replaced joint families. In this context, however, one must also examine whether the nuclear families (and the nonfamilial units) of which the ancestral links cannot be ascertained, register any familial (and not merely kinship) integration among the coresident and commensal family units and nonfamilial units.

3. The final criterion is the gradual disappearance of even the *mental image* of the nuclear family members and the nonfamilial units as belonging to joint families. As noted for the second criterion, this one also must apply to *all* coresident and commensal family units, for reasons pointed out earlier.

The sequence we have outlined will provide us with a scale to test the process of nuclearization of the joint family system—structurally, functionally and processually. The process starts at the first stage with the forming of locally functioning units, moves on to the intermediate stage which indicates the tenacity of the joint family system, and arrives finally at the last stage, in which the joint family is gone from the mental horizon of the people. The sequence, thus, denotes the broad course of nuclearization in the context of interactions between two systems: kinship and family. As noted, the context variables must therefore be systematized and integrated from the grassroots level on up, using the appropriate measure variables.

This manner of systematizing and applying a series of context variables would be appropriate, however, only when the nuclear structures are ascertained to be replacing the joint structures without any reversion to the status quo ante (vide criterion 1, above). But the nuclear families may coexist with the joint families as a matter of contingency or concomitance. In either case, the joint family system would persist even though the joint family structures break down to nuclear units and/or the latter are eventually restructured into joint families. The nuclearization of the joint family system therefore will not be registered just by any large incidence of nuclear families in society at a given point in time nor by a gradual rise in their rate of incidence over time. We must ascertain the critical point of disintegration of the system in the way coresident and commensal kin groups are formed.

The typological approach to classification cannot provide this perspective to consolidate our knowledge. Prima facie, *it cannot lead us beyond the assumption that the replacement of joint structures by nuclear ones denotes the final outcome and not a mere probability occurrence in a system of variation.* It therefore, promotes the views and counterviews already discussed on the nuclearization of the joint family system by merely shifting the polemical standpoints with reference to one *or* another context of unit characterization of the family and/or its object characterization (e.g., family *in situ* to familial integration).

The application of the population approach to classification requires, by contrast, the systemization of the relevant context variables in the first place.

These variables should refer, at one extreme, to an immutable presence of the joint family structures in order to denote the perpetuity of the joint family system, and at the other extreme, to a systematic and unequivocal breakup of the joint structures into nuclear units without any room for reversion to the status quo ante. And, in between, the contexts should refer to the depleted but persistent viability of the joint family system along with the emergence of the nuclear family system as a contingent or concomitant phenomenon.

Therefore, we shall examine next how these enumerable contexts can be formulated in the light of our prior knowledge of the dynamics of family organization in Indian society, and be systemized on that basis. Afterwards we shall indicate how the integration of the systemized series of contexts with the appropriate measure variables leads to efficient inference and effective deduction about the nuclearization of the joint family system in India. An indispensable link will thus be established between prior and subsequent knowledge in order that research on the family in India can be pursued in a precise, comprehensive, and unequivocal manner.

3   SYSTEMIZATION OF CONTEXT VARIABLES

The formation of nuclear units by the break up of the patrilineal-patrivirilocal joint structures (the commonly found composition of joint families in India) means that one or more cut-off points in the generational and collateral extension of families are in operation vis-a-vis the propagation of the patrilineal family of the men. These points can denote the course of segmentation of the joint structures but, as we shall see, only when the process reaches a *limiting condition* such that nuclearization of the joint family system can take place. On the other hand, while some cut-off points in fact enforce the operation of the joint family system, nuclear families must emerge in society under these conditions because of sex and age variations in life expectancy, marriage and fertility patterns, etc. We should therefore ascertain their *probable* incidence and relate this to the *actual* incidence of different varieties of the patrilineal–patrivirilocal joint structures and of the nuclear structures, with reference to the already mentioned demographic patterns of Indian society.

Basic to this task is the population approach to classification, which, as illustrated in Chapter 3, systematically categorizes the kinship composition of the joint and the nuclear families and locates the variations on the matrix of inter-generational and collateral distances within each kinship pattern. The utility of this approach will be demonstrated, therefore, in the course of forging an indispensable link between the known and the knowable variations in Indian family structures, with a view to leading research on the Indian family into hitherto unexplored regions of knowledge.

For this purpose we should conceive the successive family cut-off points in the proliferation of the joint family structure in the light of different explanations of the perpetuation, viability, or disintegration of the joint family system. As pointed out in Chapter 1 with reference to the measure variable of income distribution, the cut-off points that categorize the income classes must be formulated in terms of the variable contexts for classification. With respect to the measure variables of the kinship composition of family units, therefore, we may hypothesize a series of contexts in order to explore the probabilities of nuclearization of the joint family structures.

These contexts will not refer to the mere presence or absence of different forms of family structure. As we have just mentioned, research on even the strongest hypotheses about the persistence of the joint family system cannot but yield an appreciable number of nuclear families, owing to the demographic characteristics of the people concerned. This we shall demonstrate in the following pages. For the moment we may merely note that it leads us back to the essential feature of social research which we have discussed in Chapter 1, namely, that one must consider the integration (and not mere cross-classification) of the classificatory variables from the grass-roots level on up.

The context and the measure variables being thus integrated and systemized (improbable if the typological approach is adopted), the classification of families will pave the way—in theory and with reference to the empirical data—for drawing an efficient inference on the relative usefulness of the alternative explanations on the viability or disintegration of the joint family system in India.

As noted, we afterwards shall examine corresponding sets of empirical data on variations in family structures in order that the variations noticed and noticeable are categorized with reference to their relevant contexts, but in a systematic manner. This, as discussed in Chapter 2, is possible only by adopting the population approach to classification. We shall thus show how the deductions made from the classification of family structures support the inference drawn on the relative efficiency of the hypotheses constructed about the nuclearization of the joint family system. And, both ways, i.e., with respect to the deductions made from classificatory theory or the inferences drawn from the empirical data, it will be evident that the typological approach is quite inadequate to fulfill the role of classification in meeting the requirements of contemporary social research.

Pursuing this further, we may visualize the proliferation of a patrilineal-patrivirilocal joint family from its hypothetical antecedents, i.e., from the pre-joint stage of a man undergoing an effective marriage and beginning to live with his wife, whether or not the couple was ritually married earlier as frequently happens even now in India. Since the ancestors of the couple are not to be considered in this context, it may be labelled a "root couple." With respect to this couple, the family will extend generationally, but *unilaterally*, through the effective marriage of its sons, son's sons, and so on. The family will extend generationally and *collaterally* through a *set* of root couples of brothers and their wives and the couples of their married sons, son's sons, and so on. However, propagating in this manner, a family could include all possible patrilineal male realtives and their wives. There must therefore be cut-off points in the generational and collateral extension of the family in order that it not identify itself with every male in the patrilineal kinship structure of the family.

The generational extension of the joint family is limited because people die. For India, in this respect, the frequently imposed cut-off point is at the extension of a family beyond three generations, as can be deduced from the following data:

1.) The age-tables available from the Census reports, after correction for possible bias in reporting the age of an individual, show that during 1901–31 there was little chance for an individual surviving beyond the age of 64. During 1911–31, this was raised to 69 years, while before 1901 the survival rate beyond 59 was low (R. Mukherjee 1975b: 7).

2.) The National Sample Survey data point out that during 1901–61 the age of effective marriage of the two sexes and their fertility performance have remained fairly constant, irrespective of some variations by rural-urban and inter-state differences. The data show that, on average:

a.) The age difference between husband and wife is 5 years.

b.) The couple begins to cohabit when the husband is 20–24 years old, and the wife is 15–19.

c.) Two children are born to the couple when the husband is in the age group of 25–29, and the wife 20–24.

d.) Another two children are born to the couple in the subsequent 5 years.

e.) There is a sharp decline in fertility after 4 children have been born, although in two social strata of small size the fertility performance continues unabated. (See, for details, R. Mukherjee 1976a: 19-20, 24-26, 34, 51-53, etc.)

3.) The sex ratio shows a slight preponderance of males over females, and the tendency seems to have gained over 1901–61. The difference in the size of the male and female populations is, however, still so small that half the number of children born to a couple may be assumed, on an average, to be males and the other half females. Moreover, the available data show that there is no association between the birth order of children and their sex (R. Mukherjee 1975b: 10). On the average, therefore, the two children born to a husband and a wife in each of the succeeding age-groups are a son and a daughter.

On the basis of the above data, the generational extension of the patrilineal-patrivirilocal joint family of an average Indian may be schematized as follows:

1.) The family is of a 2-generation structure when the first son of the root couple brings his wife to live in the family at the age of 20-24, when his father and mother are 45–49 and 40–44 years old, respectively.
2.) The same family has a 3-generation structure when the first son's first son is born when the son is 25 to 29 years old and, correspondingly, his father and mother are 50–54 and 45–49 years old, respectively.
3.) The same family has a 4-generation structure when the first son's first son's first son is born when the husband and the wife of the root couple are 75–79 and 70–74, respectively. Since very few persons are alive in India after 69 years of age, the 4-generation joint family is only a remote possibility.

The family, however, can maintain its structural unity after the root couples of brothers and their wives all have passed away, in a collateral joint family. Under the circumstances, the links among the family members will be through those surviving couples, which emerge sequentially: namely, the couples of the sons of the deceased brothers first, the couples of the son's sons after the disappearance of the son's couples, and so on. The joint families may, in consequence, go on expanding with limited generational extension and ultimately be identified with the patrilineal kinship structure of the males in the society. But that has never been reported to be the case, even in mythologies and folk tales that eulogize large families.

The following alternative hypotheses can therefore be proposed to sequentially explain the constraints on the extension of joint family units, the formation of nuclear units in the course of segmentation of joint structures, and, ultimately, the transformation of all joint families into nuclear ones:

1.) The collateral joint family of the deceased root couples of brothers maintains its structural unity so long as at least one of their sons' couples is represented in the unit.
2.) From the collateral joint familiy formed according to Hypothesis 1, the sons of each deceased root couple will together form a separate collateral joint family.
3.) From the collateral joint family formed according to Hypothesis 2, the descendants of each deceased root couple's son who with his wife has also passed away will together form a separate collateral joint family.
4.) From the collateral joint families formed according to Hypothesis 3, the couples each form unilateral (= unilineal) joint families of three generations when they, respectively, assume the role of grandparents.
5.) From the collateral joint families formed according to Hypothesis 3, the couples form nuclear families when they, respectively, assume the role of parents, but their nuclear families turn eventually into unilateral joint families of three generations when, in due course, they assume the role of grandparents.

6.) From the collateral joint families formed according to Hypothesis 3, the sons form nuclear families (of the conjugal variety) when they begin to live with their wives, but their nuclear families (which, in due course, assume the structure of the parent(s)-child(ren) variety) turn eventually into unilateral joint families of three generations when the man and his wife assume the role of grandparents.

7.) From the nuclear families formed according to Hypothesis 5, which in due course turn into unilateral joint families of two generations, each son and his wife form a new nuclear family when they themselves become parents, except (ideally) the couple of the youngest son, who with his wife and progeny stays with the parental couple and thus maintains the joint structure of two or three generations.

8.) From the nuclear families formed according to Hypothesis 6, each son forms a nuclear family when he begins to live with his wife, except (ideally) the youngest son who with his wife and progeny stays with his parents and, thus, maintains the joint structure of two or three generations.

9.) From the nuclear families formed according to Hypothesis 5, which in due course turn into unilateral joint families of two generations, the sons and their wives form separate nuclear families when they themselves become parents, and the process is repeated in successive generations without any son's couple staying with his parental couple once he has children.

10.) From the nuclear families formed according to Hypothesis 6, each son forms a nuclear family when he begins to live with his wife, and the process is repeated in successive generations without any son's couple staying with his parental couple.

Diagram 4.1 shows the extension of a patrilineal-patrivirilocal joint family according to Hypothesis 1, based on the demographic profile of Indian society. In the diagram, the *deceased* couples are denoted by the symbol c' within brackets, those still living couples of different branches in the family are denoted by the symbol a within parentheses, and all *subsidiary* couples are denoted by the symbol s within parentheses. It is schematically assumed that all the subsidiary couples are represented by living persons, i.e., the husband and/or the wife.

We must also point out that the suffix to the symbol for each couple is the age group of the husband. For example, B2Z2 ($= a_{70}$) denotes that the couple is represented by the 65–69 year old wife of B2Z2 whose age group of 70–74 signifies (theoretically) that he is dead. Correspondingly, B2Z1Z1 ($= a_{50}$), say, would denote that the couple is represented either by the husband belonging to the age group 50–54 or his wife belonging to the age group 45–49, or both. In the same manner, the unmarried (and assumed living) family members are denoted by the previously noted symbols Z for son and D for daughter, with their

Diagram 4.1
Hypothetical Patrilineal-Patrivirilocal Joint Family Structure According to Demographic Profile of Indian Society.

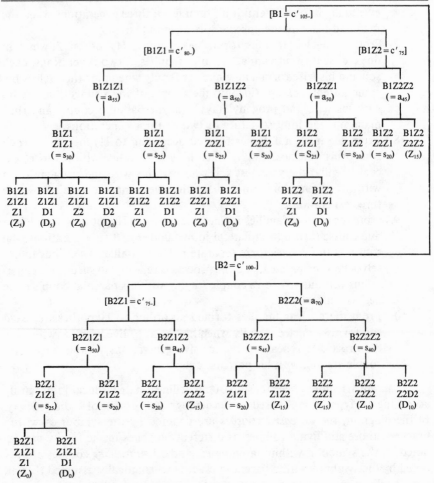

Note: c' = deceased couple [bracketed]
    a = still living principal couples
    s = living subsidiary couples
subscript n = age (by half-decades)

age suffixes, within parentheses. For example, Z_{15} would denote a male child in the age group of 15–19 years; D_0 would denote a female child in the age group of 0–4 years.

Now, it will be seen from Diagram 4.1 that Hypothesis 1 stands for the extreme possibility of retaining the joint family system in India according to the traditional image. The family would be of four generations and contain even the fourth-degree cousins related to Ego as father's father's father's father's brother's son's son's son or daughter (e.g., the relation between B1Z1Z1Z1Z1 and B2Z1Z1Z1Z1 in Diagram 4.1).

Against this maximum possible articulation of the joint family structure, which is hardly ever mentioned for the Indian family, we may describe the operation of the cut-off points according to Hypotheses 2 through 10. Diagram 4.1 will thus be employed to denote the sequential process toward nuclearization of the joint family system.

According to Hypothesis 2, three collateral joint families will be formed out of that of B1 and B2 couples in Diagram 4.1. The descendants of the deceased B1Z1 couple will form one collateral family, the descendants of the deceased B1Z2 couple will form another, while the descendants of the deceased couple B2Z1 along with those of the still existing couple of B2Z2 will form the third collateral joint family.

According to Hypothesis 3, three collateral joint families and one unilateral one will be formed out of the collateral joint family of B1 and B2 couples in Diagram 4.1. The B1Z1Z1 and B1Z1Z2 couples will together form a collateral family, the B1Z2Z1 and B1Z2Z2 couples will form a second collateral family, the B2Z1Z1 and B2Z1Z2 couples will form a third collateral family, while the B2Z2 couple will form a unilateral joint family.

According to Hypothesis 4, five 3-generational and two 2-generational unilateral joint families will be formed out of the collateral joint family of B1 and B2 couples in Diagram 4.1. The B1Z1Z1, B1Z1Z2, B1Z2Z1, B2Z1Z1, and B2Z2 couples will form 5 unilateral joint families of 3 generations each, while the B1Z2Z2 and B2Z1Z2 couples will be left to represent 2 unilateral joint families of 2 generations each.

Hypotheses 2 through 4, thus, refer to an unconditional incidence of the joint family structure but under successively more restricted extension. In other words, the joint family system remains while the joint family structures are successively attenuated. In this context, Hypotheses 2 and 3 coincide more or less with the stipulations of the ancient lawgivers like Kautilya and Manu, as we have mentioned in Chapter 3 (Shamasastry 1951: 181-182; Buehler 1886: 366-367). Hypothesis 4, on the other hand, supports the common image of the "patriarchal" (or "patripotestal") joint family in modern India.

According to Hypotheses 5 and 6, the same five 3-generational and two 2-generational unilateral joint families will be formed out of the collateral joint family of B1 and B2 as described for Hypothesis 4. In the case of these two hypotheses, however, the joint family structure will undergo a qualitative change, and not merely a formal attenuation as in the case of Hypotheses 2 through 4. The joint families break up and produce nuclear families, although the latter will eventually turn into joint families. Thus the joint family system remains viable according to these two hypotheses, while the joint family structures pass through a nuclear phase.

This, however, may create the illusion of a nuclearization of the joint family system. We notice in this context that the two possibilities conveyed by Hypotheses 5 and 6 have often been mentioned in late nineteenth and early twentieth century literature to indicate the imminent breakup of the joint family system. It will be noticed that Hypothesis 5 emphasizes the parental-filial relationship of the son to his sons more that his filial-parental relationship with respect to his own parents, and Hypothesis 6 emphasizes the conjugal relationship of this male. These two tendencies have been particularly stressed as the cause for the process of nuclearization.

Hypotheses 5 and 6, however, would appear to be inconsistent with regard to a systematic formation of nuclear families by the sons after they themselves become parents or just after their effective marriage. Prima facie it appears that if the desire of the sons in the family to form nuclear families supersedes that of their fathers to become grandfathers, the joint family system is no longer viable. On the other hand, if the desires of the fathers as grandfathers supersedes that of their sons, there would be no nuclear formation in the transition between joint family structures. The two contrary tendencies thus seem to nullify Hypotheses 5 and 6.

Incidentally, the two tendencies may not be a matter of mere mental orientation of the people in a tradition–modernity schema, which is often employed as the yardstick to explain the contradictions in Indian family organization. The two tendencies may be dictated by the objective circumstances, too, under the given social situation of marginal living conditions for the mass of the people; for example, concern for the wellbeing of the family of procreation may encourage the former tendency, and the need for survival in old age the latter (see R. Mukherjee 1976a). One observable or deducible context is thus seen to generate others, some of which may be inferential to begin with. All of them, however, should be systematically integrated into the framework of classification we have outlined in Chapter 2, which we shall briefly demonstrate later while examining the utility of the population approach to classification as an aid to deduction.

From that perspective, we should first take note of the already mentioned apparently contradictory tendencies, both of which have been noted in contemporary Indian society. Indeed, the alternative explanations for the nuclearization of the joint family in India stem from these spontaneous observations, which have three seemingly incongruent features:

1.) The sons tend to move out of the paternal joint family after becoming husbands or husbands-fathers.
2.) The parents seldom form the mere conjugal units that would more logically follow from all the sons' leaving the paternal family after becoming husbands or husbands-fathers.
3.) The parent(s) remain, instead, with one son at least, who becomes in due course a husband and a husband-father, and thus the parental

couple becomes the symbol representing the 2 or 3-generational unilateral joint family structure.

Hypotheses 7 and 8 have therefore been formulated in the light of our description of the demographic profile of Indian society and our contextual presentation of the collateral joint family of the B1 and B2 couples in Diagram 4.1. These two hypotheses, which are schematically consistent with the incongruities mentioned above, would remove any inconsistency in the formulation of Hypotheses 5 and 6 while retaining their crucial indication of the viability of the joint family system. It should, however, be borne in mind that Hypotheses 5 and 6 may not be exclusively operative in a society but that they can function along with other structures to retain the joint family system (e.g., Hypotheses 2–4) or to allow for the emergence of the nuclear family system—*conditionally* (which is germane to Hypotheses 7 and 8) or *unconditionally* (as indicated by Hypotheses 9 and 10).

According to Hypotheses 7, two 3-generational and six 2-generational unilateral joint families will be formed out of the collateral joint family of the B1 and B2 couples in Diagram 4.1, while producing simultaneously four nuclear families. The B1Z1Z1 and B2Z2 couples will form the two 3-generational unilateral joint families. The B1Z1Z2, B1Z2Z1, B1Z2Z2, B2Z1Z1, B2Z1Z2, and B2Z2Z1 couples will form six 2-generational collateral joint families, since those of their married children who have children of their own, meanwhile, the B1Z1Z1Z1, B1Z1Z2Z1, B1Z2Z1Z1, and B2Z1Z1Z1 couples, live as nuclear families.

According to Hypothesis 8, two 3-generational and three 2-generational unilateral joint families will be formed out of the collateral joint family of the B1 and B2 couples in Diagram 4.1, while it simultaneously produces ten nuclear families. The formation of 3-generational unilateral joint families will be the same as described for Hypothesis 7. Out of the six 2-generational unilateral joint families described for Hypothesis 7, however, those of B1Z2Z2, B2Z1Z2, and B2Z2Z1 couples will now turn nuclear. Of the children of these three couples, the B1Z2Z2Z1, B2Z1Z2Z1, and B2Z2Z1Z1 couples will form their own respective nuclear families. The number of 2-generational unilateral joint families will thus be reduced by three while the 4 nuclear families described for Hypothesis 7 will gain the 6 additional families to make a total of ten.

Hypotheses 7 and 8 thus denote the viability of the joint family system in the same manner as Hypotheses 5 and 6 do, but they provide, at the same time, for a systematic emergence of the nuclear family system in the society as a concomitant to the joint family system. This concomitant relationship, however, may not be appreciated because what is immediately observable is the incidence of nuclear families. It is also noticeable in this context that, as noted for Hypotheses 5 and 6, the role of a man in the family claims more (and eventually decisive) attention as a father and/or a husband rather than as a son. Various psychological, economic, or other kinds of reasons are therefore adduced to explain what is usually regarded as a clear indication of the process of nuclearization of the joint family system.

That process, however, is registered only by Hypotheses 9 and 10, which denote the systematic and unconditional replacement of the joint family system by the nuclear. In these two contexts, the disintegration of the joint family system (and not merely the breakup of joint family structures) is not a matter of assumption (as it is with Hypotheses 5 and 6) or of interpretation (as it is with Hypotheses 7 and 8). The joint families are inexorably and irrevocably turned into nuclear ones, according to Hypotheses 9 and 10.

The ten hypotheses may therefore be regarded as creating a logically consistent and sequentially arranged series of context variables which, at one extreme, explain the immutability of the joint family system (Hypotheses 2–4), pass through the intermediate stages of explaining the mutable viability of the system (Hypotheses 5 and 6) and the assured viability of the joint family system in terms of mutuality with the nuclear family system (Hypotheses 7 and 8), and terminate, at the other extreme, by explaining the unequivocal replacement of the joint family system by the nuclear (Hypotheses 9 and 10). Hence, against the context of these ten hypotheses we should examine the text of probable and actual incidences of different forms of family structure in contemporary Indian society.

4   CONTEXT AND TEXT

For each one of the Hypotheses 1–10 we can estimate the probable incidence of different varieties of the joint and nuclear family structures on the basis of a model constructed with reference to the demographic profile of Indian society (see Appendix 4A). The results are given in Table 4.1 and summarized in Table 4.2, of which the following characteristics are particularly worthy of note:

1.) Even if the "traditional" image of the Indian joint family were rigorously enforced in society (Hypothesis 1), one-tenth of all families would be nuclear.
2.) A quarter to one-third of the total family units may be nuclear, even though the joint family system operates in society without any attempt to form nuclear families (Hypotheses 2–4).
3.) More than half of the total family units may be nuclear and yet the joint family system may persist (Hypotheses 5 and 6).
4.) The incidence of even two-thirds or three-quarters of all families as nuclear does not lead to the inference that the joint famiy system is no longer viable in Indian society (Hypotheses 7 and 8).

Table 4.1.
Hypothetical Distribution of Family Structures in India

Form of family structure	Probable Incidence (in Percentages) of Family Structures According to Each Hypothesis									
	1	2	3	4	5	6	7	8	9	10
(1)	(2)	(3)	(4)	(5)	(6)	(7)	(8)	(9)	(10)	(11)
	%	%	%	%	%	%	%	%	%	%
4-generation collateral joint	4	1	–	–	–	–	–	–	–	–
3-generation collateral joint	23	23	23	–	–	–	–	–	–	–
2-generation collateral joint	45	31	31	25	–	–	–	–	–	–
1-generation collateral joint	8	3	3	2	2	–	2	–	1	–
3-generation unilateral joint	6	8	9	40	32	31	16	15	–	–
2-generation unilateral joint	3	4	4	9	12	12	18	7	15	–
Nuclear family Parent-child	6	18	18	15	44	43	56	60	65	64
of the Conjugal	1	3	3	2	4	6	3	13	16	32
variety: Sibling	4	9	9	7	6	6	5	4	3	3
Nonfamilial Unit	–	0	0	0	0	2	0	1	0	1
Total	100	100	100	100	100	100	100	100	100	100

Note: 0 denotes less than 1% incidence.

Against such inferred incidence, we should examine the actual incidence of different forms of family structure in contemporary India. Appropriate data, however, are scarce because the population approach has rarely been adopted to classify family structures, although, as elsewhere, there are many family studies from different parts of India over time. Nevertheless, we see from the sample of 59,691 families from virtually all parts of India summarized in Table 4.3 that the percentage incidence of the nuclear family among all family units varies from 35% to 65%, with a central tendency around 56%. The details given in Table 4.3 thus suggest that there is no prima facie case to infer the nuclearization of the joint family system in India in terms of forming locally functioning coresident and commensal kin groups.

We may point out once again that the fact of disintegration of the joint family system cannot be established nor the process of nuclearization assumed merely from the presence of nuclear families at any single point in time or from the *gradual* rise in that incidence over a period of time. Both developments require that critical limits of that incidence in a society be surpassed in accordance with the phenomena related to the formation and articulation of the family in a given social milieu. The processual limit in contemporary Indian society, as we find from the application of the series of context variables, is reached when only about 15% of the families remain joint (Hypothesis 9), and not before. The fact of disintegration of the Indian joint family system is

Table 4.2.
Hypothetical Distribution of Family Structures in India under Alternative Modes of Nuclearization

Possible modes of nuclearization of the Patrilineal-Patrivirlocal Joint Family System	Hypothesis	Probable Incidence (in Percentages) of Family Structures				
		Joint		Nuclear	Non-familial	Total
		Collateral	Unilateral			
(1)	(2)	(3)	(4)	(5)	(6)	(7)
		%	%	%	%	%
Extreme probability of retaining joint family system	H1	80	9	11	–	100
Unconditional presence of joint structures but of successively restricted extension	H2	58	12	30	0	100
	H3	57	13	30	0	100
	H4	27	49	24	0	100
Conditional persistence of joint structures but nuclear families in transitional life-stages	H5	2	44	54	0	100
	H6	–	43	55	2	100
Maintenance of joint family system with conditional nuclearization	H7	2	34	64	0	100
	H8	–	22	77	1	100
Unconditional and systematic nuclearization	H9	1	15	84	0	100
	H10	–	–	99	1	100
Average for all hypotheses		25	27	48	0	100

Note: 0 denotes less than 1% incidence.

established when the occurrence of joint families becomes a matter of extraneous variation around the null point of zero incidence of joint structures (Hypothesis 10). Clearly, the typological approach to classification cannot but fail to explicate this systemic relation between the relevant context and measure variables.

Table 4.3, however, does not lead us to the contrary inference that the joint family system is an immutable phenomenon in contemporary India. None of the 31 communities of people described in the table registers such a low inci-

Table 4.3
Percentage of Nuclear Families in Various Indian Areas, 1937-1966

State	Community	Sample of Family Units	Percentage of nuclear Families	Date of Enquiry
(1)	(2)	(3)	(4)	(5)
		N	%	Year
Andhra	People of 1 village	195	43	1950s
Assam	Rabhas in 2 villages	160	54	1955
Bihar	Giridih townspeople	3,453	45	1958
Delhi	All citizens of Delhi	14,644	61	1955-57
	Rampur villagers	148	45	1950s
Gujarat	Mahuva townspeople	413	47	1956-58
	Navsari townspeople	315	49	1951
	Surat District villagers	847	37	1951
Kashmir	Pandits of 1 village	84	38	1957
Kerala	Nayars in 2 census tracts	124	35	1955-60
Madhya Pradesh	Peoples of 1 city, 2 towns and 23 villages	2,314	52	1958
Madras	1 Tanjore village Brahmins	28	46	1950s
Maharashtra	Pune citizens	3,882	57	1937
	Pune citizens	4,988	56	1954
	Phalton townspeople	695	50	1961-62
	People of 23 villages	717	48	1961-62
Mysore	People of 2 towns and 16 villages	537	37	1951
	People of 39 villages	527	36	1951
Orissa	Brahmins in 1 village	155	43	1955
	Thetaris in 22 villages	151	60	1959
	Hill Bhuiyas in 6 villages	111	58	1955
Rajasthan	People of 120 villages	2,946	51	1961-62
Uttar Pradesh	Kanpur factory workers	355	50	1953-54
	People of 4 villages	380	47	1950-60
	Tharus in 33 villages	806	52	1948-50
West Bengal	Rural sector	653	50	1950
	Rural sector	547	58	1956
	Rural sector	2,626	65	1960-61
	All sectors	1,734	54	1955-56
	All sectors	4,119	62	1960-61
	All sectors	11,037	57	1965-66
Average for 31 communities		59,707	56	1937-66

Source: R. Mukherjee 1975b: 37; 1977a: 114.

dence of nuclear families as would conform to the traditional image of the Indian family according to Hypothesis 1. On the contrary, all of them indicate situations beyond the scope of the restricted but unconditional propagation of the joint family system according to Hypotheses 2-4. However, while only 11 communities demonstrate the situation between the merely conditional persistence of the joint families and their conditional nuclearization (i.e., according to Hypotheses 5 and 6, on the one hand, and Hypotheses 7 and 8, on the other), 20 communities present the situation in between the unconditional and conditional persistence of the joint structures (i.e., according to Hypotheses 2-4, on the one side, and Hypotheses 5-6, on the other).

We must also bear in mind that the percentage values in Table 4.3 may not refer exclusively to one or another of the hypotheses we have formulated. Different hypotheses may operate with reference to different social groups, all of which constitute a community, and thus produce the average values given in the table. We should therefore examine the actual incidence of different varieties of the joint and nuclear families in Indian society in the context of the variations noted with reference to the hypotheses. But that would require the adoption of the population approach to classify family structures so that a course of research could be undertaken on knowable variations in the persistence or probable disintegration of the joint family system in contemporary India.

The scope for such a course of research is indicated by some data available on the incidence of different forms of the joint and nuclear family structures in India. Table 4.4 shows that for 6 communities (2 in Mysore) from the east, south, and north of India (out of the total of 31 communities in Table 4.3) the role of Hypotheses 1-3 is virtually zero. Less comprehensive data for some other communities point to the same situation (R. Mukherjee 1975b: 39-41).

Table 4.4.
Percentage Distribution of Family Structures in Five Indian Regions, 1951-1961

Form of Family Structure	West Bengal 1960-61 (n = 4482)	Mysore 1951 (n = 1064)	Orissa Thetaris 1959 (n = 151)	Orissa Bhuiyas 1955 (n = 111)	Kashmir Pandits 1957 (n = 84)
(1)	(2)	(3)	(4)	(5)	(6)
	%	%	%	%	%
Collateral joint (total)	13	20	9	14	30
of: 4 generations	0	–	–	–	–
3 generations	3	–	–	3	12
2 generations	9	16	7	9	18
1 generation	1	4	2	2	–
Unilateral joint (total)	28	43	31	28	32
of: 4 generations	1	–	–	1	–
3 generations	22	19	21	15	21
2 generations	5	24	10	12	11
Nuclear	59	37	60	58	38
Total	100	100	100	100	100

Note: 0 denotes less than 1% incidence
Source: R. Mukherjee 1975b: 39

Moreover, from the possible emergence of different varieties of family structures according to Hypotheses 1-10, we can estimate the incidence of families recording inter-cousin relationships of successive orders of maximum distance. These estimates substantiate that Hypotheses 1-3 are of no relevance to family organization in contemporary India. The estimation procedure is the same as mentioned earlier with reference to the presence of a fourth degree inter-cousin relationship to Ego as father's father's father's father's brother's son's son's son's son, that is, F^4BZ^4 between B1Z1Z1Z1Z1 and B2Z1Z1Z1Z1 of Diagram 4.1 It is thus seen from Table 4.5, prepared on this basis, that second-degree cousins should occur in half of the joint families, according to Hypothesis 1, and in a quarter of the joint families, according to Hypotheses 2 and 3. The presence of second-degree cousins in a family, however, is now a rare phenomenon in Indian society.

Hypothesis 4 may operate to an extent, and thus indicate the occurrence of some 2-generational collateral families in Table 4.4 in the light of a negligible incidence of Hypotheses 1-3. It is likely, however, to be of minimal importance to contemporary India, as we see from the 24% incidence of nuclear families predicted from this hypothesis (vide Table 4.2) and the much higher actual incidences reported on Table 4.3.

Even so, we should recall that while Hypotheses 1-4 predict the perpetuation of the joint family system, Hypothesis 4 is clearly distinguished from Hypotheses 1-3. The first three hypotheses postulate the retention of brothers' collateral joint family of orientation with reference to the root couple, i.e., their ancestral family. Hypothesis 4, on the other hand, emphasizes the formation of unilateral joint families of procreation by breaking away from the collateral family of brothers.

We may also recall that the family of procreation, as against the family of orientation, is the motif of Hypotheses 5-10. This shift in perspective on family organization has given rise to the notion of the nuclearization of the joint family system in India. From this perspective, therefore, Hypothesis 4 acquires a distinctive meaning, and it is worthy of note that such a family process has a role to play in contemporary family organization in India, whatever may be the magnitude of that role.

Hypotheses 5 and 6 (perhaps the former more than the latter) appear to be definitely operative and probably dominate the Indian social scene. With virtually no support for Hypotheses 1-3 in contemporary family organization in India, the prevailing role of Hypothesis 5, the accompanying role of Hypothesis 6, and the attenuated role of Hypothesis 4 can yield the kind of distribution found in Table 4.3: namely, 17 out of 31 communities register 35 to 50% incidence of nuclear families, 11 communities register between 51 and 60%, but only 3 communities between 61 and 65%. Moreover, the relevance of Hypotheses 4, 5, and 6 corresponds best to the empirical data given in Table 4.4. It is also noteworthy with reference to Table 4.5 that the joint families would not involve any inter-cousin relationship, according to Hypotheses 7-9. This

Table 4.5.

Percentage Distribution of Maximum Joint-Family Collateral Extensions in Indian Families According to Various Hypotheses

Hypothesis	F^4BZ^4	F^3BZ^3	F^2BZ^2	FBZ	No inter-cousin relation	Total
(1)	(2)	(3)	(4)	(5)	(6)	(7)
	%	%	%	%	%	%
1	4	20	54	17	5	100
2			26	55	19	100
3			24	57	19	100
4				65	35	100
5				47	53	100
6				49	51	100
7, 8, 9, 10					100	100

Note: F^4BZ^4 = Father's father's father's father's brother's son's son's son's son or daughter; other inter-cousin relationships are denoted similarly.

condition is not generally met with in contemporary India, while Hypotheses 5 and 6 refer to first degree-cousins who are commonly found in present-day Indian joint families.

As we have noted, Hypotheses 5 and 6 demonstrate that the joint family system can remain viable in a society even though the joint family structures pass through a nuclear phase in between the families of orientation and procreation. In terms of the viability of the joint family system, Hypotheses 7 and 8 are allied to the preceding two, but they do not indicate the same conditions of viability. They place the joint family in a concomitant relation with the emergent nuclear family system in society (not the mere incidence of nuclear families in transit between joint family forms). The inference one may therefore draw from this application of the population approach to classification is the need for further investigation into the operation of the joint family system in contemporary India. The crucial question, however, would not be its possible but not probable disintegration in the near future, but: does the joint family system operate by itself, albeit in its most attenuated form, or by accepting a mutually supportive relationship with the nuclear family system?

We thus enter into an area of knowable variations which the typological approach to classification has failed to identify. In that perspective we find that Hypothesis 7 is probably beginning to be relevant particularly in those communities that record an overall incidence of nuclear families above 55% of the total. Out of 31 in Table 4.1, 9 communities are thus characterized. It would not be possible to account for their substantive incidence of nuclear families in terms of the decreasing role of Hypothesis 4 and the dominant role of Hypothesis 5. Hypothesis 6, and more so Hypotheses 8–10, would, however, be inapplicable to the contemporary Indian situation because the latter three hypotheses would require a preponderance of nuclear families, and all these four hypotheses refer to an appreciable incidence of old couples living alone. Neither of the two is the essential characteristic of contemporary family organization among any community of people in India.

5 CLASSIFICATION AND RESEARCH

The inference we have drawn with respect to the persistence of the joint family system in India—in some sectors of the society in the most attenuated form of the joint structures (Hypothesis 4) and by increasingly accepting mutuality with the nuclear family system in other sectors (vide Hypothesis 5 and, to an extent, Hypothesis 7)—is supported by the deductions we can make from the already mentioned large-scale sample survey data for West Bengal during 1946-66. The deductions are based on the information obtained from the 1960-61 survey, which was specifically designed to elicit variations in family structures, and the corresponding data obtained from the surveys conducted with other purposes in view during 1946-47, 1951, 1955-56, and 1965-66. All these survey data were dealt with by the population approach to classification, and a course of analysis was carried out on that basis to ascertain the essential characteristics of variations in family structures, their interrelationship with other societal phenomena, and the trend of these variations and interrelations during 1946-66 (R. Mukherjee 1977a). The study elicited the following crucial characteristics of family organization in West Bengal society:

1. More than four-fifths of the nuclear families are of the parent(s)-child(ren) variety, one-tenths of the conjugal (husband–wife) variety, and less than 2 per cent of the sibling variety. Apart from the sibling families, in all other nuclear families the role of the head of the family household—who is most frequently a male and the principal (or the only) provider for the family—is that of husband-father. In other words, the West Bengal nuclear family, the incidence of which is slightly higher than that of the extended family (Table 4.3), is the family of procreation of the male progenitor who has the privilege of running the family and the obligation to provide for the family members.

2. When the children in the nuclear families are effectively married, the daughters move out of the families in conformity with the patrilineal-patrivirilocal pattern of family organization in society. In many cases, the sons do not form separate (nuclear) families of procreation; at any rate, not all the sons. At least one of the sons continues to live in the parental family after his effective marriage. Otherwise, we cannot account for 30.82% ± 1.61 of the patrilineal-patrivirilocal joint families in 1960-61 being of the 2-generation structure, in which the role of the head is most frequently that of father.

3. Essentially, however, the patrilineal-patrivirilocal joint families of West Bengal are of a 3-generation structure; in 1960–61, 64.36% ± 1.23 of all such families. The role of the head in these families is equally likely to be in the hands of the "grandfather and father" (i.e., de facto and de jure head) or the "father and son" (i.e., de facto head). Very seldom is the "son and grandson" or any other the head. Thus the joint family in West Bengal is basically a unilateral family of procreation, in which the headship may pass from father to son when the former becomes very old.

4. One-generational patrilineal-patrivirilocal joint families, which must be collateral, occur as rarely as the already mentioned sibling variety of the nuclear family: in 1960–61, 2.24% ± 0.69 of all such joint families. In these families, the role of the head as a "brother and cousin" or only as a cousin is absolutely minimal. This means that these families represent the truncated form of the 2-generation joint families of procreation, just as the sibling families represent the truncated form of the nuclear family of procreation, with no parental couple. They thus denote variations around the central tendency to form, eventually, the 3-generation unilateral joint family of procreation.

5. The 4-generation patrilineal-patrivirilocal joint families are as rare as the 1-generation ones: in 1960–61, 2.58% ± 0.68 of all such families. Significantly, however, the role of the head in these families is predominantly as "grandfather, father, and son," which is in conformity with the form of 3-generation unilateral families of procreation.

6. Variations occur, of course, from this central tendency to form the nuclear family of procreation and then have it evolve into the unilateral joint family of procreation, or to retain the latter without any nuclear transition phase. These variations, however, do not assume any pattern or patterns. The collateral families thus formed account for one-third of the total number of patrilineal-patrivirilocal joint families. But frequently these are of a 2-generation structure, and only occasionally the role of the head in all these collateral families is as an uncle or, conversely, a nephew. This suggests that one or more brothers of the head may remain attached to the latter's joint family of procreation until the brothers set up their own families similarly.

7. As we mentioned in Chapter 3, 29% of the extended families in 1960–61 West Bengal did not conform to the patrilineal-patrivirilocal pattern, but also not to other patterns. With reference to the *core* organization as formed by their heads, we find that 44.79% ± 3.00 of them had formed the unilateral joint family of procreation of the patrilineal-patrivirilocal pattern, and 41.34% ± 3.17 the parent(s)—child(ren) variety of the nuclear family. We find, furthermore, that in more than half of these extended families the joint or the nuclear family of procreation of the heads *deviated* from that pattern

because of the presence of widowed, separated, or divorced daughters of the family, with or without their children. In the remaining families, mostly the head's or his wife's widowed mother or sister, with or without their children, were attached to the family of procreation of the heads'. All of which means that like the collateral joint families of the patrilineal-patrivirilocal pattern, these extended families also represent variations around the central tendency in West Bengal society to form patrilineal-patrivirilocal *but* unilateral joint families.

8. This tendency of family organization in West Bengal did not change over the 20 years between 1946 and 1966, a time period which covered nearly a generation just after the Second World War and saw the emergence of a new perspective on the society and the people in India and the rest of the Third World. The effort to form the joint family of procreation remained unabated, just as the association of specific social groups with the extended families held good: namely, it was most marked in that segment of the landed gentry which is composed of those literates who do not belong to the upper echelon of the caste hierarchy, and the least marked in that segment of the nonagricultural community which is composed of illiterate gentry and literate commoners. There was a slight rise in the incidence of nuclear family structures during 1946–66, but that could be accounted for as random fluctuations or because of some mobility from the category of caste-inferior landed gentry to nonagricultural categories (or to the rank of agricultural commoner) and more by the spread of literacy among the nonagricultural gentry.

9. The social structural changes over the 20 years could imply that the nuclear family organization is forced on society by economic changes and the movement of people from the rural to urban areas: for example, with the peasant proprietors becoming sharecroppers and agricultural wage laborers, and the neccesity many felt to move to urban areas where nonagricultural occupations are more available but which may also demand minimal literacy. A similar conclusion to the one drawn by Morrison from his typological study of a Maharashtrian village seemed, therefore, to be appropriate. Over the 20 years, however, the collateral joint families and the nonfamilial units (mostly males) were noticeably more present in the urban than in rural areas; but either arrangement was a stopgap for the persons concerned. The mental construct of these urban nonfamilial units and the urban collateral family members has been of the patrilineal-patrivirilocal joint family, for whose sustenance they worked in a city or town and either lived alone or with their kinsmen—each of whom had a family elsewhere. And, correspondingly, over the 20 years in rural areas, the incidence of nonfamilial units decreased, while the joint family of procreation of the heads was more pronounced during the 10 years ending in 1966 than in the previous 10 years from 1946 to 1956.

One may, therefore, deduce from these features of family organization in West Bengal that from the null incidence of persons living alone as nonfamilial units to the persistence of patrilineal-patrivirilocal joint families, passing through a phase of nuclear formation in many instances, the motif is the forming of the joint family of procreation—immediately, eventually, or potentially.

Thus, by applying the population approach to classification in order to systemize the context variables and integrate them with the relevant measure variables, we arrive at the important suggestion to include knowable variations in the Indian family. Whether or not a man is born in a joint or a nuclear family, he usually separates from his family of orientation (which is or has become a joint one) when he becomes a husband-father and occasionally when just a husband; but he forms a joint family of procreation in the course of time either with all his sons (Hypotheses 5-6) or with at least one of them, who remains with him and/or his wife, while the other sons leave this family of orientation when they become husbands-fathers in their turn (Hypothesis 7).

The suggestion, which should also incorporate Hypothesis 4 on the forming of unilateral instead of collateral joint family, leads us to inquire into the *what, how,* and *why* of the cut-off points which maintain the viability of the joint family system with conditional nuclearization. First, therefore, we ask the question: Why do the relationships referring to the family of procreation of a male play the dominant role at present instead of those referring to his family of orientation which are supposed to be traditionally ordained? Have the virtual disappearance of collateral ownership of landed property, the disintegration of a subsistence economy of agriculture and craft production, the diminishing control by the customary patrilineal family—kinship base of commercial establishments, etc., played any role in the almost total disappearance of collateral joint families except among some landlord, artisan, or large-scale business families?

We notice that the marriage of male siblings, and particularly their attainment of parenthood, set into motion divisive forces rather than other relational processes in a family unit. We ask, therefore, the follow-up questions: Does it occur because of the tension between the mother-in-law and the daughter-in-law? Equally or more important, does it refer to the sibling rivalry which is roused with the presence of wives among the siblings and reaches the critical point when the parental-filial relation emerges among them? Does that indicate that the possibility of continuing with the joint family system becomes strongest after all but one son has left the family of orientation with the attainment of parenthood?

These questions generate another set of questions: Is this course of variation in family structures dictated by a change in the cultural—psychological orientation of the people commensurate with the tradition—modernity shifts? Alternatively, or more effectively, does this course of variation denote the impact of an expanding monetized economy on the family, which affects interpersonal behavior and which spreads those cultural values associated with contractual relations rather than those determined by custom? Should we, therefore, search for those forces which operate within the joint family system and denote the diverging roles of the family as a production and a consumption unit with respect to labor force formation in a divisive but unstable economy?

The unstable nature of the economy vis-a-vis family organization in contemporary India is suggested by the fact that so long as the root couple of the unilateral joint family of procreation is represented by its husband and/or wife, the joint structure persists in however attenuated a form. To explain the latter as due to the overpowering influence of traditional values would contradict the fact of nuclearization of joint structures. On the other hand, substantive evidence is there indicating that even at the point of cutting off all its lineal and affinal ramifications, the joint family system persists because the state is not in a position to look after the old and infirm, while only a microscopic minority in India enjoys the privilege of economic security. In the patrilineally oriented society, therefore, the old and infirm parents must be looked after by at least one son (R. Mukherjee 1976a: 35-51).

All such questions and the explanations which lurk behind them should, however, be systematized as alternative sets of hypotheses to be tested for the appraisal of the prime forces in the retention of the joint family system and the prime movers for altering the system. For that purpose, we would be required to adopt the population approach to classification in order that the relevant context and measure variables be systemized and integrated from the grassroots level on up, as we have illustrated in this and the previous chapter. Undertaken in this manner, the course of research should lead us to predict probabilistically what the Indian family will be in the near future.

Basic to this understanding, however, is the confirmation of the suggestion we first made, which emerges from the rudimentary testing of hypotheses on the prevailing forms of family structure in Indian society; namely, while joint families break up, the joint family system does not disintegrate because the nuclear families formed by the breakup of joint families reemerge as joint structures. Only when these contradictory structural movements are duly deduced and inferred, may we pose further questions on what are the societal forces which produce apparently contradictory alignments of the intra-family forces and thus lead to conditional nuclearization but not to the withering away of the joint family system.

Research into the data space thus follows from the classification of knowledge at one stage of its accumulation, and, in turn, yields further knowledge for classification at the next sequential stages of the accumulation of knowledge. The population approach to classification is indispensable to this consistent and systematic endeavor, as it deals with all possible and probable variations in the known and the knowable properties of the phenomenon under investigation. The typological approach, on the other hand, would be quite inadequate in this context, primarily because it is geared to the search for information or data, and not to research in an infinite but enumerable data space.

Classification in social research is, therefore, fundamentally concerned with the relative merits of these two approaches. This is what we have examined in this volume with reference to the concepts of "classification," "social," and "research" in Chapter 1, the appropriate method of classification in social research in Chapter 2, the illustration of the method in Chapter 3, and an example in this chapter of the utility of applying the method to a course of research.

Appendix 4A.
A Probability Model to Estimate the Incidence of Family Structures

Hypothesis 1 can be represented on Diagram 4.1, which shows that the posthumous couples B1 and B2 are in age groups 105–109 and 100–104, respectively; the posthumous couples B1Z1, B1Z2, and B2Z1, and the surviving couple B2Z2 are correspondingly represented by c'_{80}, c'_{75}, c'_{75}, and a_{70}, respectively. The next possible age-determined configuration will therefore be given when the posthumous couple B1Z1 is c'_{75} and the surviving couples B1Z2, B2Z1, and B2Z2 are a_{70}, a_{70}, and a_{65}, respectively, with the posthumous couples B1 and B2 in age groups 100–104 and 95–99. Following this process of successively reducing the age group of B1 and B2, a total of 17 configurations is possible, until the posthumous couples B1 and B2 are in age groups 25–29 and 20–24. A lower age group for B1 will not leave any progeny to continue the family, as the age group of 20-24 for B2 cannot.

For some of these age distributions the direction of the family's structural development will not be given by the a couples B1Z1, B1Z2, B2Z1, and B2Z2, since the posthumous couples B1 and B2 will not be in the age groups of 45–49 years or more and, therefore, their sons will not have formed couples of their own. In these cases, unmarried males and females (denoted by m and f with relevant age suffixes) will have to indicate the direction of the family. On this basis, Table 4A.1 gives all possible age and make-up configurations of family structures for Hypothesis 1.

The configurations of rows 14–17 in Table 4A.1 would be rarely represented because families formed by young unmarried siblings and cousins are seldom found in any society. However, as we are dealing with a hypothetical situation, it is necessary to account for all possible configurations of family structures. Accordingly, we shall estimate the independent occurrence of familial directions in Indian society as denoted by the couples $a_{20}, \ldots a_{70}$, the unmarried males $m_0, \ldots m_{15}$, and unmarried females $f_0, \ldots f_{10}$. We shall not consider f_{15} because, like m_{20}, it denotes a married condition according to the demographic profile of Indian society.[1]

Table 4A.1. Configurations of Family Structure According to Hypothesis 1, with Reference to Age and Marital Status of Sons and Grandsons and Unmarried Daughters of the Deceased Root Couples formed by Brothers (B1 and B2) of a Hypothetical Indian (Joint) Family (Computed From Figures For 1941, 1951, 1961).

Configuration According to Age of B1 Couple	Family Representative (sons and unmarried daughters or grandsons)									B2
	B1Z1	B1Z2	B2Z1	B2Z2	B1Z1Z1	B1Z1Z2	B1Z2Z1	B1Z2Z2	B2Z1Z1	
(1)	(2)	(3)	(4)	(5)	(6)	(7)	(8)	(9)	(10)	
1. $(B1 = c'_{105})$	(c'_{80})	(c'_{75})	(c'_{75})	a_{70}	a_{55}	a_{50}	a_{50}	a_{45}	a_{50}	
2. $(B1 = c'_{100})$	(c'_{75})	a_{70}	a_{70}	a_{65}	a_{50}	a_{45}				
3. $(B1 = c'_{95})$	a_{70}	a_{65}	a_{65}	a_{60}						
4. $(B1 = c'_{90})$	a_{65}	a_{60}	a_{60}	a_{55}						
5. $(B1 = c'_{85})$	a_{60}	a_{55}	a_{55}	a_{50}						
6. $(B1 = c'_{80})$	a_{55}	a_{50}	a_{50}	a_{45}						
7. $(B1 = c'_{75})$	a_{50}	a_{45}	a_{45}	a_{40}						
8. $(B1 = a_{70})$	a_{45}	a_{40}	a_{40}	a_{35}						
9. $(B1 = a_{65})$	a_{40}	a_{35}	a_{35}	a_{30}						
10. $(B1 = a_{60})$	a_{35}	a_{30}	a_{30}	a_{25}						
11. $(B1 = a_{55})$	a_{30}	a_{25}	a_{25}	a_{20}						
12. $(B1 = a_{50})$	a_{25}	a_{20}	a_{20}	m_{15}						
13. $(B1 = a_{45})$	a_{20}	m_{15}	m_{15}	mf_{10}						
14. $(B1 = a_{40})$	m_{15}	mf_{10}	mf_{10}	mf_{5}						
15. $(B1 = a_{35})$	mf_{10}	mf_{5}	mf_{5}	mf_{0}						
16. $(B1 = a_{30})$	mf_{5}	mf_{0}	mf_{0}	–						
17. $(B1 = a_{25})$	mf_{0}	–	–	–						

Note: a   = principal couple   n = age by half decades
        c' = deceased couple
        m = unmarried male
        mf = unmarried male and/or female

Now:

Let P be the total population in a year, and p and and p' the male and female populations, i.e., $P = (p + p')$.

Let p_i be the male population in the ith five-year age-group. The relative incidence of males in the ith age-group is $t_i = (p_i/P)$. Correspondingly, the relative incidence of females in the ith age-group is $t'_i = (p'_i/P)$.

[1] I am indebted to Professor B. P. Adhikari of the Indian Statistical Institute for his guidance in developing the following procedure. The subsidiary conditions and the details of population data, on the basis of which the procedure has been applied to derive Table 4A.2, are not discussed or shown here as not important in the present context. These are, however, available elsewhere (R. Mukherjee 1975b: 12-23).

Let $\bar{t}_i$ and $\bar{t}'_i$ be the average values of t_i and t'_i, respectively, for the number of years for which data are available (viz. 1901–61), so that these two average values may indicate any differential mortality of males and females in the society over some long period.

Then:

The incidence of unmarried sons in the jth age group will be given by t_j for j varying from 0 to 15, and the corresponding incidence of unmarried daughters will be given by t'_j for j varying from 0 to 10.

The incidence of husbands (with or without their wives) in the jth age group will be given by t_j for j varying from 20 to 65, and the corresponding incidence of wives without their husbands will be given by $[t'_{(j-5)}(h_j)]$ for j varying from 20 to 70, where

$$h_j = \sum_{i=20}^{j-5} \bar{t}_i \bigg/ \sum_{i=20}^{65} \bar{t}_i \quad ,$$

since the probability of males (as husbands) not reaching the age level of j will be estimated by h_j and this will be zero for the particular value of $j = 20$.

It follows that the incidence of couples c_j will be given by adding the incidence of husbands with or without their wives to that of the wives without their husbands, so that the total incidence of the familial constituents in society (viz. unmarried sons and daughters and ever-married couples) will be given by

$$F = \Sigma^{15} t_j + \Sigma^{10} t'_j + \Sigma^{70} c_j \quad .$$
$$ j=0 \qquad j=0 \qquad j=20$$

The relative incidence of these familial constituents, which may be denoted by the letters u, v, and w for unmarried sons, unmarried daughters, and ever-married couples, respectively, will be given by

$$u_j = (t_j/F), \text{ for } j \text{ varying from 0 to 15,}$$
$$v_j = (t'_j/F), \text{ for } j \text{ varying from 0 to 10,}$$
$$w_j = (c_j/F), \text{ for } j \text{ varying from 20 to 70.}$$

Each of these familial constituents may occur in society in two ways. It may represent a specific component of the family such as an a couple (as shown in Diagram 4.1) or as the corresponding unmarried son or daughter with parents dead, or it may form a part of the familial segment represented by an a couple. In the former capacity, the familial constituents will be related to the non surviving ($= c'$) parental couples in either of two ways:

1. If the husband of an a couple is the first son of his parents (or if the first-born son or daughter is still unmarried), the nonsurviving parental ($= c'$) couple would belong to the $j + 25$ age-group with reference to the jth age group of this husband, son, or daughter.

2. If the husband, son, or daughter as above is the second son or daughter of a c' couple, that c' couple would belong to the $j + 30$ age group.

Now, since for the present schema the first and the second sons (and daughters) are born when the father is in the age group 25–29 and 30–34, respectively, each category of the familial constituent will be of the "first son/daughter type" or the "second son/daughter type" in the proportion of t_{25} to t_{30}, for each age group j. Hence, in the light of the assumption (validated by the available population data) that the average age composition will be the same at different times in the past, each of the proportions u_j, v_j, and w_j will have to be partitioned in the ratio $t_{25} : t_{30}$.

We find, at the same time, that the probability of a c' couple not reaching the respective age group of $(j + 25)$ or $(j + 30)$—after the husbands have passed the age group of 25–29 or 30–34 in order for them to have produced the first or the second set of sons and daughters—will be given by e_j or e'_j, respectively, where

$$e_j = k \left(\sum_{i=25}^{j+20} \bar{t}_i \right) \left(\sum_{i=25}^{j+15} \bar{t}'_{(i-5)} \right),$$

$$e'_j = k \left(\sum_{i=30}^{j+25} \bar{t}_i \right) \left(\sum_{i=30}^{j+20} \bar{t}'_{(i-5)} \right),$$

k being a constant of probability.

Therefore, the proportion of those familial constituents who are, on the one hand, first son/daughter or second son/daughter types and have, on the other, already lost both parents, will be obtained by multiplying each of the numbers u_j, v_j, and w_j by $(k' \bar{t}_{25} e_j)$ and $(k' \bar{t}30 e'_j)$, respectively. Let the resultant numbers be denoted as u'_j, v'_j, and w'_j.

The constants k and k', however, may be ignored because our ultimate objective is to estimate the distribution of the relative incidence of the a couples and the corresponding unmarried sons and daughters in the society. Hence, the incidence of the these familial constituents, designated as the first- or the second-son type (= Z1 or Z2) and as the first- or second-daughter type (= D1 or D2) of the c' couples, will be given by

$\mathbf{u}'(\mathbf{Z1})_j = \mathbf{u}_j \ (\bar{t}_{25}) \ e_j$, for j varying from 0 to 15,

$\mathbf{u}'(\mathbf{Z2})_j = \mathbf{u}_j \ (\bar{t}_{30}) \ e'_j$, for j varying from 0 to 15,

$\mathbf{v}'(\mathbf{D1})_j = \mathbf{v}_j \ (\bar{t}_{25}) \ e_j$, for j varying from 0 to 10,

$\mathbf{v}'(\mathbf{D2})_j = \mathbf{v}_j \ (\bar{t}_{30}) \ e'_j$, for j varying from 0 to 10,

$\mathbf{w}'(\mathbf{Z1})_j = \mathbf{w}_j \ (\bar{t}_{25}) \ e_j$, for j varying from 20 to 70,

$\mathbf{w}'(\mathbf{Z2})_j = \mathbf{w}_j \ (\bar{t}_{30}) \ e'_j$, for j varying from 20 to 70,

and the total of the incidence of all these familial constituents in the society will be given by R.

It follows that the relative incidence in the society of u'_j as m_j, of v'_j as f_j, and of w'_j as a_j, will be given by:

$$m_j(Z1) = [u'(Z1)_j/R], \qquad m_j(Z2) = [u'(Z2)_j/R],$$
$$f_j(D1) = [v'(D1)_j/R], \qquad f_j(D2) = [v'(D2)_j/R],$$
$$a_j(Z1) = [w'(Z1)_j/R], \qquad a_j(Z2) = [w'(Z2)_j/R].$$

The independent occurrence of the *a* couples and the corresponding unmarried sons and daughters in the society can thus be estimated. This is shown in Table 4A.2 with reference to the years 1941, 1951 and 1961 (the empirical data on variations in family structures in Indian society hardly ever refer to a period earlier than 1941). It will be seen from the table that the corresponding values for the three years are so close that their averages given in columns 8 and 9 of the table can satisfactorily represent the situation for the period 1941–61.

Now, we have seen from Table 4A.1 that for Hypothesis 1 the couples denoted by $a_{70}, \ldots, a_{60}$ and $a_{40}, \ldots, a_{20}$, which are further distinguished as of Z1 and Z2 types, occur twice, respectively. Those unmarried sons and daughters who correspond to all *a* couples also occur twice, respectively. The $a_{55}(Z1)$ couples, on the other hand, occur 3 times, but $a_{55}(Z2)$ only twice; $a_{50}(Z1)$ couples occur 5 times but $a_{50}(Z2)$ only 3 times; and $a_{45}(Z1)$ couples occur twice but $a_{45}(Z2)$ 5 times. Since each of these familial constituents will occur with equal chance in relevant configurations of family structure, its rate of occurrence is obtained by dividing its estimated value in Table 4A.2 by its number of occurrences under different configurations. Table 4A.3 has been prepared on this basis to reproduce the configurations shown in Table 4A.1. The data for this table refer to the average values given in columns 8 and 9 of Table 4A.2 for 1941–1961.

For configuration 1 in Table 4A.3, the minimum value recorded is 0.0034. To this extent, therefore, the family structure left by the couples B1 and B2 will maintain its structural unity at the maximum possible coverage of generational and collateral extension. That is, by representing all the family lines denoted by the *a* couples of B2Z2 (a_{70}), B1Z1Z1 (a_{55}), B1Z1Z2 (a_{50}), B1Z2Z2 (a_{45}), B2Z1Z1 (a_{50}), and B2Z1Z2 (a_{45}), the family will comprise 4 generations and register the fourth degree of inter-cousin relationship. It will, however, be seen from the table that this minimum value is represented by the branch headed by

Table 4A.2.
Independent Probability of First and Second Son and Daughter Born to Couples of Various Ages in India, 1941, 1951, 1961

Age of Family Constituents	1941		1951		1961		Average 1941/1951/ 1961	
	Z1/D1	Z2/D2	Z1/D1	Z2/D2	Z1/D1	Z2/D2	Z1/D1	Z2/D2
(1)	(2)	(3)	(4)	(5)	(6)	(7)	(8)	(9)
a_{70}	.0108	.0066	.0108	.0066	.0114	.0069	.0110	.0067
a_{65}	.0269	.0165	.0284	.0174	.0285	.0173	.0279	.0171
a_{60}	.0377	.0231	.0395	.0241	.0387	.0235	.0386	.0236
a_{55}	.0496	.0303	.0510	.0311	.0504	.0306	.0503	.0307
a_{50}	.0605	.0370	.0620	.0378	.0606	.0368	.0610	.0372
a_{45}	.0709	.0444	.0701	.0439	.0689	.0428	.0700	.0437
a_{40}	.0726	.0478	.0720	.0473	.0711	.0462	.0719	.0471
a_{35}	.0725	.0479	.0699	.0460	.0698	.0457	.0707	.0465
a_{30}	.0639	.0429	.0612	.0411	.0621	.0415	.0624	.0418
a_{25}	.0488	.0334	.0478	.0328	.0488	.0331	.0485	.0331
a_{20}	.0322	.0226	.0332	.0233	.0340	.0237	.0331	.0232
m_{15}	.0230	.0165	.0243	.0174	.0250	.0178	.0241	.0172
m_{10}	.0138	.0104	.0137	.0103	.0144	.0107	.0140	.0105
m_5	.0044	.0037	.0041	.0033	.0044	.0037	.0043	.0036
m_0	.0000	.0000	.0000	.0000	.0000	.0000	.0000	.0000
f_{10}	.0124	.0093	.0128	.0097	.0137	.0102	.0130	.0097
f_5	.0041	.0035	.0040	.0031	.0042	.0035	.0041	.0034
f_0	.0000	.0000	.0000	.0000	.0000	.0000	.0000	.0000

Source: See R. Mukherjee 1975b: 12-23.

the couple B2Z2, and the next higher value is represented by the branches headed by the couples B1Z2Z2 and B2Z1Z2. The difference between the two values (= 0.0054) will therefore point away from the branch headed by the couple B2Z2, removed by demographic exigencies from representing the ancestral family. Proceeding in this manner, and thus successively eliminating the branches headed by B1Z2Z2, B2Z1Z2, B1Z2Z1, B2Z1Z1, and B1Z1Z2, we find that the difference between the highest and the next lower value (= 0.0044) will designate as the representative of the ancestral family the 3-generation joint family of procreation of B1Z1Z1.

The procedure is applicable to all other configurations shown in Table 4A.3, so that the last of the successively subtracted values for each configuration may refer exclusively to the family of procreation of one of the deceased original brothers, and denote thereby: (1) the collateral joint family formed by the sons or grandsons of that deceased brother, (2) the unilateral joint family of procreation of only one of the sons or grandsons, (3) the nuclear family of procreation formed by that son or grandson, (4) the nuclear family of the conjugal variety formed by a son or grandson with his wife only, or (5) the nuclear family formed by a set of unmarried siblings.

Table 4A.3
Probable Occurrence of Surviving Married Sons (and Grandsons) and Unmarried Sons/Daughters of the Deceased Root Couples of Brothers (B1 and B2) under Variable Configurations of Family Structures Shown in Table 4A.1 for Hypothesis 1 (Computed from Figures for 1941, 1951, 1961).

Configurations	Family Representative (See Table 4A.1)									
	B1Z1	B1Z2	B2Z1	B2Z2	B1Z1Z1	B1Z1Z2	B1Z2Z1	B1Z2Z2	B2Z1Z1	B2Z1Z2
(1)	(2)	(3)	(4)	(5)	(6)	(7)	(8)	(9)	(10)	(11)
1	–	–	–	.0034	.0168	.0124	.0122	.0088	.0122	.0088
2	–	.0033	.0055	.0085	.0122	.0087				
3	.0055	.0086	.0140	.0118						
4	.0139	.0118	.0193	.0154						
5	.0193	.0153	.0167	.0124						
6	.0168	.0124	.0122	.0087						
7	.0122	.0087	.0350	.0235						
8	.0350	.0236	.0360	.0233						
9	.0359	.0232	.0353	.0209						
10	.0354	.0209	.0312	.0165						
11	.0312	.0166	.0243	.0116						
12	.0242	.0116	.0165	.0086						
13	.0166	.0086	.0121	.0101						
14	.0120	.0101	.0135	.0035						
15	.0135	.0035	.0042	.0000						
16	.0042	.0000	.0000	–						
17	.0000	–	–	–						

Source: See R. Mukherjee 1975b: 12-23.

Thus, the method evolved to exhibit the operational application of a hypothesis shows that although according to Hypothesis 1 the sons of the deceased couples of the original brothers will sustain the ancestral collateral family, various forms of family structure are bound to emerge in Indian society and some of them will be nuclear. The method is applicable to all hypotheses which may be formulated to specify the cut-off points in the propagation of the patrilineal-patrivirilocal joint family structures in India, and with appropriate computation it can be employed for all variations in the kinship composition of family units in any society. We may therefore employ this method to ascertain the relative incidence of different forms of family structure that are expected to emerge in Indian society according to Hypotheses 2–10 and, for this purpose, use only the average values for 1941–61 as employed to construct Table 4A.3.

For Hypothesis 2, there may be 16 different configurations of family structures, as seen from Table 4A.4, which also gives the rate of incidence of the *a* couples and of the corresponding unmarried sons and daughters for each configuration.

Table 4A.4
Configurations of Family Structure According to Hypothesis 2 and Probabilities of Surviving Married Sons and Grandsons and Unmarried Sons/Daughters of the Deceased Root Couples of Brothers (B1 and B2) (Computed from 1941, 1951, 1961 Averages)

Configurations	Family Representative (B1's or B2's Sons, Grandsons, and Unmarried Daughters)			
	Z1	Z2	Z1Z1	Z1Z2
(1)	(2)	(3)	(4)	(5)
1.	(c'_{75})	a_{70} (.0067)	a_{50} (.0305)	a_{45} (.0219)
2.	a_{70} (.0110)	a_{65} (.0171)		
3.	a_{65} (.0279)	a_{60} (.0236)		
4.	a_{60} (.0386)	a_{55} (.0307)		
5.	a_{55} (.0503)	a_{50} (.0372)		
6.	a_{50} (.0305)	a_{45} (.0218)		
7.	a_{45} (.0700)	a_{40} (.0471)		
8.	a_{40} (.0719)	a_{35} (.0465)		
9.	a_{35} (.0707)	a_{30} (.0418)		
10.	a_{30} (.0624)	a_{25} (.0331)		
11.	a_{25} (.0485)	a_{20} (.0232)		
12.	a_{20} (.0331)	m_{15} (.0172)		
13.	m_{15} (.0241)	mf_{10}(.0202)		
14.	mf_{10}(.0270)	mf_{5} (.0070)		
15.	mf_{5} (.0084)	mf_{0} (.0000)		
16.	mf_{0} (.0000)	–		

Source: See R. Mukherjee 1975b: 12-23.

For Hypothesis 3, the first age-determined configuration will be represented only by column 3 of Table 4A.4, and there will be an additional configuration given by the *a* couples in columns 4 and 5 of Table 4A.4. Otherwise the configurations of family structure according to this hypothesis will be the same as for Hypothesis 2.

For Hypothesis 4, each *a* couple for which *j* varies from 50 to 70 will form unilateral joint family of 3 generations, and each a_{45}(Z2) couple will form a 2-generation unilateral joint family. The incidence rates of these couples, as also for the similar ones of the following hypotheses, will be obtained from Table 4A.2. The remaining *a* couples and the corresponding unmarried sons and daughters will form the configurations 7–16 of Table 4A.4.

For Hypothesis 5, each *a* couple in the age groups 50 to 70 will form a 3-generation unilateral joint family, each a_{45} couple will form a 2-generation unilateral joint family, each *a* couple in the age groups of 25 to 40 will form the parent-child variety of nuclear family, and each a_{20}(Z2) couple will form the conjugal variety of nuclear family. The a_{20}(Z1) couples and the unmarried sons and daughters will form the configurations 12–16 of Table 4A.4.

For Hypothesis 6, the arrangement for Hypothesis 5 will hold except that: (1) each a_{20} (Z1) couple will form the conjugal variety of nuclear family, (2) each m_{15}(Z2) son will be reduced to a nonfamilial unit as having no kin or affines to form a nuclear family or a patrilineal-patrivirilocal joint family, and (3) the remaining unmarried sons and daughters will form configurations 13-16 of Table 4A.4.

For Hypothesis 7, each a couple in the age groups 55 to 70 will form a unilateral joint family of 3 generations, each a_{50} and a_{45} couple will form a 2-generation unilateral joint family, each a couple in the age groups 25 to 40 will form a nuclear family of the parent-child variety, each $a_{20}(Z2)$ couple will form the conjugal variety of nuclear family, and the $a_{20}(Z1)$ couples and the unmarried sons and daughters will form configurations 12-16 of Table 4A.4.

In addition, for this and subsequent hypotheses, more and more subsidiary couples denoted in Diagram 4.1 by the symbol s will lead to different forms of family structure. Thus, in accordance with Hypothesis 7, each $s_{45}(Z1)$ couple will form a unilateral joint family of 2 generations, and each $s(Z1)$ couple in the age groups 25 to 40 will form a nuclear family of the parent-child variety. The incidence of $s(Z1)$ couples of the jth age group will be the same as the incidence of $a(Z1)$ and $a(Z2)$ couples in the age group $j + 25$, for j varying from 25 to 45.

For Hypothesis 8, each a couple in the age groups 55 to 70 will form a unilateral joint family of 3 generations, each a_{50} couple will form a 2-generation unilateral joint family, each a couple in the age groups 25 to 45 will form a nuclear family of the parent-child variety, each a_{20} couple will form a nuclear family of the conjugal variety, each $m_{15}(Z2)$ son will form a nonfamilial unit, and the remaining unmarried sons and daughters will form configurations 13-16 of Table 4A.4. In addition, each $s(Z1)$ couple in the age groups 25 to 45 will form a nuclear family of the parent-child variety, and each $s_{20}(Z1)$ couple will form the conjugal variety of a nuclear family. The incidence of $s(Z1)$ couples for j varying from 25 to 45 will be the same as indicated for Hypothesis 7, but the incidence of $s_{20}(Z1)$ couples will be the sum of the incidence of $a_{45}(Z1 + Z2)$ and $s_{45}(Z1)$ couples.

For Hypothesis 9, each a couple in the age groups 55 to 70 will form a nuclear family of the conjugal variety, each a_{50}, a_{45}, and $s_{45}(Z1)$ couple will form a 2-generation unilateral joint family, each a couple and s couple in the age groups 25 to 40 will form nuclear families of the parent-child variety, each $a_{20}(Z2)$ couple will form the conjugal variety of nuclear family, and the $a_{20}(Z1)$ couples and the unmarried sons and daughters will form configurations 12-16 of Table 4A.4.

For Hypothesis 10, each a couple in the age groups 50 to 70 and each a_{20} and s_{20} couple will form the conjugal variety of nuclear family, each a couple and s couple in the age groups 25 to 45 will form nuclear families of the parent-child variety, $m_{15}(Z2)$ sons will form respective nonfamilial units, and the remaining unmarried sons and daughters will form configurations 13-16 of Table 4A.4. We may note that $s_{45}(Z2)$ couples cannot occur according to the present schema while the incidence of $s(Z2)$ couples for j varying from 20 to 40 will be the sum of the incidence of $a(Z1)$ and $a(Z2)$ couples in $j + 30$ age groups.

References Cited

Amin, S.
1978 *The Arab Nation.* London, ZED Press.

Andrews, F.M.; Morgan, J.N.; Sonquist, J.A.; Klem, L.
1973 *Multiple Classification Analysis.* Ann Arbor, The University of Michigan (Institute for Social Research).

Ariga, K.
1956 'Introduction to the Family System in Japan, China and Korea', pp. 199–207 in: *Transactions of the Third World Congress of Sociology.* Vol. IV. London, International Sociological Association.

Arrighi, G.
1978 *The Geometry of Imperialism: The Limits of Hobson's Paradigm.* London, New Left Books.

Bailey, F.G.
1960 *Tribes, Caste, and Nation.* Manchester, Manchester University Press.

Barnes, J.A.
1960 'Marriage and Residential Community', *American Anthropologist* 62(5) : 850–866.
1972 'Comment' on Mukherjee, R. 'Concepts and Methods for the Secondary Analysis of Variations in Family Structures', *Current Anthropology* 13 (3-4) : 417–443.

Bettelheim, C.
1978 *Class Struggle in the USSR: First Period, 1917–23.* New York, Monthly Review Press.

Birnbaum, A.
   1970   'A Perspective for Strengthening Scholarship in Statistics', *New York Statistician* 22 (1) : 1–2.

Born, Max.
   1956   *Physics in My Generation: A Selection of Papers.* London, Pergamon Press.

Braverman, H.
   1974   *Labor and Monopoly Capital.* New York, Monthly Review Press.

Brenner, R.
   1977   'The Origins of Capitalist Development: A Critique of Neo-Smithian Marxism', *New Left Review,* July-August, pp. 25–92.

Bühler, G.
   1886   *The Laws of Manu.* Oxford, Clarendon Press.

Carr, E.H.
   1964   *What is History?* London, Pelican.

Carstairs, G.M.
   1970   'Overcrowding and Human Aggression', pp. 751–764 in: Graham, H.D.; Gurr, T.D. (eds.) *Violence in America.* New York, Bantam.

Chattopadhyay, K.P.
   1961   'On Definitions, mainly of Family Types', pp. 75–86 in: Madan, T.N.; Sarana, G. (eds.). *Indian Anthropology.* Bombay, Asia Publishing House.

Comte, A.
   1848   *A General View of Positivism.* Stanford (California), Academic Reprints.

Daalder, H.
   1973   'Building consociational nations', pp. 14–31 in: Eisenstadt, S.N.; Rokkan, S. (eds.). *Building States and Nations.* Vol. II. Beverly Hills, Sage.

Davis, H.T.
   1941a   *The Analysis of Economic Time Series.* Bloomington, Principia Press.
   1941b   *The Theory of Econometrics.* Bloomington, Principia Press.

Desai, I.P.
   1964   *Some Aspects of Family in Mahuva.* Bombay, Asia Publishing House.

Deutsch, K.W.
   1963   'Some problems in the study of nation-building', pp. 1–16 in: Deutsch, K.W.; Foltz, W.J. (eds.). *Nation-Building.* New York, Atherton.

Dobzhansky, Th.
   1962   'Comment' on Wiercinski, A.; Bilicki, T. 'Issues in the Study of Race: Two Views from Poland, with Discussion', *Current Anthropology.* 3 (1) : 26–27.

Dube, L.
   1969   *Matriliny and Islam.* Delhi, National Publishing House.

Dublin, L.I.; Lotka, A.J.
1936 *Length of Life: A Study of the Life Tables.* New York, Ronald.

Dutt, N.K.
1931 *Origin and Growth of Caste in India.* Vol. I, London, Kegan Paul, Trench, Truebner.

Einstein, A.
1916 'Obituary' on Ernst Mach, *Phys. Z.,* Vol. 17, p. 101 (quoted in Born, Max, *op cit.,* p. 90).

Ember, M.
1964 'Comment' on Naroll, R. 'Ethnic Unit Classification', *Current Anthropology* 5 (4) : 296.

Emmanuel, A.
1972 *Unequal Exchange.* New York & London, Monthly Review Press.

Engels, F.
1939 *Herr Eugen Dühring's Revolution in Science (Anti-Dühring).* New York, International Publishers.

Everitt, B.
1974 *Cluster Analysis.* London, Heinemann.

Fernand Braudel Center
1979 *The Household and Labor-Force Formation in the Capitalist World Economy.* Binghamton (N.Y.), State University of New York at Binghamton.

Fisher, R.A.
1949 *The Design of Experiments.* London, Oliver and Boyd.

Fortes, M.
1949 *The Web of Kinship among the Tallensi.* London, Oxford University Press.

Frank, A.G.
1970 *Latin America: Underdevelopment or Revolution.* New York, Monthly Review Press.
1972 *Lumpen Bourgeoisie: Lumpen Development.* New York, Monthly Review Press.
1975 *On Capitalist Underdevelopment.* Bombay, Oxford University Press.

Froebel, F.; Heinrich, J.; Kreye, O.
1980 *The New International Division of Labour.* Cambridge (U.K.); Cambridge University Press.

Fuchs, F.
1964 'Comment' on Wiercinski, A.; Bielicki, T. 'Issues in the Study of Race: Two Views from Poland', *Current Anthropology* 3 (1) : 27–28.

Galtung, J.
n.d. 'On the Definition and Theory of Development in relation to Balance-Imbalance Indicators of Human Resources Components', pp. 147–183 in: Gostkowski, Z. (ed.). *Toward a System of Human Resources Indicators for Less Developed Countries.* Warsaw, Ossolineum (Institute of Philosophy and Sociology, The Polish Academy of Sciences).

Ganguli, M.; Sanyal, S.K.
  1968   'Compensation for loss of Real Income: Graded Rates based on Income Elasticity', *Economic and Political Weekly* (Bombay) 3 (21) : 811–814.

Garn, S.M.
  1962   'Comment' on Wiercinski, A.; Bielicki, T., 'Issues in the Study of Race: Two Views from Poland', *Current Anthropology* 3 (1) : 27–28.

Genovese, E.D.
  1974   *Roll, Jordon, Roll: The World the Slaves Made.* New York, Pantheon.

Glick, P.C.
  1957   *American Families.* New York, Wiley.

Goldthorpe, J.H.; Hope, K.
  1974   *The Social Grading of Occupations: A New Approach and Scale.* Oxford, Clarendon Press.

Goody, J. (ed.)
  1958   *The Development Cycle in Domestic Groups.* London, Cambridge University Press.

Gough, K.; Schneider, D.M. (eds.)
  1962   *Matrilineal Kinship.* Berkeley, University of California Press.

Habib, I.
  1963   *The Agrarian System of Mughal India, 1556–1707.* Bombay, Asia Publications.

Hallen, G.C.; Theodorson, G.A.
  1961/   'Changes and Traditionalism in the Indian Family', *Indian Journal of Social Research*
  1965   (Meerut) 2 (2) : 51–59; 4 (1) : 105–110; 1964; 1965 (3) : 208–211.

Hayakawa, M.
  1951   'The application of Pareto's Law of Income to Japanese data', *Econometrica* 19 (2) : 174–183.

Hiernaux, J.
  1962   'Comment' on Wiercinski, A.; Bielicki, T., 'Issues in the Study of Race: Two Views from Poland', *Current Anthropology,* 3 (1) : 29–30.
  1965   'The application of the Concept of Race to the Human Species', *International Social Science Journal* 17 (1) : 112–114.
  1965   'Problems of Race Definition', *International Social Science Journal* 17 (1) : 115–117.

Hope, K. (ed.)
  1972   *The Analysis of Social Mobility: Methods and Approaches.* Oxford, Clarendon Press.

International Labor Office
  1949   *International Standard Classification of Occupations.* Geneva, International Labor Office.
  1958   *International Standard Classification of Occupations.* Geneva, International Labor Office.

Kapadia, K.M.
  1947   *Hindu Kinship.* Bombay, Popular Book Depot.

Karve, I.
1953 *Kinship Organisation in India.* Pune, Deccan College (Monograph Series No. 11).

Kendall, M.G.; Stuart, A.
1966 *The Advanced Theory of Statistics, Vol. 3, Design and Analysis, and Time-series.* New York, Hafner.

Kirkpatrick, C.
1953 *The Family: as Process and Institution.* New York, Ronald.

Kothari, R. (ed.)
1970 *Caste in Indian Politics.* New Delhi, Orient Longman.

Kumarappa, J.C.
1951 *Gandhian Economic Thought.* Bombay, Vora.

Kunstadter, P.
1963 'A Survey of the consanguine or matrifocal family', *American Anthropologist* 65 : 56–66.

Laslett, P.
1965 *The World We Have Lost.* New York; Scribner.

Lazarsfeld, P.F.; Menzel, H.
1961 'On the Relation between Individual and Collective Properties', pp. 422–440 in: Etzioni, A. (ed). *Complex Organizations: A Sociological Reader.* New York, Holt, Rinehart and Winston.

Lenin, V.I.
1951 'The Marxian Doctrine: The Materialist Conception of History' in *Marx, Engels, Marxism.* Moscow, Foreign Languages Publishing House.

Lewis, O.
1951 *Life in a Mexican Village: Tepoztlan Restudied.* Urbana (Illinois); University of Illinois Press.

Linton, R.
1956 *Culture and Mental Disorder.* New York, Thomas.

Linz, J.
1973 'Early State-Building and Late Peripheral Nationalisms against the State: The Case of Spain', pp. 32–116 in Eisenstadt, S.N.; Rokkan, S. (eds.). *Building States and Nations: Analyses by Region,* Vol. II. Beverly Hills, Sage.

Luxemburg, R.
1951 *The Accumulation of Capital.* London, Routledge and Kegan Paul. (First German edition, 1913).

Maclachlan, M.D.
1972 'Comment' on Mukherjee, R. 'Concepts and Methods for the Secondary Analysis of Variations in Family Structures', *Current Anthropology* 13 (3–4) : 435–436.

Mahalanobis, P.C.
  1950 'Why Statistics?' (Address of the General President), *Proceedings of the 37th Indian Science Congress, Poona.* Calcutta, Indian Science Congress.
  1960 'Method of Fractile Graphical Analysis', *Econometrica* 28 : 325–351.

Majumdar, D.N.
  1955 'Demographic Structure in a Polyandrous Village', *Rural Profiles.* Lucknow, Ethnographic and Folk Culture Society.

Marcuse, H.
  1969 *An Essay on Liberation.* London, Penguin.

Marx, K.
  1853 'British Rule in India', *New York Daily Tribune,* 25 June.
  1942 *The German Ideology.* London, Lawrence & Wishart.
  1964 *Pre-capitalist Economic Formations.* London, Lawrence & Wishart.

Morgan, L.H.
  1964 *Ancient Society.* Cambridge, Massachusetts, The Belknap Press of Harvard University Press. (First edition, New York).

Morrison, W.A.
  1959 'Family Types in Badlapur: An Analysis of a Changing Institution in Maharashtrian Village', *Sociological Bulletin* (Bombay) 8 (2) : 45–67.

Morton, A.L.
  1951 *A People's History of England.* London, Lawrence & Wishart.

Moser, C.; Hall, J.
  1954 'The Social Grading of Occupations', pp.29–50 in: Glass, D.V. (ed.). *Social Mobility in Britain.* London, Routledge and Kegan Paul.

Mshvenieradze, V.V.
  1964 'Objective Foundations of the Development of Society: Critical Study of Some Sociological Theories', pp.33–37 in: *Transactions of the Fifth World Congress of Sociology,* Vol. 3. Louvain, International Sociological Association.

Mukherjee, P.
  1974 'Toward Identification of Untouchable Groups in Ancient India as enumerated in Sanskrit Lexicons', *Journal of the Asiatic Society* (Calcutta) 16 (1–4) : 1–14.
  1978 *Hindu Women: Normative Models.* Calcutta, Orient Longman.

Mukherjee, R.
  1957 *The Dynamics of a Rural Society.* Berlin, Akademie-Verlag.
  1959 'A Note on the Classification of Family Structures', pp.133–140 in: *Proceedings and Papers: Regional Seminar on Techniques of Social Research.* Calcutta, Unesco Research Centre.
  1964 'Comment' on Naroll, R. 'Ethnic Unit Classification', *Current Anthropology* 5 (4) : 301.
  1965a *The Sociologist and Social Change in India Today.* New Delhi, Prentice-Hall.
  1965b 'On Major Stocks, Grand-Races, Hauptrassen', *International Social Science Journal* 17 (1) : 124–125.
  1972 'Concepts and Methods for the Secondary Analysis of Variations in Family Structures', *Current Antrhopology* 13 (3–4) : 417–443.

Mukherjee, R. *(contd.)*

1974   *The Rise and Fall of the East India Company.* New York, Monthly Review Press.

1975a   *Social Indicators.* New Delhi, Macmillan.

1975b   'Family in India: A Perspective', pp.1–64 in: Narain, D. (ed). *Family, Kinship and other Essays in Commemoration of K.M. Kapadia.* Bombay, Thacker.

1976a   *Family and Planning in India.* New Delhi, Orient Longman.

1976b   'The Value-base of Social Anthropology: The Context of India in Particular,' *Current Anthropology* 17 (1) : 71–95.

1977a   *West Bengal Family Structures: 1946–66.* New Delhi, Macmillan.

1977b   'Some Introductory Remarks,' pp.11–23 in: International Sociological Association (sponsor) *Scientific-Technological Revolution: Social Aspects.* London, Sage.

1977c   *Trends in Indian Sociology.* Beverly Hills, Sage.

1979   *What Will It Be? Explorations in Inductive Sociology.* New Delhi, Allied Publishers.

1980   "Commentary" on Bach, R.L. "On the Holism of a World-System Perspective," pp.314–316 in: Hopkins, T.K.; Wallerstein, I. (eds.). *Processes of the World-System.* Beverly Hills, Sage.

1981   "Realities of Agrarian Relations in India," *Economic and Political Weekly* (Bombay) 16 (4): 109–116.

Mukherjee, R.; Bandyopadhyay, S.

1964   "Social Research and Mahalanobis' D^2," pp. 259–282 in: Rao, C.R. (ed.). *Contributions to Statistics.* Calcutta, Statistical Publishing Society.

Mukherjee, R.; Rao, C.R.; Trevor, J.C.

1955   *The Physical Characteristics of the Ancient Inhabitants of Jebel Moya, Sudan.* Cambridge (U.K.), Cambridge University Press.

Müller, M.

1919   *The Six Systems of Indian Philosophy.* London, Longmans, Green & Co. (reprint: The Chowkhamba Sanskrit Studies, Vol. XVI. Varanasi, The Chowkhamba Sanskrit Series Office).

Murdock, G.P.

1949   *Social Structure.* New York, Macmillan.

Murdock, G.P.; Ford, C.S.; Hudson, A.E.; Kennedy, R.;
Simmons, L.W.; Whiting, J.W.M.

1950   *Outlines of Cultural Materials,* Vol. I. New Haven, Human Relations Area Files.

Nagata, S.

1972   "Comment" on Mukherjee, R. "Concepts and Methods for the Secondary Analysis of Variations in Family Structures," *Current Anthropology* 13 (3–4) : 436–437.

Narrol, R.

1964   'Ethnic Unit Classification', *Current Anthropology* 5 (4) : 296.

Nie, N.H.; Powell, Jr. G.B.; Prewitt, K.

1969   'Social Structure and Political Participation: Developmental Relations', *American Political Science Review* 63 (2) : 361–378; (3) : 808–832.

Nimkoff, M.F.

1959   'Some Problems Concerning Research on the Changing Family in India', *Sociological Bulletin* (Bombay) 8 (2) : 32–38.

Ogburn, W.F.; Nimkoff, M.F.
1955 *A Handbook of Sociology.* London, Routledge and Kegan Paul.

Ossipov, G.V.; Kolbanovsky, V.V.
1974 *Social Indications and Indicators of the Social Development Planning.* Moscow, Soviet Sociological Association.

Parsons, T.
1954 *Essays in Sociological Theory.* Glencoe (Ill.), Free Press.

Parsons, T.; Bales, R.
1956 *Family: Socialization and Interaction Process.* London, Routledge and Kegan Paul.

Perlin, F.
1981 *Some Central Problems Concerning the Proto-Industrialization Thesis and Pre-Colonial South Asia.* Rotterdam, Erasmus University (History Department).

Peter, Prince
1963 *On Polyandry.* Paris and 'S Gravenhage, Mouton.

Pocock, D.F.
1963 'Review' of *Indian Anthropology* (eds.). Madan, T.N.; Sarana, G., *Man* (London) 63, October, Review No. 216.

Radcliffe-Brown, A.R.
1922 'Some Problems in Bantu Sociology', *Bantu Studies,* October.
1959 *Structure and Function in Primitive Society.* London; Cohen and West.

Redfield, R.
1956 *Peasant Society and Culture.* Chicago, The University of Chicago Press.

Ridge, J.M. (ed.)
1974 *Mobility in Britain Reconsidered.* Oxford, Clarendon Press.

Rivers, W.H.R.
1926 *Social Organisation.* London, Kegan Paul.

Robbins, L.
1932 *The Nature and Significance of Economic Science.* London, Macmillan.

Rosch, E.; Mervis, C.B.; Gray, W.; Johnson, D.; Boyes-Braem, P.
1976 'Basic Objects in Natural Categories', *Cognitive Psychology 8:* 382–439.

Rostow, W.W.
1962 *The Stages of Economic Growth: A Non-Communist Manifesto.* Cambridge (U.K.); Cambridge University Press.

Roy Burman, B.K. (ed.)
1967 *Socio-Economic Survey Report on Chetlat Island.* New Delhi, Census of India (Monograph Series, Part VI).

Royal Anthropological Institute of Great Britain and Ireland
1954 *Notes and Queries on Anthropology.* London, Routledge and Kegan Paul.

Safa, H.T.
1965 'The Family Based Household in Public Housing: A Case Study in Puerto Rico', *Human Organization* 24 (2) : 135-139.

Seal, B.N.
1958 *The Positive Sciences of the Ancient Hindus.* Delhi, Moti Lal Banarsi Das.

Service, E.R.
1960 'Kinship Terminology and Evolution', *American Anthropologist* 62 (5) : 747-763.

Shamasastry, R.
1951 *Kautilya's Arthasastra.* Mysore.

Singh, Y.
1977 'Cultural and Social Contents of Scientific and Technological Revolution', pp. 131-146 in: International Sociological Association (sponsor) *Scientific-Technological Revolution: Social Aspects.* Beverly Hills, Sage.

Srinivas, M.N.
1966 *Social Change in Modern India.* Bombay, Allied Publishers.

Stannard, J.
1965 'Method and Logic in PreSocratic Explanation', pp.107-131 in: Tymieniecka, Anna-Teresa (ed.). *Contributions to Logic and Methodology.* Amsterdam, North-Holland Publishing Company.

Statistical Office of the United Nations
1968 *International Standard Industrial Classification of All Economic Activities.* New York, United Nations (Statistical Papers, Series M, No. 4).

Sutcliffe, B.
1972 'Conclusions' in: Owen, R.; Sutcliffe, B. (eds.). *Studies in the Theory of Imperialism.* London, Longman.

Swartz, B.K., Jr.
1965 'Comments', p. 117 in: Vore, P.L. (ed.). *The Origin of Man.* Chicago, Wenner-Gren Foundation for Anthropological Research.

Sweezy, P.M.
1946 *The Theory of Capitalist Development.* London, Dennis Dobson.

Tsurumi, K.
1977 'Some Potential Contributions of Latecomers to Technological and Scientific Revolution: a Comparison between Japan and China', pp. 147-174 in: International Sociological Association (sponsor) *Scientific-Technological Revolution: Social Aspects.* London, Sage Publications.

Wallerstein, I.
1974 *The Modern World-System.* New York, Academic Press.
1979 *The Capitalist World-Economy.* Cambridge (U.K.), Cambridge University Press.

Warner, W.L.
1958 *A Black Civilization.* New York, Harper.

Weber, M.
   1958   *The Religion of India*. Glencoe (Ill.), The Free Press.
   1965   *The Sociology of Religion*. London, Methuen & Co.

Weldon, W.F.R.; Pearson, K.; Davenport, C.B.
   1901   'Editorial', *Biometrika* 1 : 1-6.

Zensho, E.
   1936   'The Family System in Korea', pp. 222-230 in: *Transactions of the Third World Congress of Sociology*. Vol. IV. London, International Sociological Association.

Name Index

Subject Index